SHall I compare thee to a Summers day?
Thou art more louely and more temperate:
Rough windes do shake

the darling buds of Maie,

And Sommers lease hath all too short a date:
Sometime too hot the eye of heauen shines,
And often is his gold complexion dimm'd,
And euery faire from faire some-time declines,
By chance,or natures changing course vntrim'd:
But thy eternall Sommer shall not fade,
Nor loose possession of that faire thou ow'st,
Nor shall death brag thou wandr'st in his shade,
When in eternall lines to time thou grow'st,
So long as men can breath or eyes can see,
So long liues this,and this giues life to thee,

**The Sonnets
belonging to
William Shakespeare
explained at last**

by

Ben Alexander

BAIL

Published by BAIL (B A Interim Ltd) 2004
Copyright © Ben Alexander 2004

Ben Alexander has asserted his right under the
Copyright, Designs and Patents Act 1988
to be identified as the author of this work.

First published in Great Britain by
(BAIL) B. A. Interim Ltd
Reg: 2938603
1 Crown Street
Stockport
Greater Manchester
SK6 7JH

British Library Cataloguing in Publication Data
A catalogue record for this book is available from the British
Library

ISBN 0-9548474-0-7 (hbk)

Printed by Deanprint, Stockport, Cheshire.

father

I would like to thank all those who have had faith;
especially
my wife
my daughter
and my mentor.
All three have tested me to near destruction,
but not quite!

I would like to thank the help given to me by:
The staff of the Records Office in Warwick,
Brenda Newell of Arbury Hall, Warwickshire
Tim and Liz Richards of Gawsworth Hall, Cheshire
Friends at the Folger in Washington,
Staff at the Wallace Collection, London.
The National Portrait Gallery, London.
Leslie & Nola Miles

I would like to acknowledge the remarkable research of,
Margaret Hannay (Philip's Phoenix)
Sheila T Cavenagh (Cherished Torment)
Leslie Hotson (The First Night of Twelfth Night)
Katherine Duncan Jones (The Ardern Shakespeare's Sonnets)
Kari Boyd McBride (Aemelia Lanier).

And again to my mentor,
Michael Leete,
who untangled my many thoughts,
thank you.

March-October 2004

Contents

Chapters

Appendices

PRINCIPAL RELATIONSHIPS

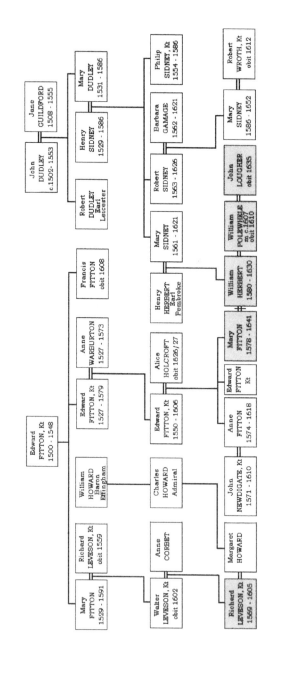

THE DARLING BUDS OF MAIE

*Sinc distanc bares me from so great hapenes as I can seldom
hear from you, which when I do is so welcom as I esteme nothing
more worthie, and for your love which I dout not of shall be
equaled in ful mesure, but lest my lines to tedius weare, and time
that limets all thinges bares me of wordes, which eles could
never ses to tel howe dear you ar, and with what zele I desire
your retorne, than can wish nothing more then your hartes
desire, and wil ever contineu; your afectina sister. . .* Mary
phytton

Letter from Mary Fitton to Anne Newdigate, her married sister.

CHAPTER ONE

THE MYSTERIES

The story could be told in one paragraph. It started about the year 1600
when it appears that an adolescent courtier had a fleeting infatuation for an
older, married woman. In the heat of his passion he composed poetry, in the
form of sonnets, expressing his wild thoughts, anger, and his many emotions.
In the end he was frustrated and, on the rebound, he wooed one of Queen
Elizabeth's Maids of Honour. The Maid became pregnant but he refused to
make an honest woman of her, despite *her* composing a sequence of sonnets
imploring him to take a wife. The Queen, furious that the man had
impregnated and then refused to marry her ward, expelled them both from
Court. The baby died soon after birth and the woman left London in disgrace.
Exiled, she wrote a poem titled *A Lover's Complaint* describing her seduction
by the courtier and, during the next few years created a diary of sonnets
expressing her ever fluctuating feelings for the man. In 1609 all this poetry was
brought together and published in a small book. Her sonnets, seamlessly
followed by those of the courtier, were concluded with the poem about the
seduction. The poetry is, at worst, excellent and, at best, brilliant. It is a true
gift. It is a gift that, at the time, in itself, cried out to be published. The book
was and is called *Shake-Speares Sonnets.*[1]

---

[1] A sonnet is a fourteen-line poem, each line of ten syllables having varied rhyming patterns but
with up to seven different sound endings, for example, abab-cdcd-efef-gg. Usually the sense is
made up in three Quatrains, blocks of four lines, ending with a slightly dispassionate two-line
Couplet. There is often a logical change after line-eight. The text of the poetry in this book is an
amalgam from various sources. Various editions differ slightly because one has to contend with
modern spelling, differing punctuation and sense. When in doubt, I have referred back to the
original 1609 printing held in the Huntingdon Library on line through the Internet. Other help
has come from the *Norton Shakespeare; A Shakespeare Glossary* by C. T. Onions; *A Dictionary of
Shakespeare's Sexual Puns and their Significance* by Frank Rubinstein; the Ardern, the Cambridge and

The Mysteries

Here is Sonnet Seventeen, the Maid of Honour, pregnant with his baby, writes to the Courtier:

Who will believe my verse in time to come
If it were filled with your most high deserts?
Though yet, heaven knows, it is but as a tomb
Which hides your life and shows not half your parts.

If I could write the beauty of your eyes,
And in fresh numbers[2] number all your graces,
The age to come would say, *This poet lies;*
Such heavenly touches ne'er touched earthly faces.

So should my papers, yellowed with their age,
Be scorned, like old men of less truth than tongue,
And your true rights be termed a poet's rage
And stretched metre of an antique song.

But were some child of yours alive that time,
You should live twice in it, and in my rhyme.

The book of poetry was a gift that has never yielded its full enjoyment because nobody has ever understood the context in which the 154 sonnets and the poem had been written. This book gives that understanding and, when the verses are read in their proper context, you will find that the poetry is so personal, and at times so lascivious, derogatory or scandalous that the work could only have been published if the identities of the characters were obscured or obliterated. In Sonnet 135; the petulant courtier, believing himself in love, jealous, frustrated, feeling neglected and very angry with the married woman, became grossly insulting;

Whoever hath her wish, thou hast thy *Will,*
And *Will* to boot, and *Will* in overplus;
More than enough am I that vex thee still,
To thy sweet will making addition thus.

Wilt thou, whose will is large and spacious,
Not once vouchsafe to hide my will[3] in thine?
Shall will in others seem right gracious,
And in my will no fair acceptance shine?

The sea, all water, yet receives rain still,
And in abundance addeth to his store;
So thou, being rich in *Will,* add to thy *Will*
One will of mine to make thy large *Will* more.

Let no unkind no fair beseechers kill,
Think all but one, and me in that one *Will.*

---

the New Penguin series of plays; and *Shakespeare, the Invention of the Human* by Harold Bloom.

[2] Here a *number* is a verse or poem.

[3] A *will* in this context can be either sexes' genitalia.

The Mysteries

The names of the Courtier, the Maid of Honour and the Married Lady and the true nature and context of Shake-Speares Sonnets with its additional poem, *A Lover's Complaint,* have been the greatest mysteries of English literature. This book unravels the mysteries and explains the background so, at last, one can enjoy fully the remarkable passions of the Sonnets.

In 1600 a member of the Elizabethan nobility or gentry would have been considered somewhat vulgar to have his poetry or play published in print under his own name. It was *not* the done thing! Publishing the works of one's own pen was seen to be the domain of the lower-class and social-climbing wordsmiths, exclusively male, who prostrated, importuned or climbed over each other to gain notice, attention and advancement through the system of patronage. It should be noted that the early *Shakespeare* plays neither had an author's name nor contained a dedication. If the male head of the great family was not approachable, a well worn, circuitous, but obsequious route was to dedicate their works to his wife. One woman in particular, Mary Sidney Herbert,[4] Countess of Pembroke, wealthy in her own right and a great patron of the literary arts, was the recipient of some hundreds of fawning dedications as begetters of poems, plays and books displayed their wares.

For the ennobled, publishing anonymously or under a pseudonym circumvented such vulgarity – but still ran the risk of discovery and exposure. Five great lords, Derby, Leicester, Oxford, Pembroke and Southampton are now believed to have been exceptional poets. The acceptable way of sharing one's ability and entertaining others was by circulating or reciting hand-written verses to friends. But it was not just the nobility who had cause to obscure their identity; for a woman to publish her own work under her own name was unheard of, it would have been tantamount to soliciting. It was not until 1611, with King James I on the throne and eight years after the death of Queen Elizabeth, that the first ever collections of verses composed by women started to be published; those of Aemelia Bassano Lanier (published 1611) and Mary Sidney Wroth (in 1621).[5]

It was in London, on 20th May 1609 that the 154 sonnets with the 329-line poem, *A Lover's Complaint,* were registered at the Company of Stationer's Hall[6] and soon published in the eighty page book titled *Shake-Speares Sonnets.* It was prefaced by an apparently clumsy or strange dedication [PLATE 7];

---

[4] Mary Sidney was her maiden name. She married Henry Herbert.

[5] Mary Sidney Wroth was Countess Pembroke's niece by her brother Robert Sidney, later 1st Earl of Leicester, second creation. The first 1st. Earl was the Countess's uncle, her mother's brother, Robert Dudley. Previously, the Countess had completed her poet brother's unfinished poetry, and his translations of the Psalms.

[6] The Stationers' Register gives *20 May; Tho. Thorpe. Entered for his copie under the handes of master Wilson and master Lownes Wardenes a booke called Shakespeares sonnettes vjd.*

The Stationers Hall in London and its Register was the accepted way of copyrighting a literary work or register ownership of property. To prevent theft of plagiarism authors would exhibit and register a document, often before completion and pending publication. One would assume the document would have been marked as having been shown to the Stationer's clerk.

The Mysteries

TO.THE.ONLIE.BEGETTER.OF.
THESE.INSVING.SONNETS.
M^r.W.H. ALL.HAPPINESSE.
AND.THAT.ETERNITIE.
PROMISED.
BY.
OVR.EVER-LIVING.POET.
WISHETH.
THE.WELL-WISHING.
ADVENTVRER.IN.
SETTING.
FORTH.
T. T.

The title page says *"never before imprinted "* but two of the sonnets had appeared ten years earlier in a booklet of twenty-one poems *by W Shakespeare*[7] called *The Passionate Pilgrim*. In fact, six of the poems in *The Passionate Pilgrim*[8] have been identified as the work of other poets, two of the six are by a Richard Barnfield. Three had appeared in the Shakespeare play, *Loves Labour Lost*, and three others in the William Shakespeare poem *Venus and Adonis*. No one has been able to attribute authorship to the remaining seven.

The first *Shakespeare* works, as they later became known, started to appear around 1590[9] but no author's name was ascribed until 1598, other than for the two narrative poems *Venus and Adonis* (registered April 1593) and *The Rape of Lucrece* (1594). *Venus and Adonis* was described by the author as *"the first heir of my invention"* – a curious epithet seeing that the three plays, *Henry VI Parts 1, 2 and 3* had already been performed. Only in 1598 was a play, *Richard II*, registered for the first time against William Shakespeare's name, and the same year Shakespeare was clearly named by a third party in lines from a poem again attributed to Richard Barnfield:

> *And Shakespeare thou, whose hony-flowing Vain,*
> *(Pleasing the World) thy Praises doth containe.*
> *Whose Venus, and whose Lucrece (sweet, and chaste)*
> *Thy Name in fames immortall Book have plac't.*

The last Shakespeare plays, *Henry VIII* and *Two Noble Kinsmen,*[10] were produced in 1613. Three years later an actor, William Shakespeare, died aged 52 and was buried in the market town of his birth, Stratford-upon-Avon in Warwickshire. In 1623 the *first folio* of *Mr William Shakespeares Comedies, Histories and Tragedies* was published. The book was dedicated to two

---

[7] Printed by Thomas Judson for William Jaggard.

[8] The twenty-one poems of *The Passionate Pilgrim* are given at Appendix 2.

[9] Registered in the Stationer's Register of 1594 are plays without authors' names which appear to be Shakespeare's; at 4039 The First Part of the Contention betwixt the Houses of York and Lancaster; 4042 The True Tragedy of Richard III; 4039 The famous Victories of Henry V; containing the honourable Battle of Agincourt.

[10] Thought to be collaborations.

The Mysteries

brothers, William and Philip Herbert, sons of the late Henry, 2nd. Earl
Pembroke (died 1601) and his dowager Countess, Mary Sidney Herbert, (died
1621). William Herbert was then the 3rd. Earl of Pembroke. On the title page of
the First Folio is a portrait, engraved by Martin Droeshout,[11] (typeset as Dro
es hout) of a moustached man whom one *assumes* to be William Shakespeare
[PLATE 7]; one sees an oversized head stuck on to a tailor's dummy.[12] The
facing page contains this short poem *To the Reader*, by Ben Jonson:

> This figure, that thou here seest put,
> It was for gentle Shakespeare cut:
> Wherein the Graver had a strife
> With Nature, to outdo the life:
> O, could he but have drawn his wit
> As well in brass, as he hath hit
> His face, the Print would then surpass
> All, that ever was writ in brass.
> But, since he cannot, Reader look
> Not on his Picture, but his Book.

Twenty-eight years earlier, in 1595, a highly intelligent, literate, passionate
and beautiful lass from the northern English county of Cheshire turned her
back on her black-and-white timbered country home. Escorted by her much
respected father she rode out of his large estate and steadily travelled south to
a new life in London. Aged seventeen, she had been appointed to be one of
Queen Elizabeth's Maids of Honour. Her father was to entrust his daughter to
the care of his friend, one Sir William Knollys, then Treasurer of the Queen's
household, before making the equally long journey back to Cheshire. At Court,
if not quite the Queen's favourite,[13] the young lady appears over time to have
become the leader of a group of talented and attractive young women.[14] This
Maid of Honour could write poetry and, as it was not possible to publish her
verses under her own name, research has led me to posit that she used a man's
name or, more likely, appended her best poems to those of a man with whom
she was acquainted – the aforementioned Richard Barnfield.

---

[11] An anagram of Martin Dro es hout is I'st Our Man The Dor (Door)? A Dor is a Jest.

[12] The First Folio was printed by Isaac Jaggard and Ed. Blount.

[13] The Queen's favourite Maid of Honour then was Margaret Radcliffe, depicted in *Twelfth Night*
as Viola. After hearing of the awful death of her twin brother, Alexander, (Sebastian in the play)
in a skirmish in Ireland in August 1599, Margaret became anorexic and her life wasted away. In
her last days she was nursed by the Queen, and died in the Queen's arms that November. Ben
Jonson wrote a poignant epitaph for the tombstone in Westminster Abbey. The name Sebastian
conjures up the image of St. Sebastian whose body was pierced by many arrows. In *Twelfth Night*
the twins confirm their identities, by saying their father died on their thirteenth birthday. In
reality, Sir John Radcliffe of Ordsall in Salford, Lancashire, died in 1590 on what could very well
have been their fifteenth birthday. On Twelfth Night 1601, a year after the twins died, they
reappeared like spirits, to the delight of the Court, in the play, *Twelfth Night*, Act 5.1, l-232 Viola
says, *"If spirits can assume both form and suit, you come to fright us."* Sebastian replies, *"A spirit I am
indeed, . . ."*

[14] Chapter Five, section 5.19 explains this further.

The Mysteries

The Court in London was a community of nearly two thousand people. At its head was the Queen served by her administrators and her immediate staff, including a hierarchy of maids and servants each with their own function in the massive beehive. Closest to the Queen were the Maids of Honour, daughters of the gentry, skilled in the arts of music, song, recitation, dance, cards and sewing. They were, effectively, wards of the Queen, there to look after the Queen and help keep her entertained. They had a reputation of being virtuous (although some were not) and acted almost like foster-daughters who would have made the ageing Queen feel youthful.

Over the five years she lived at Court under the Queen's protection, care and close scrutiny, the Maid of Honour from Cheshire became a great success. She watched, perhaps with envy, as some of her friends and colleagues married well; then in 1600 she fell in love with the young, handsome and gifted son of the most notable earl of England. He too composed verse – brilliantly, and they shared this love of poetry. One can romanticise that he may have presented her with an early, if not the first, copy of *The Passionate Pilgrim* which he had compiled to impress the married woman who had just rejected him! The compilation of love poems probably included some written by himself and there is a slight possibility that the two "Barnfield" poems[15] may have been written by the young lady.[16] The young lady, two years his senior, steadfastly resisted the pressure of the young man's tokens of love, and his persistent sexual advances. But, only after his having *sworn his troth* – that he would marry her – did she finally succumb to his voluminous tears and to his one vital promise. The sex was good[17] but, oh dear, she became pregnant.

Promises! Puh! He refused to marry her – or anyone else for that matter; this was the fourth marriage proposal that had been put to him, and he was not yet twenty-one.[18] The Queen was exceedingly angry, not only had her Maid of Honour been defiled, but the young courtier was defiant of her and would not marry. The woman was put under house arrest and the child died very soon after birth; he may have infected her with a venereal disease.[19] The man was locked away in the Fleet Prison and was only released after three months when his doctor certified he was ill. It was at about this same time his father died and he became the new Earl, but he still remained exiled from the Court and was unable to return until after Queen Elizabeth died in 1603.

Behind the scenes, however, during these last years of the old Queen's reign, the young Earl showed his political astuteness by currying favour with the heir to the English throne, James VI of Scotland who became James I of England. Plague was rampant in London as the new king made the long

---

[15] PP8 & PP21 at Appendix 2.

[16] PP18 could also be a Barnfield poem. Although PP19 seems to complement PP18, it was written by Thomas Weelkes.

[17] *A Lover's Complaint,* Appendix 1, Stanza 43.

[18] Elizabeth, daughter of Sir George Carey; Bridget Vere daughter of the Earl of Oxford; 1599, a niece of Charles Howard, Lord Nottingham. Edward Hyde, Lord Clarendon later wrote that the man was, "immoderately given up to women." Source: *Ardern Sonnets.*

[19] See Appendix 1, *A Lover's Complaint,* stanza 43, line 301, *"He poisoned me..."*

The Mysteries

journey southwards to claim his throne so the Earl, for two months, entertained him, and his extensive Court, at his country home. The now twenty-three year old Earl was immediately rewarded for his loyalty when King James made him a Knight of the Garter. At the coronation he was one of the Earls who held up the canopy over the King's head during the ceremony and, after formally swearing his allegiance, he demonstratively greeted his King James with a kiss on the face, or on the lips – it certainly took all the other courtiers by surprise. King James was to remain very fond of him and his brother, the Earl's future was assured and his fortune was to be made during the next decade through tin and tobacco. In 1604 the Earl finally married – a noble woman with a huge dowry[20] and a sizeable estate. The marriage was not a happy one and the Earl and his Countess were to live apart.

The young lady, ostracised, vilified and shamed, returned to her parent's home one hundred and sixty miles away. Her parents, especially her mother, were profoundly embarrassed. She then seemed to become nomadic and moved around the country. For a while she lived in the Rectory next to her parent's home in Cheshire, then with her sister in Warwickshire; there is evidence of her being in Wales and Shropshire and at some time she lived in a second-cousin's property in Staffordshire where, around 1606, she finally settled, married and had children.

During the time she was estranged from her former lover, or in exile, she privately composed sonnets expressing her emotions, writing them into the copybook he had given her. Somehow between 1605 and 1609 it appears that the Earl obtained the copybook. In 1609, when the *Sonnets* and *A Lover's Complaint* were published, the former lovers were married to others so authorship used the Earl's family's secret pen-name, that of Shake-Speare. In Stanzas 7 and 8 of *A Lover's Complaint* we can read that Mary tore up the letters she had received from William. So the identities of the man and the two women were lost, not to be properly identified for nearly four hundred years.

And four hundred years have passed and, although many have tried, the mysteries of Shake-Speares Sonnets have never been resolved to anyone's satisfaction. Who were the people involved? What was the background? Who actually wrote them? When were they written? Are they homoerotic? The answers and explanations are about to unfold. When you follow the real life story that inspired these fantastic verses I hope that you will enjoy poetry in a way you have never experienced poetry before. You are about to enter the minds of two very gifted people, a man in lust and a woman in love.

Why am I so convinced that here are the solutions? The answer is that everything fits, but there will be a final twist in the tail of this story. Clearly, there were no obvious statements as to whom the protagonists were – otherwise there would not be a mystery. There were no deliberate clues – otherwise a hundred and fifty years of investigation by some brilliant scholars

---

[20] The dowry was then £3,000, equivalent to over £1m today.

The Mysteries

would have found them. In fact, we will read that the protagonists went out of their way to preserve anonymity; from Sonnet 76:

> Why write I still all one, ever the same,
> And keep invention in a noted weed,
> That every word doth almost tell my name,
> Showing their birth and where they did proceed?

The both had brilliant minds, better than nearly all of the investigators that have tried to expose them. The woman even hid her sex. It has needed a number of accidents to stumble across who they were, lots of determination, and a mind that for forty years has applied itself to professional logistics and amateur historical research. The thread of the story, as you will read, can be traced through the Sonnets. The Shakespeare plays, and other contemporary documents, fill in and help confirm the detail. Two of the three protagonists in the Sonnets are the authors themselves. The third also became a notable poet.

For many months I have been reading books and articles about all the various theories, hoping, in a way, to disprove myself because the responsibility of being right is simply enormous. Nothing has presented itself that cannot be explained within the framework of this book nor refuted with little more than a simple argument. Hard facts are still appearing and every one now adds to the body of evidence. For instance, the woman and her family used to make wordplays on the family name such as in the family motto or on tombstones. I had confidently expected to see one very obvious wordplay in the Sonnets – but it was not there. Yet, if I knew the woman's mind after "living" with her so long within the Sonnets, it would have been something she could not have resisted. Recently another sonnet has emerged that would have been written when she was still a teenager – and there was the very wordplay I had expected. The woman knew she could not use it again in the Sonnets as it would have easily identified her.

This book will create many questions. In March 2004 I knew nothing about the poetry in the Sonnets; all I knew was that H. E. Bates had used *The Darling Buds of May* as the title of a book. Now I find their content breathtaking, and they must be even more so for a woman. I have always marvelled at the Shakespeare plays and the analysis, research and development of the body of knowledge that has been derived from the plays themselves is a tribute to some great minds; no other secular body of text gives us a better understanding about our selves. The big BUT is that, to best understand Shakespeare one needs to know what the writer intended, just as it helps to know about Mozart or Beethoven to better enjoy their music. We would like to know the real background within which the plays and poetry were written. For instance, how can one explain how the magnificent frivolity of *Twelfth Night* be can be so closely followed by the sombre, psychological genius of *Hamlet*?

This is not an easy book to read. It is a mixture of history, forensics, facts, probabilities and possibilities – but nowhere does conjecture or whim transmute into "fact". There are two academics whom I must single out. Margaret Hannay, Professor of English at Siena College, for her book *Philip's*

The Mysteries

Phoenix, and Sheila Cavanagh, Associate Professor of English at Emory University for her *Cherished Torment*. I read their books trying very hard to find evidence to disprove what I had found. The quality of their research is astounding and has helped me understand so much about the lives of the protagonists. I resisted the temptation to abstract huge tracts from their works to block-fill the background; this is essentially a book about Shake-Speares Sonnets. I'm sure, when the two American professors read these lines, it would not have been lost on them that their books were about two women of the same maiden name, Mary Sidney, aunt and niece.

I have climbed to the top of Ludlow Castle in Shropshire and looked down on the castle and across the river into Wales. It is not hard for me to imagine three siblings, Philip, Mary and Robert Sidney [PLATE 3] doing the same a long time ago when William Shakespeare was a boy; this was their childhood home. High up there, shaken by rough winds, one can be *King of the Castle*, enjoying a brief delusion of power that lasts only until the descent into reality. The Sidney family had no such delusion of power. They were powerful; but they also were very human and the family's great passion was drama and literature. I am wondering if the two professors, as they wrote their books, sensed that Mary Sidney (Herbert) and Mary Sidney (Wroth), through their inspiration of others, were perhaps the greatest of all influences on English Literature and the English language – other than the King James' Bible.

Truth is a very interesting commodity. If you add or mix truth with truth you get truth. If you add truth to a lie, or a lie to truth, you get a lie. Given the truth one can face a lie. Given a lie one cannot face truth.

Ladies, how many of you have proposed marriage to a man in a Leap Year? A strange question? The relevance of this question, and many others, will be explained and answered. Believe me, this really is a fantastic and fascinating story. So, after four hundred years, yes – four hundred years, let's blow the cover and let in the light!

Here we go!

CHAPTER TWO

THE PROTAGONISTS

The young man who in 1600 seduced the Maid of Honour was William Herbert [PLATE 5], son of Henry, 2nd. Earl of Pembroke, and the Countess Pembroke, Mary Sidney Herbert. Indeed, many people had already come to a conclusion that William Herbert was the object of William Shakespeare's homosexual love. The first twist in this tale, however, is that it was William Herbert who wrote Sonnets 127-154. The second twist is that it was a woman's love that poured forth from Sonnets 1-126.

The Maid of Honour was Mary (Mall) Fitton of Gawsworth, Cheshire, [PLATE 1], known to some Shakespeare devotees as the model for Olivia in *Twelfth Night*.[21] [22] Many people had already associated Mary Fitton with the *Dark Lady of the Sonnets*, although the *Dark Lady's* eyes were described as black and Mary's eyes were a slate-blue.[23] More pertinent is that the *Dark Lady* was married and Mary Fitton, when she had her affair with William Herbert, was not. Our third twist is that it was Mary Fitton who wrote Sonnets 1-126 and the poem *A Lover's Complaint*.[24] The final twist is that my findings indicate that Mary's character, or story, appears in some Shakespeare plays written during or after 1599.

The woman with whom it appears William Herbert was infatuated before he met Mary Fitton, the woman now famously known as the *Dark Lady of the Sonnets*, for reasons you will read in the next chapter, was probably Aemelia (Bassano) Lanier. In the modern era she has been identified as the first English feminist writer, publishing her excellent poetry in 1611. If she was the woman, this might have been, in part, a reaction to what was published about her in Shake-Speares Sonnets in 1609.

In 1601 William Herbert became the 3rd. Earl of Pembroke. He lived until 1630 and died two days after his fiftieth birthday. He was a gifted man with many titles including Lord Warden of the Stanneries of Devon & Cornwall,[25] Governor of Portsmouth, Knight of the Garter and a member of the King's

---

[21] Leslie Hotson's *The First Night of Twelfth Night* provides an excellent analysis of the play. Mary Fitton would then have been six month's pregnant. At Act-1 iii we find, *"Are they to take dust like Mistress Mall's picture?"*

[22] Mary Sidney Wroth's 1621 allegory, *The Countess of Montgomery's Urania* (referred to as *Urania*), recounts her knowledge of the two lover's adult lives. They are the characters *Antissia* and *Amphilanthus*. Mary Wroth was William's first cousin, lover and mother of two children by him. *Antissia* means *Opponent*. [*Cherished Torment* by Sheila T. Cavanagh, although the first identification of Mary Fitton as *Antissia* was by Josephine A Roberts]. The Countess of Montgomery was the wife of William Herbert's brother, Philip.

[23] Olivia's eyes in *Twelfth Night,* Act 1.5, are grey.

[24] The 1609 printing of the poem is titled "A Louers Complaint BY William Shake-Speare."

[25] Tin mines.

The Protagonists

Privy Council. From 1615 to 1625 he was Lord Chamberlain.[26] When Chancellor of Oxford University the name of Broadgate Hall was changed to Pembroke College, which he helped fund. He successfully speculated in the Virginia Company,[27] and helped finance the establishment of Bermuda and Newfoundland. He married a daughter of the Earl of Shrewsbury, Mary Talbot, but their one child died shortly after birth.[28] His wife survived him and lived until 1649 with little, if any, distinction. His brother Philip succeeded him. Hugh Sanford, William Herbert's tutor, had predicted that William Herbert would not live beyond his fifty-first year and this prediction is repeated in a document of his that describes the Earl's character: *He mends his mind to follow the means to attain riches with a little covetousness, but on honourable occasion shall spend from it. He is vigilant and apt to fall into quarrel by hastiness. He is of a lofty mind —delights in magnanimity . . . Courteous and affable to his friends but cannot bear injury or cross in his reputation. He is bountiful to his friends . . because of his regard for honour and reputation . . shall be very dainty in the choice out of jealousy and suspicion.*[29]

The remains of William, Philip and their parents lie together under the choir[30] in Salisbury Cathedral near to the family home of Wilton in Wiltshire, through whose grounds flow tributaries of a nearby river called the Avon. One of the other frequently used Pembroke family homes was at Ivychurch, a few miles away, which is by the same Wiltshire Avon.[31] This is evidently the same river Avon that Ben Jonson writes about in his First Folio dedication *To the memory of my beloved the author, Mr William Shakespeare and what he hath left us,* and says *"Sweet Swan[32] of Avon! What a fight it were, to see thee in our waters yet appear, and make those flights upon the banks of Thames, that so did take Eliza and our James!"*

Mary Fitton, twice widowed, died in more humble circumstances in Staffordshire in 1641, aged 63. Three children of her eight recorded

---

[26] One of the Lord Chamberlain's duties was licenser of plays in the City of London, Westminster and other areas. His brother, Philip took over from him.

[27] 1607, tobacco - Virginian car number plates already show they will celebrate 400 years in 2007. Pembroke was the second largest (adventurer) single stockholder of several hundreds.

[28] Mary Talbot, 24 year old daughter of Gilbert, 7th Earl of Shrewsbury and Mary Cavendish, has been said to be malformed. That Mary Talbot failed to produce an heir is not surprising as the Shrewsburys and the Pembrokes had a long history of intermarriage. The dau. of 4S, Anne, marries 1P; Catherine, dau. of 6S marries 2P and Mary dau. of 7S marries 3P. Another Mary Talbot married Thomas Holcroft, Mary Fitton's cousin in the 1600's.

[29] Hannay, op .cit. page 211.

[30] The floor of the choir is covered by yellow, sandstone paving. Hidden beneath the pulpit in the choir is a brick vault containing several generations of the family. On the opposite wall is a modern dedication to the Pembrokes below which is an epithet to Mary Sidney Herbert.
Underneath this sable herse / Lies the subject of all verse, / SIDNEY's sister, PEMBROKE's mother; / Death! ere thou hast slain another, / Learn'd and fair, and good as she, / Time shall throw a dart at thee.

[31] The Stratford *Avon* flows into the Severn River; the Wiltshire *Avon* into the English Channel.

[32] The swan is considered to be mute.

pregnancies survived her. She requested that she should be buried in the delightful, country church at Gawsworth, Cheshire, [PLATE 8] where she was brought up, but this may not have happened. In the church is a touching memorial to her father. The tomb originally had Alice, his wife, seated alongside, with Sir Edward's head resting on her hand, and at each corner kneeling effigies of their four children [PLATE 8]. Today's visitors to the church can still see the weary face of Alice Fitton, her two sons in knight's armour to the front of her, and behind her the attractive sisters, Anne and Mary, dressed in black robes of mourning – the sleeping statue of her husband is missing.

We are not looking at a love affair between rustics. The door has been opened and we can catch sight of the very movers and shakers of that era. William's father, Henry Herbert, the 2nd. Earl Pembroke, was thought to be the wealthiest man in England and Wales. William's mother was the sister of Sir Philip Sidney, who completed her brother's work *Astrophel and Stella* which described Philip's passion for the teenage Penelope Devereux Rich. Penelope was the beautiful daughter of the beautiful Letitia Knollys, sister of Sir William Knollys of whom we shall read more. William Herbert's aunt, Katherine, married Lord Huntingdon. Another aunt, Frances, Countess of Sussex, left £5,000 in her will to found Sidney Sussex College at Cambridge. Philip and Mary Sidney's uncle was Robert Dudley, Earl of Leicester whose third wife was the same Letitia Knollys whom he scandalously married in secret, to the chagrin and great anger of the Queen. Power, wealth, influence and intrigue hovered, malevolently interwoven around these two lovers.

The 154 Shake-Speare Sonnets are generally recognised to be in four sections or themes; Sonnets 1-17, 18-126, 127-152 and 153-154.

The word *begetter* in the Dedication, *the only begetter of these ensuing sonnets,* can have a number of interpretations but basically it means either the person who wrote the Sonnets or the person who inspired their being written. The Shake-Speare Sonnets are a *combination* of these two meanings. Although it is not sufficient to say, *trust the dedication on face value,* one can do so, and logically one should be able to do so. Following the *macho* sonnets, 127-152, are two, softer, pivotal sonnets, 153-154. These link William Herbert to Mary Fitton whose sonnets are 1-17 and 18-126. In other words, William Herbert, when emotionally involved with the *Dark Lady* and prior to his relationship with Mary Fitton, (sonnets 138 & 144 were published in 1599), gave birth to 127-154; his affair with Mary Fitton inspired Mary to create Sonnets 1-17 imploring him to marry; and she continued with 18-126 expressing her love and emotions for him. It is not news to say that William Herbert was the love object. It is news to say that he was the object of the love of a *woman*, Mary Fitton. Shake-Speare was simply the pen name under which the book of poetry was published.

Since the first sonnets composed were William Herbert's, 127-154, they are the ones that should be the first read. The last two of these sonnets, 153-154, are

The Protagonists

almost an interact as the whole tone changes from lust and frustration to softness and love. These two sonnets are so similar in composition, it is as if the poet could not make up his mind which one to use to finish, or for some reason wanted to have twenty-eight sonnets instead of twenty-seven. It must have been a delight to William Herbert, and a great bond between them, when Mary Fitton also started to express her own strong feelings for him through the same medium of sonnets.[33]

What happened next appeared to be the seduction. This was described by Mary in her poem, *A Lover's Complaint*, although a few years may have passed before it was written. Chronologically, Sonnets 1-17 follow *A Lover's Complaint*. These cleverly throw all sorts of reasons and arguments at the adolescent William Herbert, imploring him to marry and have children. If one tries reading them wearing different people's hats one could posit that they could have been composed by one of a number of people, William's mother, his cousin Mary Sidney (Wroth), Aemelia Lanier, his sister, aunt or uncle, certainly someone with great poetic ability who knew, cared for and loved him. However common sense and certain nuances favour them to be from the pen of a young, unmarried woman – and it was unlikely to be William's younger sister, who was then only thirteen.

Mary Fitton, who loved William Herbert almost to distraction, was the author of the 108 sonnets (18-125) which form the core of the Sonnets and also Sonnet / Poem 126. It is hard to reconcile Mary not being the author of Sonnets 1-17. They are very clearly the writings of a woman pining at a distance for her lover. When Sonnets 127-154 have been switched to the front, Sonnet 126 becomes the last to have been composed; it appears to be incomplete – missing its couplet and having only twelve lines – as if to say this is the end of the story. But it is complete, that was Mary Fitton firmly saying, "here *is* the *End of the Story*." So, the chronological sequence in which the poetry should be read is:

Sonnets 127-154,
    A Lovers Complaint, [34]
        Sonnets 1-17,
            Sonnets 18-125,
                Poem 126.

By not printing the blocks of sonnets in the correct chronological order, and subsequently appending the poem, *A Lover's Complaint*, the publisher made it impossible to make overall sense of a story-line which ranks as highly as any Shakespeare play. After publication, the *Shake-Speares Sonnets* appear to have had only modest circulation but thirteen copies of the original still exist. The

---

[33] There was a tradition of sonnet writing in the Sidney family starting with Philip Sidney, then his sister Mary, followed by her son William. By composing in sonnet format, Mary Fitton demonstrated that she could compose as well as any Sidney. However, sonnet-writing was not unique to the Sidneys, it was just a family trait.

[34] *A Lover's Complaint* was written, I believe, in South Wales around 1602, but the core events described in it happened immediately after Sonnets 127-154.

The Protagonists

Sonnets were not reprinted until 1640 when a small number were excluded. Curiously this was the same year that Mary Fitton made her will.

There must have been good reasons why the book was published in 1609. The reasons may be firstly – as one can read – Mary's poetry cried out to be published for its own sake; secondly, Mary wanted the verses to survive for posterity; thirdly, publishing was a way to ensure editorial control and ownership of the intellectual property; fourthly, in 1609 William Herbert may have heard that Mary Fitton's husband was dying and, if the poetry fell into the wrong hands, it could have caused considerable damage to him and to his family.[35]

The poet Richard Barnfield's name has been mentioned five times. It also has been mentioned that Mary Fitton may have hidden or published poetry behind his name. Chapter Four discusses Barnfield in some depth. Some poetry attributed to him is said to be as good as *Shakespeare's* – and, as if having a dual personality, a lot of his poetry was not. After leaving Oxford in 1592 he appears to have produced small books of poetry in 1594, 1595, 1598 and an enlarged second printing of his 1598 works in 1605. Barnfield's 1594 book was a translation from Latin of homoerotic verse and it is improbable that Mary studied Latin which was the preserve of young men at Oxford and Cambridge. However, Barnfield's later work *was* influenced by Mary Fitton, as will be explained; how extensively I shall leave to the experts. Mary simply may have helped him, or, on the other hand, inserted whole poems. It makes no difference to the story if Mary did not publish under Barnfield's name. Whether she did or not, Mary Fitton of Gawsworth should soon take her place amongst the great English poets, and certainly the first woman.[36]

At least two people wrote the *Shake-Speare Sonnets*. Yet, time and time again I wavered, having recurring thoughts that Richard Barnfield, who was in the right place at the right time, had a hand in writing them. Indeed, it is most unlikely that he was unknown to Mary – and most likely that they knew each other very well; they could have been childhood sweethearts in Staffordshire, they were probably very good friends in London; later they could have been adult lovers in Staffordshire. Each time I had doubt I would churn over the evidence and side with Mary. I sensed that Mary's monogram was stamped on her work and then finally, in a monumental moment, I saw her, at least I saw her name, peeping out from the corner of one of her creations, as if winking at me to confirm all my convictions.

It was two years after the death of Mary Sidney Herbert, dowager[37] Countess of Pembroke, William's mother, when the *First Folio* of Shakespeare

---

[35] There are times during Mary's sonnets when one feels that the affair was still going on, even after William had married Mary Talbot. This love affair seems to have resonance in Shakespeare's *Hamlet* and *Twelfth Night,* and I look on Rosalind in *As You Like It* as having a similar character to Mary Fitton's.

[36] Mary Sidney Herbert's work was done in collaboration with others.

[37] She had then been a widow for 20 years.

The Protagonists

plays was printed. The Folio brought together all but two of the thirty-seven scripts for the plays that had been performed by a wide range of companies over thirty years.[38] It did not include Shake-Speares Sonnets.

A few words about William's mother, as I believe that the publishing of the *First Folio* only two years after her death was not coincidental. Thirty-seven years earlier, in 1586, in the space of six months, the Countess had tragically lost her father, mother and favourite brother, the famous poet, courtier, soldier and scholar, Sir Philip Sidney. All this had followed the death in 1584 of her three year old daughter, Katherine. For two years she mourned, remaining at the Pembroke family seat at Wilton. Then one day with great style and flamboyance[39] she came out of mourning and in the next few years, with the encouragement of her husband, assembled at Wilton what effectively was a college of literary[40] and musical excellence capable of producing, as Polonius half-jests in the *Hamlet, Prince of Denmark, tragedy, comedy, history, pastoral, pastoral-comical, historical-pastoral, tragical-historical, tragical-comical-historical-pastoral, scene individable, or poem unlimited.[41]* The Countess was known to be the very capable director of all this literary effort[42] but it seems that the known output falls far short of the capacity. There is something missing and that is *Drama*, drama that the Sidneys and the Herberts were known to enjoy.

Two years ago in a BBC television programme to identify the greatest Briton my first vote went automatically to William Shakespeare of Stratford-upon-Avon. The reason was that I believed Shakespeare was the supreme genius who single-handedly had given us all these fantastic plays, and through them had so richly improved the English vocabulary and our way of talking to each other. My perception has changed! Despite this, I still love and am enthralled by the Shakespeare plays. Now, however, I believe Shake-Speare is a pen name, the origin of which will be explained later, and that the Works of William Shakespeare should be interpreted in the genitive – meaning *ascribed-to* or *owned-by*. The W, as in William, probably derives from the emblem of the Sidney family. The emblem is known as a *pheon* [PLATE 3] which is a vertical arrowhead or spearhead like a letter V with a vertical line through the middle making it look somewhat like W. The Sidney arrowhead was retained as an emblem[43] after their marriages by both William's mother, Mary Sidney Herbert, and later his cousin, Mary Sidney Wroth, both of whom produced literary works. Recalling that publishing was considered vulgar, if

---

[38] It begs the question of who could have identified the plays and also obtained all the scripts some of which had not been published.

[39] A huge procession left Wilton to take up residence at Baynards Castle, the home the Pembrokes kept and used in London. It was on the Thames in the area of Blackfriars.

[40] The Countess was patron to, at one time or another, Edmund Spencer 1552-99, Samuel Daniel 1562-1619, Nicholas Breton 1555-1625, Thomas Moffat; Thomas Nashe 1567-1601, Gabriel Harvey 1555-1631; John Donne 1572-1631, Ben Jonson 1572-1637, and others.

[41] *Hamlet* 2.2.

[42] Margaret P Hannay - *Philip's Phoenix*.

[43] Known in heraldry as a *charge*.

The Protagonists

the Countess was the driving force,[44] and I believe she was, it appears that all the artists involved respected a code of silence, whether out of loyalty or in their own self interest – they had much to lose and little to gain from losing their reputation, their patrons and their livelihood. Publishing historical plays also had a political edge and carried added risk. I deleted the following paragraph, and later reinstated it to illustrate that two great playwrights died in strange circumstances during that period.

There is still great controversy about the death in 1593 of the brilliant playwright, Christopher Marlowe.[45] This followed his (false) betrayal under torture by another playwright, Thomas Kyd.[46] Marlowe, like Kyd, had been accused of promoting atheism. A warrant had been issued for his arrest and, if caught, he would certainly have been tortured and hanged. A week after the warrant was issued, Marlowe was either stabbed to death at a house in Deptford or he escaped England, and another cadaver was put in his place – probably that of his Cambridge colleague, John Penry. Penry had been hanged two days earlier, just a few miles away, for printing satirical documents called the Mar-prelate Tracts that had attacked the hierarchy of the established Protestant Church. Had Marlowe been tortured, who knows what secrets he would have spilled or invented about the Wilton college. Aside from his own play-writing he had a connection to the Herberts and Sidneys through his patron, Thomas Walsingham whose cousin was Frances Walsingham, Mary Sidney Herbert's sister-in-law.[47] In the last hundred years documents have been discovered that disprove the story that he was killed in a brawl in a tavern, and the circumstances of the events would indicate either a state assassination or a plot that allowed him to escape.

Without question, reading Sonnets 127-154 first works. It was then tempting to try to re-order the other sonnets to improve sense but I resisted. Since the plays of the First Folio *were* corrected before going to print one would expect the Sonnets to be edited in the same way. However, I concur with analysts who have concluded that, because they contained so many mistakes, they were not emended. There may be a good reason for this. I believe that the lines contain many cryptic clues and riddles and the person who had them published knew that to change a letter or a word might destroy hidden meaning; Sonnet 66 reads just like a crossword. As they stand, therefore, they appear to have their original integrity although the compositors of the printed pages may have corrected some spelling. The numeracy identified with the Sonnets should be

---

[44] In places the Shakespeare plays are so sexually explicit and vulgar that it is easy to understand why neither nobility nor a woman would append his or her name as author.

[45] His works include the plays Tamburlaine, Dr. Faustus, the Jew of Malta, and Edward II, and an unfinished poem, Hero and Leander.

[46] Kyd never recovered from the torture and died the following year.

[47] I give little credence to the story that a fifteen year old Christopher Marlowe impregnated Mary Sidney Herbert at Canterbury in 1579; nor that Marlowe returned to England and was hidden at Wilton. When in 1592 Marlowe was sent back a prisoner to England by Countess Pembroke's brother, Robert Sidney, Governor of Flushing in Holland, Robert states that Marlowe, a scholar, claimed he is known to the Earl of Northumberland and to Lord Strange.

The Protagonists

respected – it is as if Mary Fitton said to herself, *this is Sonnet number 60 in the copy book, I'll use the number of minutes in an hour as a motif*. It is clear that some poets put mathematical store into their work. Numbers were important in those days – but it is always easy to see numerical relationships where none were intended.

For a better understanding of the Elizabethan text I recommend the paperback *The Arden Shakespeare – Sonnets* edited by Katherine Duncan-Jones; she has an academic brilliance I would, but never could, aspire to. Invaluable reading has been Margaret P. Hannay's book, *Philip's Phoenix, Mary Sidney, Countess of Pembroke* in which I sense she senses that many other original manuscripts went through the Countess's hands.[48] Here are some of the players;

Queen Elizabeth I 1533-1603
Monarch from 1558, (The Reindeer)

Sir William Knollys, 1547- 532
Member of the Privy Council
(The Clown, parodied in Shakespeare's *Twelfth Night* as Malvolio)
In 1595, Comptroller of the Queen's Household, later Lord Banbury
He was supposed to look after Mary Fitton but fell in love with her.

Mary Sidney Herbert, Countess Pembroke
1561-1621 mother of William (below) and a great patron of the arts
Her father was Lord President of Wales and Lord Deputy of Ireland
Her uncle was Robert Dudley, First Earl of Leicester.

Sir Richard Leveson – Vice Admiral
Licensed pirate, and Privy Councillor, 1569-August 1605.
Leveson and Mary Fitton, who a common great-grandfather.
were lovers and had two children, William and Anne.
He was born and buried in Staffordshire.

The musician and poet, Aemelia Bassano Lanier 1569-1645
A feminist in her mature years, born and buried in London;
from 1592-1596 the mistress of Henry Carey,
Lord Hunsden, the Lord Chamberlain until he died.
William Herbert was infatuated with her.

Richard Barnfield, Oxford graduate, translator and writer of poetry
Probably a friend of Mary Fitton and Richard Leveson
1574-1627; born and buried in Staffordshire

---

[48] I read Philip's Phoenix specifically for new information that would prove me *wrong*. All I found was a superb and wonderfully researched book which has helped explain some small detail, for instance in October 1600 William mother's secretary reported, *"My Lord Harbert is practising at Greenwich . . . He leapes, he daunces, he singes . . . he makes his horse runne with more speede . . ."*

The Protagonists

Mary Fitton (The White Doe) 24/6/1578– 19/9/1641
daughter of Sir Edward Fitton, Deputy President of Ireland
Born in Ireland or London, her baptism [49] is registered at Gawsworth,
Cheshire, She fell in love with William Herbert and suffered the scandal.
Once an exuberant young lady, she died aged 63 at
Tettenhall in Staffordshire and her burial was registered there.
Her will asked that she should be buried at Gawsworth.
There is no evidence that this happened.

William Herbert, 3rd. Earl Pembroke, 8/4/1580 – 10/4/1630
Lord Chamberlain; founder of Pembroke College, Oxford;
Helped finance the development of Virginia and Newfoundland
was born in London and buried in Salisbury Cathedral alongside his parents.
The first Folio of Shakespeare plays is dedicated to him and his brother.
He was once a vain and precocious adolescent.

Mary Sidney Wroth, 1586-1652.
Daughter of Robert Sidney, 2nd Earl of Leicester.
In 1621 she published a massive allegory of contemporary court life in which
Mary Fitton is depicted as *Antissia,*[50] William Herbert as *Amphilanthus.*
She always loved William Herbert, her first cousin,
lived with him while he was still married
and bore him two children.

In a contemporary court lampoon[51]

The Reindeer was embossed,[52]
The White Doe[53] *she was lost,*
Pembroke struck her down,
And took her from the Clown.

Research is never exhaustive but as my research discovered new, hard
facts they each fitted into the jigsaw without effort. I have never had to
disregard, bury or eliminate a fact that was uncomfortable or did not fit. There
has been no explanation from which I have shied away. When one meets the
truth, or is close to seeing the full picture, the pieces of the jigsaw easily fit on
each other; Cinderella's slipper after all the twisting, turning and contortions
comfortably fits to a tee. I do promise that I have tried my very best to prove
myself wrong; being right is an awesome responsibility. I do expect at best a

---

[49] The record of her baptism is interpolated into the register at Gawsworth Church. [Raymond
Richards - *The Manor of Gawsworth, Cheshire*]. The date will be correct but her birth may have
been either in Dublin or London. The Register entry for 1578 reads:
   Mary Fitton, daughter of Edward Fitton Esquire was christned June 24th.
[50] It has been suggested that *Antissia* (Mary Fitton) suffered from post-traumatic stress.
[51] C C Stopes - *Life of Henry, 3rd. Earl of Southampton.*
[52] Foaming with anger
[53] Or White Hind

The Protagonists

modicum of antagonism. I leave open to others the opportunity to help consolidate the facts here uncovered.

On reading the Sonnets one realises that there was an understanding between the two lovers to hide their names and identities; four hundred years is a reasonable measure of their success. However much a rogue William appeared, I dispassionately believe that he loved Mary Fitton for many years and liken the situation to the ambivalence portrayed between the characters Ophelia and Hamlet where one never can tell whether Hamlet loved Ophelia.

So many people have been so close to the truth. To some, who have been researching the early poetry of female writers, I owe a debt; I really am grateful. Without their research I would never have got to the corner of the right street. We all seem to have been there at one time or another. I just happened to see a much misread sign that made me turn that last corner into the winding alley of Time. What I find hard to believe is that nobody has suggested that the Sonnets were written by a woman; then again, perhaps someone did and, in what used to be a male dominated, academic world, got laughed out of court. One thing they are not – they are not homoerotic literature, even if they can be read that way.

My skin creeps when I think that nearly twenty years ago I enjoyed watching *Twelfth Night* in the open air theatre at Gawsworth Hall, Mary Fitton's childhood home [PLATE 8]. The play was set against the backcloth of the picturesque, timbered, Elizabethan manor house, but I only remember it was Twelfth Night because, during what was supposed to be a humorous scene between Olivia and Viola, a black cat walked across the lawn behind them, turned his back on the audience, squatted and defecated in a flower bed. The two actors enthused by the laughter little realised that it was for the cat's delivery, not theirs. That evening at Gawsworth were the very ghosts of Sir William Knollys (Malvolio in his cross-gartered, yellow stockings), Margaret Radcliffe (Viola), Mary Fitton (Olivia), and by extension, as I will explain later, Ophelia in *Hamlet*, the Jailor's Daughter in *Two Nobel Kinsmen* and the most magnificent Rosalind in *As You Like It*.

Mary Fitton's poem, *A Lover's Complaint*, is printed in full at Appendix 1. It was published in 1609 in the same book as the Shake-Speare Sonnets. The 329-line poem has forty-seven seven-line stanzas and relates the story of a courtship between a woman and a younger male whose;

Small show of man was yet upon his chin;
His phoenix down began but to appear
Like unshorn velvet on that termless skin [54]

---

[54] Stanza 14. Knowing that he was the most eligible bachelor at Court, William Herbert knew that unmarried women would throw themselves at him and that some married women would also like to have enjoyed his charms.

The Protagonists

Here is a brief summary of the poem:

An unseen commentator watches an old man approach an unhappy younger woman. He sees that the woman is beginning to lose her good looks and he witnesses her destroying reminders, letters and trinkets, mementoes of a love affair, taking them out of a basket and throwing them into a stream. The old man sits near her and asks if she would like to tell him what is the matter. She relates that she had allowed herself to be seduced by a young man of handsome looks, well brought up, well dressed and a very competent horseman. Many women sought him out, but she had fallen for him even though he had told her that he was promiscuous. However, she would not give herself up to him and he started to court her. He denied ever having loved another woman; the many gifts women had given him meant nothing and he offered them all to her. He even told of a nun that had yielded herself up to him. At last he admits that the woman has defeated him and that he has fallen in love with her; there is a great outpouring of tears and he promises to marry her. She was seduced, then with his back-word on marriage, she realises what really has happened, and that this has been the cause of her sadness over all the years. In the end, however, she admits she would still succumb to a man of such charms as this is the very nature of women. In stanza 12 she tells of; *A youthful suit; it was to gain my grace; Of one by nature's outwards so commended, That maidens' eyes stuck over all his face.* The object of this *youthful suit* was William Herbert.

CHAPTER THREE is dedicated to the famous *Dark Lady of the Sonnets*, probably Aemelia Bassano Lanier who was a very interesting and capable lady.

An outline biography by Kari Boyd McBride is given at Appendix 3. In addition, however, I gently draw your attention to Robert Greene's *Groats-Worth of Wit* posthumously published in 1592. *Groats-Worth of Wit* is a story of two brothers. The elder one seeks retribution after their father left his fortune to the younger, naive son. The worldly wise son takes his brother to a courtesan who is beautiful, sings sweetly, plays the lute, is cultured, lives in a good suburb and is named Lamilia. She fleeces the younger brother of the family fortune so both brothers are the losers.

The short work can be downloaded from the Internet. Interestingly it also contains what is thought to be the first written reference to Shakespeare, *"Yes, trust them not: for there is an upstart crow, beautified with our feathers ..... supposes he is well able to bombast out a blank verse as the best of you: and being an absolute Johannes fac totum, is in his own conceit the only Shake-scene in a countrey."*

It is clear from the context that the author was talking about an actor, not an author, and there must have been a number of actors who could shake the scenery with their bombasts; but is Lamilia a reference to Aemelia Bassano at

The Protagonists

the age of twenty-three just before she became the mistress of the sexagenarian Lord Hunsden, conceived his child and was forced to marry her cousin? A few years later Simon Forman, Aemelia's astrologer and gynaecologist, would have us believe she indeed *was* a woman of easy virtue; but then both Robert Greene and Simon Forman had the most wicked and scurrilous natures.

CHAPTER FOUR examines the works of Richard Barnfield. CHAPTER FIVE gives background to Mary Fitton, extracted from a nineteenth century book in which she and her sister Anne Newdigate are the subjects. The text contains many golden nuggets of historical fact. The sections are numbered for cross reference. I do not subscribe to all of the editor's interpretations.

CHAPTER SIX presents the opening seventeen sonnets, almost certainly written by Mary Fitton.

CHAPTER SEVEN shows connections between the Sonnets and the two plays, *Hamlet* and *Two Noble Kinsmen*.

CHAPTER EIGHT contains Mary Fitton's Sonnets 18-126. There are a also number of allusions to the play *As You Like It*. CHAPTER NINE summarises.

It would have been very much smoother for me to write this story as a blockbuster novel, but I don't have that particular ability. Even if I did, to do so would have required me to conjure up or invent some new folklore in order to fill in gaps of knowledge and time. To do this would have been quite inappropriate when the very object has been to strip away the old paint and find out what is underneath. It would also have taken at least another couple of precious years, before then having to find an agent who was totally committed to accepting the work, and a publisher to publish and sell it. So, please excuse my style and my impatience to share with you the pathos, the passions, and these discoveries.

Finally, I have discovered a huge number of *small* bits of evidence that support what I am putting forward which I have *not* included – for three reasons. Firstly, they would clutter the text and you might think I am trying to make an impression by simply throwing everything at you. Secondly, I am leaving them to be rediscovered, helping consolidate the findings in other people's minds and promote new research into how the Shakespeare plays evolved. Thirdly, this book and its passions will speak for itself.

As I discovered what had been happening, real-life of four hundred years ago turned into a drama, almost like a modern soap. There is so much we will never know about Mary Fitton, but we do know she outlived at least two lovers and two husbands, and it is thought she tried to have one killed.

Do, please, enjoy it.

CHAPTER THREE

THE DARK LADY SONNETS, 127-154

Sonnets 127-154 provide us with the thoughts and passions of a young man infatuated and believing himself in love with, and lusting after an older woman. The woman has been given the title, *The Dark Lady of the Sonnets,* the name coming from the first four lines of Sonnet 127.

> In the old age black was not counted fair,
> Or if it were, it bore not beauty's name;
> But now is black beauty's successive heir,
> And beauty slandered with a bastard shame

This theme of darkness repeats occasionally during the twenty-eight sonnets, her black eyes, her being in mourning, her bad character and his dark or foul moods. Finally, in Sonnets 153-154, we find the man seems to come to terms with the futility, recording that his attention had been drawn to a *Maid of Dian,* whom he calls *Mistress.* This indication that the woman was a Maid of Honour of Queen Elizabeth is resonated when history confirms the affair between William Herbert, Mr. W. H., and the Maid of Honour, Mistress Mary Fitton. We now have a link in a chain, the two Sonnets, 153-154, connect the *Dark Lady,* on one end, with the Maid of Honour (Mary Fitton), on the other.

On one end of the link, William Herbert gave birth to (begot) Sonnets 127-154 and, on the other end, he was the begetter, here meaning inspirer, of Sonnets 1-126. His actions also gave rise to, that is begot, through Mary Fitton, the poem *A Lover's Complaint.* In today's world of political spin one could say that William Herbert was the *only* begetter and mean something else but there is no reason to mistrust the Dedication, *TO THE ONLY BEGETTER OF THESE ENSUING SONNETS, M^R. W. H.;* it would be crass to suggest it was a lie. Sonnet 77 goes on to tell us that there were empty pages left in the copybook in which Mary Fitton was writing *her* Sonnets, 1–126. One could imagine William Herbert filling in some of those empty pages with his own *Dark Lady* sonnets, before the book was passed on to the printers.

I have not been able to link the *Dark Lady* with Aemelia (Bassano) Lanier although *her* candidature, by others, as the *Dark Lady of the Sonnets* is the most compelling. Aemelia Lanier was Mediterranean-looking, married, played the virginal,[55] was not shy of men or noblemen, and was close to the Court where she entertained the Queen and the courtiers. She was cultured, and years later demonstrated literary ability with some excellent poetry. All these elements fit Aemelia's being the *Dark Lady* – although there were other candidates, from courtiers to alehouse-keepers to prostitutes, and as many theories, including Oscar Wilde's and George Bernard Shaw's, all of which

---

[55] An early piano that looks like a small writing desk.. See Sonnet 128.

break down under analysis.[56] One interesting and uncanny fact is that amongst the very first English women to have their poetry or works published and acclaimed, and almost certainly the most significant, were Mary Sidney Herbert – William Herbert's mother; Mary Fitton (under the pen name of Shake-Speare) – William's lover; Aemelia Lanier – whom it appears William lusted over; and Mary Sidney Wroth – the first cousin of the adulterous William, who loved and at times lived with him in London, from 1615 to his death in 1630.

Aemelia Bassano was born in 1569 of an Italian-French background. Her father was a court musician and she played the virginal.[57] In the Sonnets the lady had dark skin when the fashion at court was paleness. She had been the mistress of Henry Carey, Lord Hunsden, 45 years her senior and Lord Chamberlain but, when she conceived his child in 1592, it was arranged that she marry Alphonse Lanier, her cousin. The child was christened Henry Lanier and he, in turn, became a Court musician. Lord Hunsden died in July 1596 when Aemelia was 26 leaving her with an annual pension of £40. Both the Bassano and the Lanier families were musicians and years later a Nicholas Lanier set some of William Herbert's verses to music.

Simon Forman[58] was not only an astrologer to the London gentry but also a man of medicine who dealt with gynaecological matters. He knew who was sleeping with whom. Aemelia Lanier first consulted him in 1597. Forman found Aemelia seductively attractive but she refused his overtures and would not halek[59] with him. According to the Sonnets, she was not a beauty but was very sexy and had a seductive voice. Simon Forman tells of her having a mole in the hollow of her throat. She admitted to Forman that she had been "brave" in her younger days but her consultation with him was only to find out whether the stars and the dice predicted financial success for her husband's military activities. Her husband then was serving as a gentleman volunteer in the *Essex Islands Voyage*[60] in what proved an unsuccessful attempt to improve his fortune. Forman also wrote of a mysterious gentleman who consulted him as to whether the time was auspicious to visit Aemelia Lanier and leads us to understand that she did, in fact, receive this gentleman.[61] The last record of her

---

[56] The historian A. L. Rowse examined the many theories and concluded that the *Dark Lady* was Aemelia Lanier in *Simon Forman, Sex and Society in Shakespeare's Age*.

[57] Abstracts about Aemelia Lanier from a biography by Kari Boyd McBride.

[58] A. L. Rowse; *Simon Forman, Sex and Society in Shakespeare's Age*, 1974. Simon Forman's notes and his diary still exist so his clientele is known.

[59] A word Forman created meaning to *copulate* or *copulation*. One gets the impression that some of Forman's female clients, attractive or not, could have the fee waived if they chose to accommodate him.

[60] State-sanctioned piracy against the Spanish, the privateers being given a percentage of the booty by the Crown. This expedition to the Spanish islands was led by the Earl of Essex. Previously, on 28th March 1595 Lady Margaret Hawkins, wife of Admiral Sir John Hawkins, asked Forman to visit her on what proved to be the eve of her husband's last expedition.

[61] This is not meant to imply the gentleman was William Herbert as A. L. Rowse may have wanted his reader to think. The fact is that Aemelia Lanier, a married woman, was receiving a gentleman during her husband's absence.

The Dark Lady Sonnets, 127-154

in Forman's diary was on 7th January 1600 when Forman writes that he wants to know, *Why Mrs Lanier sent for me today; what will follow, and whether she intendeth any more villainy.*

The character Rosaline in the play *Love's Labour's Lost* is imbued with the same darkness of complexion as the *Dark Lady of the Sonnets.* Some people, therefore, assume them to be one and the same, and that William Shakespeare was enjoying Aemelia Lanier as his mistress in 1594-5 when she already was Lord Hunsden's mistress. I don't think so. Lord Hunsden was then Lord Chamberlain and his players were the Chamberlain's Men in which William Shakespeare of Stratford was an actor and shareholder. Was the actor's libido so out of control that he would risk having an affair with the mistress of the most powerful person in the theatrical world? I think not! An interpretation is that around 1595 Aemelia Lanier was probably written into *Loves Labours Lost* to please Lord Hunsden, and five years later it was William Herbert who went weak at the knees over her.

William Herbert, born just before midnight on 8th April 1580, was given the courtesy title, Lord Herbert of Cardiff, at birth. He was eleven years younger than Aemelia Lanier. After private education under tutors at Wilton he was sent to Oxford at the age of twelve. He first appeared at Court, albeit briefly, at the age of fifteen, the same year as Mary Fitton, and returned again aged seventeen. Herbert and Fitton were such high-profile characters that it is almost certain that they knew each other from that time, if not before, and there are indications that the number seventeen is significant to their subsequent relationship. However, 1597 may have been premature for the puppy love of an over-sexed, precocious, seventeen-year-old youth for a twenty-eight-year-old, married mother. 1599 seems a better year for the passion – by then William had had time to write more poetry, make more conquests and believe himself more skilled in the language of seduction – as Mary Fitton attests in *A Lover's Complaint,* (Appendix-1, Stanza 30), where we read of the young man's *deep-brained sonnets.*

The writer of the *Dark Lady* sonnets was so intense that he hardly found time for any contemporary reference. In fact, the word *time* is totally absent making them very distinct from Sonnets 1-126 where *time* alone appears fifty-three times.[62] Here, and in the present, the poet, often in a frenzy,[63] is describing his experiences, emotions and thoughts; whether for private ingestion, or to share with his lover, or his friends – we do not know – although two *Dark Lady* sonnets were published in 1599 in the *Passionate Pilgrim.* William Herbert was caught in this emotional situation with this married woman to the point he admits he completely deluded himself.

During 1598 Aemelia Lanier was pregnant with a daughter, Odillya, born in the December but who survived only ten months. From Sonnet 153 one would be led to understand that the *Dark Lady* sonnets were written (by William

---

[62] Time; times; hour; hours; minutes; days; years appears ninety-seven in Sonnets 1-126 and only three times in Sonnets 127-154.
[63] An element of onanism being interpreted by commentators.

The Dark Lady Sonnets, 127-154

Herbert) just before he was involved with Mary Fitton (in 1600). We know that Sonnets 138 & 144 were published in 1599-1600,[64] although modified for the 1609 printing. Therefore, on this evidence, the broadest time-window for the writing of the *Dark Lady Sonnets* is between 1595, when William Herbert was first presented at Court, and late 1599 into early 1600 when *The Passionate Pilgrim* was published. Common-sense would point to the second half of 1599 after Odillya had died. That November, on the 11th, the Court mourned the tragic death of the Queen's favourite Maid of Honour, Margaret Radcliffe, so these two deaths could link up with Sonnet 132. The timing of Aemelia Lanier's last visit to Foreman on 7th January 1600 raises an unanswerable question – was the *villainy* at all connected with William Herbert?

In 1611, Aemelia Lanier published the first feminist, semi-religious English text and poetry called *Salve Devs Rex Ivdaeorum, (Praise God, the King of the Jews)*, at times repenting her early years. Just before reading the *Dark Lady Sonnets*, here is an abstract from *Salve Deus Rex Judaeorum* where Aemelia Lanier praises William's mother in a poem entitled – *The Authors Dreame to the Ladie Marie, the Countesse Dowager of Pembrooke*. Aemelia appears to have been arriving at a Pembroke home in the countryside,[65] possibly Wilton:

> ME Thought I pass'd through th'Edalyan Groues,
> And askt the Graces, if they could direct
> Me to a Lady whom Minerva chose,
> With her in height of all respect.
> Yet looking back into my thoughts again,
> The eie of Reason did behold her there
> Fast ti'd unto them in a golden Chain,
> They stood, but she was set in Honors chair.
> And nine faire Virgins sate vpon the ground,
> With Harps and Vialls in their lilly hands;
> Whose harmony had all my sences drown'd,
> But that before mine eyes an object stands,
> Whose Beauty shin'd like Titons cleerest raies,
> She blew a brasen Trumpet, which did sound
> Throgh al the world that worthy Ladies praise,
> And by Eternal Fame I saw her crown'd.
> Yet studying, if I were awake, or no,
> God Morphy came and took me by the hand,
> And wil'd me not from Slumbers bowre to go,
> Til I the sum of all did understand.
> When presently the Welkin[66] that before
> Look'd bright and cleere, me thought, was ouercast,
> And duskie clouds, with boyst'rous winds great store,
> Foretold of violent storms which could not last,

---

[64] The calendar year then ended on 24th. March.
[65] Baynards Castle, the Pembroke London Home, was a medieval castle beside the Thames.
[66] Welkin - celestial sphere - she quotes from the Fairie Queene by Edmund Spenser.

The Dark Lady Sonnets, 127-154

And gazing up into the troubled skie,
Me thought Chariot did from thence descend,
Where one did sit repleat with Majestie,
Drawn by four fierie Dragons, which did bend
Their course where this most noble Lady sate,
Whom all these virgins with due reverence
Did entertain, according to that state
Which did belong unto her Excellence.

A dozen years after Aemelia's alleged brief affair, if it even was an affair, with William Herbert there was nothing but deep respect for his mother. Any relationship between William and Aemelia appears to have been very short-lived, a month perhaps, and I believe it was no more than a mild flirtation. It may only have existed in William Herbert's mind, Aemelia not even knowing about it. From Sonnet 142 we can read that he thought the woman a flirt as she is constantly making eye-contact with other men.

Be it lawful I love thee as thou lov'st those
Whom thine eyes woo as mine importune thee.

What has been a pleasant surprise was discovering that the Sonnets contain what look like plays on words, riddles, double entendres and cryptic clues, precursors to the art of crosswords. Take Aemelia's first line (above),

ME Thought I pass'd through th'Edalyan Groues,

there is a mal adroitness – it could simply read, *Methought* or *I thought*. So look again, I hope you can see a signature, *M-E-lya*.

I briefly had to consider whether Aemelia had written all the remaining Sonnets. One can see she certainly had the ability but I would question whether she had the wildness of spirit; but it is clear that there were two women, one married (Aemelia Lanier) and the other a virgin (so Mary Fitton protests in *A Lover's Complaint*). For the avoidance of doubt I believe that William Herbert was Mary Fitton's first lover on the night of 16th June 1600.[67]

I also considered the possibility that the *Dark Lady* was Mary Sidney Wroth, William Herbert's first cousin. In Ben Jonson's 1606 *Masque of Blackness* Mary Wroth had performed with the James' Queen, Lady Anne, William Herbert's sister, and other ladies of the Court, all made up as Negresses. Mary Wroth had both the genius and capability to have written the Sonnets. Her history, however, made an awkward fit as she did not suffer exile from the Court, although she did lead a separate lifestyle to that of her husband. William, it seems, had a predilection with the name Mary. His wife whom he married in November 1604, six weeks after his cousin Mary Sidney married Sir Robert Wroth, was Mary Talbot. William part financed his cousin's dowry and Sir Robert never knew that the first £200 he received was a wedding gift *to the bride* from the officers of the army in Holland, commanded by his father-in-law, Robert Sidney. William's £1,000 (of £3,000) was not

---

[67] The date is explained in Chapter Five.

forthcoming until he himself had married.[68] In 1621, in her allegorical *Duchess of Montgomery's Urania,* Mary Wroth tells the story, amongst many others, of Pembroke (*Amphilanthus*) and Fitton (*Antissia*). By then Mary Wroth had been living with Pembroke for six years with their two children and she would have known the Mary Fitton story as William chose to tell it.

Enough! It is time for the first of Shake-Speare's Sonnets! At the head of each is written a line of explanation or continuity.

Sonnets 127-154

127 William Herbert admires her made-up face – beauty being in the eye of the beholder.

> In the old age black was not counted fair,
> Or if it were, it bore not beauty's name;
> But now is black beauty's successive heir,
> And Beauty slandered with a bastard shame;[69]
> For since each hand hath put on Nature's power,
> Fairing the foul with Art's false borrowed face,
> Sweet beauty hath no name, no holy bower,
> But is profaned, if not lives in disgrace.
> Therefore my mistress' eyes are raven black,
> Her eyes so suited, and they mourners seem
> At such who, not born fair, no beauty lack,
> Sland'ring creation with a false esteem.
> Yet so they mourn, becoming of their woe,
> That every tongue says beauty should look so.

128 He admires her music playing.

> How oft, when thou, my music, music play'st
> Upon that blessed wood whose motion sounds
> With thy sweet fingers when thou gently sway'st,
> The wiry concord that mine ear confounds,
> Do I envy those jacks[70] that nimble leap
> To kiss the tender inward of thy hand,
> Whilst my poor lips, which should that harvest reap,
> At the wood's boldness by thee blushing stand.
> To be so tickled they would change their state
> And situation with those dancing chips,
> O'er whom thy fingers walk with gentle gait,
> Making dead wood more blest than living lips.
> Since saucy jacks so happy are in this,
> Give them thy fingers, me thy lips, to kiss.

---

[68] A factor of 250 would indicate current values.

[69] Henry Carey's, the Lord Chamberlain's, bastard child?

[70] Keys of a musical instrument.

129 He muses about lust and its power and fascination for men

Th' expense of spirit in a waste[71] of shame
Is lust in action; and, till action, lust
Is perjured, murdrous bloody, full of blame,
Savage, extreme, rude, cruel, not to trust,
Enjoyed no sooner but despised straight,
Past reason hunted, and, no sooner had
Past reason hated, as a swallowed bait,
On purpose laid to make the taker mad;
Mad in pursuit, and in possession so,
Had, having, and in quest to have, extreme;
A bliss in proof and proved a[72] very woe;
Before, a joy proposed; behind, a dream.
All this the world well knows, yet none knows well,
To shun the heaven that leads men to this hell.

130 but he admits to her failings and his being besotted.

My mistress' eyes are nothing like the sun;
Coral is far more red than her lips red;
If snow be white, why then her breasts are dun;
If hairs be wires, black wires grow on her head.
I have seen roses damasked, red and white,
But no such roses see I in her cheeks;
And in some perfumes is there more delight
Than in the breath that from my mistress reeks.
I love to hear her speak, yet well I know
That music hath a far more pleasing sound.
I grant I never saw a goddess go,
My mistress when she walks treads on the ground.
And yet, by heaven, I think my love as rare
As any she belied with false compare.

131 He lusts after her although she is not a beauty.

Thou art as tyrannous, so as thou art,
As those whose beauties proudly make them cruel;
For well thou know'st to my dear doting heart
Thou art the fairest and most precious jewel.
Yet, in good faith, some say that thee behold
Thy face hath not the power to make love groan.
To say they err I dare not be so bold,
Although I swear it to my self alone;
And to be sure that is not false I swear,
A thousand groans, but thinking on thy face,

---

[71] waste = waist, alluding to her body.
[72] At times the original text known as Quarto (Q) is used; here a = and

The Dark Lady Sonnets, 127-154

One on another's neck do witness bear
Thy black is fairest in my judgment's place.
In nothing art thou black save in thy deeds,
And thence this slander, as I think, proceeds.

132 He admires her during a period of mourning

Thine eyes I love, and they as pitying me,
Knowing thy heart torment me with disdain,
Have put on black, and loving mourners be,
Looking with pretty ruth [73]upon my pain;
And truly not the morning sun of heaven
Better becomes the grey cheeks of the east,
Nor that full star that ushers in the even
Doth half that glory to the sober west,
As those two mourning eyes become thy face.
O, let it then as well beseem thy heart
To mourn for me since mourning doth thee grace,
And suit thy pity like in every part.
Then will I swear beauty her self is black,
And all they foul that thy complexion lack.

133 – 134 then finds she has taken a friend of his, who was supposed to speak to her on his behalf, to her bed.

Beshrew that heart that makes my heart to groan
For that deep wound it gives my friend [74] [75] and me!
Is't not enough to torture me alone,
But slave to slavery my sweet'st friend must be?
Me from my self thy cruel eye hath taken,
And my next self thou harder hast engrossed.
Of him, my self, and thee, I am forsaken,
A torment thrice threefold thus to be crossed.
Prison my heart in thy steel bosom's ward,
But then my friend's heart let my poor heart bail;
Who e'er keeps me, let my heart be his guard;
Thou canst not then use rigour in my jail.

[73] Ruth = Pity. The Court was in mourning for the burial on 10th November 1599 of Margaret Radcliffe, the Queen's favourite Maid of Honour. If the theme of mourning here reflects this event, it almost pinpoints the dates of the composition of the *Dark Lady* Sonnets.

[74] It makes interesting reading if his friend is his penis who has a mind of his own.

[75] Arthur Marlowe's *Shakespeare - Digging for the Truth,* part 3, identifies that when Francis Fitton (Mary Fitton's great-uncle) died in 1608 he left in his will, *certain writings and books meant for no-one else's eyes but my dear friend William Herbert, son of Sir Edward Herbert, deceased. William Herbert now Knight.* This William Herbert, born 1573, had married Francis Fitton's stepdaughter, Lady Eleanor Percy, before 1600. Marlowe presents him as a candidate for Mr.W.H. because of this Fitton connection. Indeed, in this sonnet he could have been the *friend* of the Pembroke W.H., but it was the Pembroke W.H. who impregnated Mary Fitton. Francis Fitton's writings and books could have been either religious or pornographic.

And yet thou wilt; for I, being pent in thee,
Perforce am thine, and all that is in me.

134

So, now I have confessed that he is thine,
And I my self am mortgaged to thy will,
My self I'll forfeit, so that other mine
Thou wilt restore to be my comfort still.
But thou wilt not, nor he will not be free,
For thou art covetous, and he is kind.
He learned but surety-like to write for me
Under that bond that made him as fast doth bind.
The statute of thy beauty thou wilt take,
Thou usurer that putt'st forth all to use,
And sue a friend came debtor for my sake;
So him I lose through my unkind abuse.
Him have I lost; thou hast both him and me;
He pays the whole,[76] and yet I am not free.

135 – 136 Has she had her way with him and he with her?

Whoever hath her wish, thou hast thy *Will*,
And *Will* to boot, and *Will* in overplus;[77]
More than enough am I that vex thee still,
To thy sweet will making addition thus.
Wilt thou, whose will is large and spacious,
Not once vouchsafe to hide my will in thine?[78]
Shall will in others seem right gracious,
And in my will no fair acceptance shine?
The sea, all water, yet receives rain still,
And in abundance addeth to his store;
So thou, being rich in *Will*, add to thy *Will*
One will of mine to make thy large Will more.
Let no unkind no fair beseechers kill,
Think all but one, and me in that one *Will*.

136

If thy soul check thee that I come so near,
Swear to thy blind soul that I was thy *Will*,
And will, thy soul knows, is admitted there;
Thus far for love my love-suit, sweet, fulfil.
Will will fulfil the treasure of thy love,
Ay, fill it full with wills, and my will one.
In things of great receipt with ease we prove

---

[76] Hole / *whole*. His friend pays for her and so does he.

[77] This sonnet is the object of many different interpretations, for instance, was she servicing three Williams? Another that her will is her sexual organ, to boot - his friend her slave, and the author who is over-sexed. Clearly, he was not writing about a virgin.

[78] A sexual act; *will* can mean either a male or female sexual organ.

Among a number one is reckoned none[79].
Then in the number let me pass untold,
Though in thy store's account I one must be;
For nothing hold me, so it please thee hold
That nothing me, a something sweet to thee.
Make but my name thy love, and love that still,
And then thou lov'st me for my name is *Will*.

137 He is angry with himself for what has happened;

Thou blind fool Love, what dost thou to mine eyes
That they behold and see not what they see?
They know what beauty is, see where it lies,
Yet what the best is take the worst to be.
If eyes, corrupt by over-partial looks,
Be anchored in the bay where all men ride,
Why of eyes' falsehood hast thou forged hooks
Whereto the judgment of my heart is tied?
Why should my heart think that a several plot,
Which my heart knows the wide world's common place?
Or mine eyes seeing this, say this is not
To put fair truth upon so foul a face?
In things right true my heart and eyes have erred,
And to this false plague[80] are they now transferred.

138 – 139 admitting he deludes himself in his infatuation.[81]

When my love swears that she is made of truth
I do believe her, though I know she lies,
That she might think me some untutored youth
Unlearned in the world's false subtleties.
Thus vainly thinking that she thinks me young,
Although she knows my days are past the best,
Simply I credit her false-speaking tongue;
On both sides thus is simple truth suppressed.
But wherefore says she not she is unjust?
And wherefore say not I that I am old?
O, love's best habit is in seeming trust,
And age in love loves not to have years told.
Therefore I lie with her, and she with me,
And in our faults by lies we flattered be.

139

O call not me to justify the wrong
That thy unkindness lays upon my heart;

---

[79] "I don't count if I am just one of a stream of men with whom you have coupled."
[80] Plague = mistress
[81] Another version of Sonnet 138 appears in *The Passionate Pilgrim* (1599). As well as a number of other changes, at line-6 *days* has replaced *years* in the original.

Wound me not with thine eye, but with thy tongue,
Use power with power, and slay me not by art;
Tell me thou lov'st elsewhere, but in my sight,
Dear heart, forbear to glance thine eye aside;
What need'st thou wound with cunning when thy might
Is more than my o'erpressed defence can bide?
Let me excuse thee: Ah, my love well knows
Her pretty looks have been mine enemies,
And therefore from my face she turns my foes,
That they elsewhere might dart their injuries.
Yet do not so; but since I am near slain,
Kill me outright with looks, and rid my pain.

140 He accuses her of playing around with his emotions

Be wise as thou art cruel; do not press
My tongue-tied patience with too much disdain,
Lest sorrow lend me words, and words express
The manner of my pity wanting pain.
If I might teach thee wit, better it were,
Though not to love, yet love to tell me so;
As testy sick men, when their deaths be near,
No news but health from their physicians know.
For if I should despair I should grow mad,
And in my madness might speak ill of thee.
Now this ill-wresting world is grown so bad,
Mad slanderers by mad ears believed be.
That I may not be so, nor thou belied,
Bear thine eyes straight, though thy proud heart go wide.

141-142 He tries to rationalise his situation.

In faith, I do not love thee with mine eyes,
For they in thee a thousand errors note;
But 'tis my heart that loves what they despise,
Who in despite of view is pleased to dote.
Nor are mine ears with thy tongue's tune delighted,
Nor tender feeling to base touches prone,
Nor taste nor smell desire to be invited
To any sensual feast with thee alone;
But my five wits, nor my five senses can
Dissuade one foolish heart from serving thee,
Who leaves unswayed the likeness of a man,
Thy proud heart's slave and vassal wretch to be.
Only my plague thus far I count my gain,
That she that makes me sin awards me pain.

The Dark Lady Sonnets, 127-154

142 Angered and spiteful, he accuses her of being promiscuous.

Love is my sin, and thy dear virtue hate,
Hate of my sin grounded on sinful loving;
O, but with mine compare thou thine own state,
And thou shalt find it merits not reproving;
Or if it do, not from those lips of thine,
That have profaned their scarlet ornaments
And sealed false bonds of love as oft as mine,
Robbed others' beds' revenues of their rents.
Be it lawful I love thee as thou lov'st those
Whom thine eyes woo as mine importune thee.
Root pity in thy heart, that, when it grows,
Thy pity may deserve to pitied be.
If thou dost seek to have what thou dost hide,
By self-example mayst thou be denied!

143 He finds he is dependent on her, just like a child

Lo, as a careful housewife runs to catch
One of her feathered creatures broke away,
Set down her babe, and makes all swift dispatch
In pursuit of the thing she would have stay;
Whilst her neglected child holds her in chase,
Cries to catch her whose busy care is bent
To follow that which flies before her face,
Not prizing her poor infant's discontent;
So runn'st thou after that which flies from thee,
Whilst I, thy babe, chase thee a far behind;
But if thou catch thy hope, turn back to me
And play the mother' part; kiss me, be kind.
So will I pray that thou may'st have thy *Will*,
If thou turn back and my loud crying still.

144[82] and is caught emotionally, but rationally, between two stools.

Two loves I have of comfort and despair,
Which like two spirits do suggest me still;
The better angel is a man right fair,
The worser spirit a woman coloured ill.
To win me soon to hell my female evil
Tempteth my better angel from my side[83],
And would corrupt my saint to be a devil,
Wooing his purity with her foul pride.
And whether that my angel be turned fiend,
Suspect I may, yet not directly tell,

---

[82] Also in *The Passionate Pilgrim* but with only minor changes.
[83] Q *sight.*

But being both from me, both to each friend,
I guess one angel in another's hell.
Yet this shall I ne'er know, but live in doubt,
Till my bad angel fire my good one out.

145 He is very upset because he misheard something she said [84]

Those lips that love's own hand did make
Breathed forth the sound that said *'I hate'*
To me that languished for her sake;
But when she saw my woeful state,
Straight in her heart did mercy come,
Chiding that tongue that ever sweet
Was used in giving gentle dome,
And taught it thus a new to greet:
'I hate' she altered with an end
That followed it as gentle day
Doth follow night, who, like a fiend,
From heaven to hell is flown away.
'I hate' from hate away she threw,
And saved my life, saying *'not you.'*

**146 and telling himself to stop wasting his time
and to pull himself together.**

Poor soul, the centre of my sinful earth,
My sinful earth these rebel powers that thee array,
Why dost thou pine within and suffer dearth,
Painting thy outward walls so costly gay?
Why so large cost, having so short a lease,
Dost thou upon thy fading mansion spend?
Shall worms, inheritors of this excess,
Eat up thy charge? Is this thy body's end?
Then, soul, live thou upon thy servant's loss,
And let that pine to aggravate thy store;
Buy terms divine in selling hours of dross;
Within be fed, without be rich no more.
So shalt thou feed on death, that feeds on men,
And death once dead, there's no more dying then.

147 She has abandoned him, he is desolate and angry.

My love is as a fever, longing still
For that which longer nurseth the disease,
Feeding on that which doth preserve the ill,
Th' uncertain sickly appetite to please.

---

[84] This sonnet has only eight syllables per line perhaps reflecting his anger and his haste to compose or has he borrowed this from previous work?

My reason, the physician to my love,
Angry that his prescriptions are not kept,
Hath left me, and I desperate now approve
Desire is death, which physic did except.
Past cure I am, now reason is past care,
And frantic-mad with evermore unrest;
My thoughts and my discourse as mad men's are,
At random from the truth vainly expressed;
For I have sworn thee fair, and thought thee bright,
Who art as black as hell, as dark as night.

148 – 149 He starts to understand the reality ...

O, me! What eyes hath love put in my head,
Which have no correspondence with true sight,
Or if they have, where is my judgement fled,
That censures falsely what they see aright?
If that be fair whereon my false eyes dote,
What means the world to say it is not so?
If it be not, then love doth well denote
Love's eye is not so true as all men's. No,
How can it? O, how can love' eye be true,
That is so vexed with watching and with tears?
No marvel then though I mistake my view;
The sun itself sees not, till heaven clears.
O cunning love, with tears thou keep'st me blind,
Lest eyes well-seeing thy foul faults should find.

149

Canst thou, O cruel, say I love thee not,
When I against my self with thee partake?
Do I not think on thee when I forgot
Am of myself, all tyrant, for thy sake?
Who hateth thee that I do call my friend?
On whom frown'st thou that I do fawn upon?
Nay, if thou lour'st[85] on me, do I not spend
Revenge upon my self with present moan?
What merit do I in myself respect,
That is so proud thy service to despise,
When all my best doth worship thy defect,
Commanded by the motion of thine eyes?
But love hate on, for now I know thy mind:
Those that can see thou lov'st and I am blind.

---

[85] Scowls at

150 ... and his own behaviour.

Oh, from what power hast thou this powerful might
With insufficiency my heart to sway,
To make me give the lie to my true sight,
And swear that brightness doth not grace the day?
Whence hast thou this becoming of things ill,
That in the very refuse of thy deeds
There is such strength and warrantise of skill
That in my mind thy worst all best exceeds?
Who taught thee how to make me love thee more,
The more I hear and see just cause of hate?
Oh, though I love what others do abhor,
With others thou shouldst not abhor my state.
If thy unworthiness raised love in me,
More worthy I to be beloved of thee.

151 He philosophises on love . . .

Love is too young to know what conscience is;
Yet who knows not conscience is born of love,
Then, gentle cheater, urge not my amiss,
Lest guilty of my faults thy sweet self prove.
For thou betraying me, I do betray
My nobler part to my gross body's treason,
My soul doth tell my body that he may
Triumph in love; flesh stays no farther reason,
But, rising at thy name, doth point out thee
As his triumphant prize. Proud of this pride,
He is contented thy poor drudge to be,
To stand in thy affairs, fall by thy side.
No want of conscience hold it that I call
Her love for whose dear love I rise and fall.

152 . . . finally blaming himself for his own stupidity.

In loving thee thou know'st I am forsworn;
But thou art twice forsworn, to me love swearing;
In act thy bed-vow broke, and new faith torn
In vowing new hate after new love bearing.
But why of two oaths' breach do I accuse thee,
When I break twenty? I am perjured most,
For all my vows are oaths but to misuse thee,
And all my honest faith in thee is lost;
For I have sworn deep oaths of thy deep kindness,
Oaths of thy love, thy truth, thy constancy,
And to enlighten thee gave eyes to blindness,
Or made them swear against the thing they see.

For I have sworn thee fair: more perjured eie,[86]
To swear against the truth so foul a lie.[87]

153-154 Now he writes of the time he met Mary Fitton.

Cupid laid by his brand[88], and fell asleep.
A maid of *Dian's*[89] this advantage found,
And his love-kindling fire did quickly steep
In a cold valley-fountain of that ground;
Which borrowed from this holy fire of love,
A dateless lively heat, still to endure,
And grew a seething bath, which yet men prove
Against strange maladies a sovereign cure.
But at my mistress eie loves brand new fired,
The boy for trial needs would touch my breast,[90]
I, sick withal, the help of bath desired,
And thither hied, a sad distempered guest,
But found no cure: the bath for my help lies
Where *Cupid* got new fire; my mistress eye.

154

The little Love-God lying once asleep,
Laid by his side his heart inflaming brand,
Whilst many nymphs that vowed chaste life to keep[91]
Came tripping by; but in her maiden hand
The fairest votary[92] took up that fire
Which many legions of true hearts had warmed;
And so the General of hot desire
Was sleeping by a virgin hand disarmed.
This brand she quenched in a cool well by,
Which from love's fire took heat perpetual,
Growing a bath and healthful remedy
For men diseased; but I, my mistress' thrall,[93]
Came there for cure and this by that I prove:
Love's fire heats water, water cools not love.

It is thought these last two sonnets derive from a sixth-century, six-line epigram literally translated – *Here beneath these plane trees, exhausted love was sleeping softly. He had entrusted his torch to the nymphs but the nymphs*

---

[86] Punning on "I"
[87] The greatest lie of all would be to lie against the truth. He admits again that he loves her.
[88] Puts down his torch (penis). Cupids work is done and the goddess of chastity puts out the fire. *Brand* appears twelve times Shakespeare, four times in these two sonnets.
[89] A Maid of Honour of the Queen who in Sonnet 154 is described as *the fairest.*
[90] Lines 9-10 are discussed below.
[91] The Queen's Maids of Honour.
[92] votary - a devoted follower.
[93] slave

The Dark Lady Sonnets, 127-154

said to one another, "Come on, why are we waiting? Let's put out the torch and with it quench the fire in human hearts." But the torch set light even to the waters, and the Nymphs of Love have filled the bath with hot water ever since.[94]

It was practise to embed cryptic clues into verses to help increase intellectual content, better hold people's attention and induce the reader to revisit the words and look for further meanings. In Sonnet 153, lines 9-10; with eie (I) suggesting *first*, then a cryptic clue of **eie Love's brand** new **fired**, calls up an anagram of **L, brand** and **fired** to give R Barnfield – the boy, the homosexual[95] – whose male-gender love poems, his Mistress suggests, would touch his breast.[96] I have yet to find an explanation for the presence of the word *boy*. Consider lines 11-14 in Sonnet 77:

> Those **children** nurst, deliuerd **from** thy **braine**, To take a new acquaintance of thy minde. These offices, so oft as thou wilt looke, Shall **profit thee**, and much **in-rich** thy booke.

Take the words **children** and **braine** and find an **"f"** from somewhere and rearranged, out emerges *Richarde Barnfield*. In line 14 we have **fit thee an,** followed by And Much In Rich (MARIEE FITTHEAN) and the *booke* looks like the ending of Pembroke. Who knows whether this is what the author intended but it is clear that the writer is saying *if you look closer at the words and think in a new dimension you will get more out of thy book;* that is, *this book I am writing for you, or the copybook you gave me.* Sonnet 42.10 has; *"Both finde each other, and I loose both twaine,"* which, dissected using the operational words of *both, each, lose* and *twain,* generates the elements of Fi; t; her; an; bo; th – making her-bo-t and fi-th-an.

The two sonnets cover four themes. William introduces a Maid of Dian (Maid of Honour of the Queen) as having aroused him. He is also playing around with the metaphors of hot baths used to cure venereal diseases which cause a burning sensation when urinating. There is also an introduction by the Queen's Maid, Mary Fitton, to the homoerotic poetry of her friend, Richard Barnfield, which William Herbert finds exciting and finally, there appears to be an attempt to write pornography in the style of the Italian, Pietro Aretino (1492-1556), but without being too explicit.[97]

The essence of William Herbert's twenty-eight sonnets was an infatuation for an older woman. There are 392 lines, just over 3,000 words – a month's composing at most, very much less for a very highly intelligent, passionate, young man stirred by such a craving. Mary Fitton later writes of William Herbert's charm, and guile, in these two stanzas from *A Lover's Complaint:*

---

[94] The Ardern Shakespeare, Sonnets.
[95] *Boy* is usually used as the catamite - passive homosexual partner. Richard Barnfield is discussed in Chapter Four.
[96] B*reast* is sometimes used as a sexual pun for *buttocks*.
[97] Pietro Aretino is mentioned again in Chapter Five

18 So on the tip of his subduing tongue
All kind of arguments and question deep,
All replication prompt, and reason strong,
For his advantage still did wake and sleep.
To make the weeper laugh, the laugher weep,
He had the dialect and different skill,
Catching all passions in his craft of will,

25 For further I could say " this man's untrue",
And knew the patterns of his foul beguiling;
Heard where his plants in others' orchards grew;
Saw how deceits were gilded in his smiling;
Knew vows were ever brokers to defiling;
Thought characters and words merely but art,
And bastards of his foul adulterate heart.

At the end his sonnet-writing William Herbert, discarded by Aemelia Lanier, was immediately captivated by the expansive character of Mary Fitton,[98] two years his elder and eight years younger than Aemelia. Fortunately or unfortunately, Mary fell deeply in love. The next chapter is about the poetry of Richard Barnfield and includes an introduction to Sir Richard Leveson, a second cousin of Mary Fitton's. It reaches a number of conclusions, in particular that after Mary Fitton arrived in London she and Richard Barnfield collaborated in writing poetry. There is a definite overlap with an amorous, Barnfield poem, dedicated to *"R. L."* whom I believe to be Richard Leveson. Sir Richard Leveson had a passion for Mary Fitton and was her lover and protector from some time after she left London in 1601 to when he died, a Vice-Admiral of the Fleet, in 1605.

---

[98] Around 1599 Mary's father, Sir Edward Fitton, has correspondence with Sir Robert Cecil about her marriage portion. Mary may have been a little nervous at this time about her future and William Herbert would have looked a more attractive prospect.

CHAPTER FOUR

RICHARD BARNFIELD

Only scholars of Elizabethan or homoerotic poetry are likely to have read the works of Richard Barnfield, the poet mentioned in the previous three chapters. It would have been easy to draw a veil and hide his existence but to do so would have been wrong. This chapter identifies that Richard Barnfield and Mary Fitton were friends, and collaborated in London; there is evidence that they remained close friends after they left London and lived in Staffordshire. However, to justify including this chapter, I needed to have solid answers to the following question. What differences did Richard Barnfield make? The answers, based on a balance of probability, are as follows.

Without Richard Barnfield, Mary Fitton would not have had an outlet for her poetry or developed as a poet. The late Elizabethan predilection with same-sex love, part fuelled by Barnfield's gentle, homoerotic poetry, may not have taken place. Plays such as *Twelfth Night* and *As You Like It* may never have been written or been as good as they are, and we might never have had the pleasure of meeting the characters of the majestic Olivia and the dominant Rosalind. Fitton's and Barnfield's poetry and literary ability would not have come to the notice of William Herbert who would never have had a passion for Mary Fitton. Hamlet would never have reached its psychological heights and there would have been no Ophelia, the Lady of the Flowers.

Shake-Speare in his Sonnets, and Barnfield in his early works, shared a unique common fact. They were the *only* Elizabethan poets who wrote what appeared to be male-male love poems. I needed to satisfy myself whether or not Shake-Speare and Barnfield were one and the same person. Exploring this particular avenue was either luck – or a reward for a dogged persistence to get back to basics. I was to discover pieces of a lost jigsaw, which I here share with you, that gradually began to fit together. Yes, there were two poets but the two poets were linked in a way no one could ever have expected.[99] My misfortune was that the extra dimensions made research and understanding that much harder. Fortunately facts have emerged, and are still emerging, that greatly add to our body of knowledge. The conclusion was that both Richard Barnfield *and* Mary Fitton *were* poets, and that they knew each other well, probably very well.

If Barnfield had not translated and written *homoerotic* poetry he might never have been known to posterity. Perhaps he only came to be noticed in the nineteenth century, when people started to study William Shakespeare's

---

[99] I expected Barnfield to know Shakespeare - who knew William Herbert - who knew Mary Fitton. What I found was that Barnfield knew Mary Fitton *very* well and that he or his poetry may well have been known to William Herbert.

Richard Barnfield

works, because, in 1598, he was the first person to name and praise Shakespeare in the last six lines of the following poem. The poem[100] could be hinting at his knowledge of the literary college at Wilton in an attempt to get there himself, as the people mentioned were, at some time or other (except William Shakespeare of Stratford-upon-Avon) thought to be connected with the Mary Sidney Herbert's patronage.

> Live Spenser[101] ever, in thy Fairy Queen:
> Whose like (for deepe Conceit) was never seen.
> Crownd mayst thou bee, unto thy more renown,
>   As King of Poets with a Lawrell Crown.
> And Daniell[102], praised for thy sweet-chast Verse:
> Whose fame is grav'd on Rosamonds[103] black Herse.
> Still mayst thou live: and still be honored,
> For that rare Work, The White Rose and the Red.
> And Drayton[104], whose well-written Tragedies,
> And Sweet Epistles, soare thy fame to skies.
> Thy learned Name, is aequall with the rest;
> Whose stately Numbers are so well addrest.
> And **Shakespeare** thou, whose hony-flowing Vaine,
> Pleasing the World thy praises doth obtaine.
> Whose Venus, and whose Lucrece (sweet, and chaste)
> Thy name in fames immortall Book have plac't.
> Live ever you, at least in Fame live ever:
> Well may the Body dye, but Fame dies never.

Nearly three hundred years were to pass before Barnfield again achieved some recognition. This was probably for his generally bland, homoerotic poetry which was coloured by occasional flashes of genius. He was then, and still remains a figure in the shadows with very little biographical flesh to dress the bones of his literature.

Richard Barnfield was four years older than Mary Fitton. He was born to Mary Skrymsher Barnfield and baptised at Norbury in Staffordshire on 13th June 1574. His mother died during his childhood while giving birth to his sister – who survived. From a poem dedicated to his aunt[105] it is thought that the children were brought up by his mother's sister, Elizabeth Skrymsher, at Johnson's Hall in nearby Eccleshall. Richard was an undergraduate at Brazenose College, Oxford, from 1589-1592 and started but did not complete his

---

[100] This is one of *The Diverse Poems* that follow The *Encomion of Lady Pecunia*.

[101] Edmund Spenser c1552-1599; *Fairie Queene* was published 1596.

[102] Samuel Daniel, 1562-1619, a highly commended poet and sometime tutor at Wilton wrote *A History of the Civil Wars between York and Lancaster (The White Rose and the Red)*. The first *Shakespeare* Plays were Henry VI (1-2-3) and Richard III.

[103] Rosamond contains the name Sam(uel Daniel).

[104] Michael Drayton, 1563-1631; like William Shakespeare, a Warwickshire man, born at Hartshill, a few miles from Arbury, the year before William Shakespeare.

[105] In the 1605 reprint of Pecunia with other works.

masters degree. At the age of 20, still a minor, he appears to have had the ability, finance, contacts and influence to produce and publish anonymously his first booklet of poems.

Four small books, the last an enlarged repeat of the third, are now attributed to Barnfield:

> 1594 The tears of an Affectionate Shepheard. Containing the Complaint of Daphnis for the love of Granymede; dedicated to Lady Penelope Rich. London: Printed by John Danter for T. G. and E. N. 54 p. Published anonymously; TG is Thomas Gubbin and EN (sic) is Thomas Newman.

> 1595 Cynthia with Certain Sonnets (20) and The Legend of Cassandra; dedicated to William Stanley, Earl of Derby[106]. London: Printed for Humfrey Lownes [107]70 p.

> 1598 The Encomion[108] of Lady Pecunia: Or, The praise of Money; with some Poems of Diverse Humours. London Printed by G. S(haw). for John Jaggard 62 p.[109]

> 1605 (repeat) Lady Pecunia, or The praise of Money. Also A Combat betwixt Conscience and Couetousnesse. Together with, The complaint of Poetry, for the death of Liberality. Newly corrected and inlarged, by Richard Barnfield London: Printed by W. I(aggard). and are to be sold by John Hodgers 54 p.

The Affectionate Shepheard is a translation from a Roman Latin homoerotic text. Both Daphnis and Ganymede were males; a Ganymede was a catamite, the passive partner of a homosexual relationship. No author's name is subscribed, perhaps to create a mystery – or because the subject was homoerotic. The footnote to Sonnet 153 in the previous chapter indicates that Barnfield was known to William Herbert as a "boy", that is, a homosexual. [110]

The 1605 *Cynthia* and *The Legend of Cassandra* includes a Commendation[111] by TT. Included in the book are twenty sonnets in iambic pentameter (similar in style to Shake-Speares Sonnets), continuing the homoerotic theme of the love of Ganymede of his first book, *The Affectionate Shepheard*. It finishes with an Ode that draws a conclusion on the other homoerotic poems.

Later in the chapter I will explain why I think that the 1598 *Pecunia,* was dedicated, or addressed to Lady Margaret Hawkins,[112] the widow and second

---

[106] Written, perhaps to celebrate his wedding to Elizabeth de Vere 26/6/1594, sister of Susan, wife of Philip Herbert.

[107] Lownes later published for Dowland.

[108] Encomium = high-flown expression of praise.

[109] In 1599 two of the poems were printed in the *Passionate Pilgrim.*

[110] Less convincingly - he could have been an actor who played female roles but by now he would be about twenty-six years old.

[111] The Commendation is given in full later in the chapter.

[112] Margaret Vaughan Hawkins, daughter of Charles Vaughan and Elizabeth Baskerville, was

Richard Barnfield

wife of Sir John Hawkins [PLATE 5]. Sir John died at sea in 1595 having accumulated massive wealth, firstly through piracy and later as the first trader in African slaves. During the threat of the Spanish Armada in 1588 he had served as a notable naval commander under Lord High Admiral, Charles Howard, Lord Nottingham. Lady Margaret, was to play an important role during Mary Fitton's pregnancy.

With *Pecunia* were *diverse* other verses including two pieces which reappeared a year later in *The Passionate Pilgrim* –a sonnet, dedicated to *Maister R.L. –In Praise of Musique and Poetrie,* and an Ode, both of these are printed in this chapter.[113] New to the 1605 repeat of *Pecunia* was *A Combat betwixt Conscience and Covetousness* given in full at Appendix 4 which will be discussed later in the chapter.

Before looking at Barnfield's poetry for clues, let me introduce two names which have slender links in the various chains; Sir Richard Leveson and Sir Francis Leigh.

Vice-Admiral Sir Richard Leveson and Mary Fitton had common great-grandparents; Mary's father and Richard Leveson's mother were first cousins. Leveson was born in 1569 and, in 1588, the year of Spanish Armada, he married Lady Margaret Howard, daughter of Charles Howard, the Lord High Admiral. He was then serving under his father-in-law as a volunteer on the fleet's flagship, the Ark Royal.[114] After the victory over the Spanish, Howard was created 1st. Lord Nottingham and went on to serve the Queen as a most eminent privy councillor and foreign diplomat. The Levesons' marriage, however, did not produce progeny. A child was born but did not survive and Lady Margaret became insane. It was arranged that she lived apart from her husband, at Oxley Hall near Wolverhampton. Leveson rose through the ranks, was knighted in 1596, after serving at the siege of Cadiz, again under his-father-in-law, and in 1604 was promoted to Vice-Admiral of the Fleet. The same year he attended the peace conference in Madrid between England and Spain.

One of the Leveson's homes was at Lilleshall which is six miles from Norbury where Barnfield was baptised, and when the Fitton and Leveson families travelled the thirty miles to visit each other they would have passed by the imposing manor house, Johnson Hall, at Eccleshall a few miles from Norbury, where Barnfield was thought to have been brought up. Mary Fitton was

brought up in Wales and had been a Lady of The Bed Chamber to the Queen. Hawkins' first wife had died in 1591 and he died off Puerto Rico on 12 November 1595.

[113] Another sonnet from *Pecunia* praises the poetry of the Scottish King. This poem and Barnfield's name are noted by a Francis Meres in his *Palladis Tamia* of 1598 which appears to list the books he owned or had read. Worthy of note is that James VI fancied himself as a poet. Shakespeare's *Venus and Adonis* and *Rape of Lucrece* had had been reprinted several times by 1598 when Meres also lists twelve plays as Shakespeare's, eleven of which whose author had hitherto been unknown. The exception was Love Labours Lost.

[114] Sir John Hawkins was the next senior commander and was in charge of the Vidory.

Richard Barnfield

probably brought up at Gawsworth,[115] just south of Macclesfield. It is almost certain that the Fittons and Levesons, who were related, also knew the Skrymshers and Barnfields, both families being notable gentry in adjacent counties.

Sir William Knollys (*Malvolio*, to whom Sir Edward Fitton had entrusted his daughter on her arrival in London), and Richard Leveson (younger by twenty years) were contemporaneous members of King James' Privy Council, as was Charles Howard, Leveson's father-in-law. Knollys and Leveson both corresponded with Mary Fitton's married sister, Anne, wife of John Newdigate, who lived at Arbury Hall near Nuneaton in Warwickshire. Arbury Hall, [PLATE 8] set in a delightful estate, is still the family home of the Newdigates[116] and portraits of Mary Fitton [PLATES 1 & 2], Anne Newdigate [PLATE 2], Richard Leveson and Charles Howard can be seen there. A portrait of Leveson is found in PLATE 5. When Leveson died in August 1605, Mary was living at Perton, near Wolverhampton in Staffordshire, in a house rented from him on a long lease. A bronze of Leveson can be found in the parish church of Wolverhampton. There exists a correct accusation[117] that Leveson sired two bastards by Mary Fitton – even though he was spending considerable time at sea and in London. Two days before he died in 1605 he made a financial arrangement with Sir Edward Fitton and others, concerning a lease which would raise £10,000, a massive amount of money. In his will he left a financial provision for an unnamed person and others whom one can guess to be Mary Fitton and their two children;[118]

> Which said sum of one hundred pounds yearly during the continuance of the foresaid lease . . . shall be employed by them to such uses and purposes and such person and persons as I shall appoint unto them by some private instruction from myself.

One should note that Leveson's father-in-law, Charles Howard (1534-1624) was married to Catherine Carey (died 1602) daughter of Henry Carey, the first Lord Hunsden, whose mistress was Aemelia Lanier. Charles Howard maintained the company of stage players known as the Admiral's men.

Other sets of family connections need to be noted. The first concerns Juliana and Alice, daughters of Sir Francis Leigh of Newnham Regis in Warwickshire. Juliana Leigh married Mary Fitton's nephew, Richard Newdigate. Alice Leigh, Juliana's sister married Richard Barnfield's first

[115] At the time of her birth her father was Lord President of Munster in Ireland and her grandfather was buried, in state, in Dublin Cathedral.
[116] The family home of Viscount Daventry.
[117] Papers of Sir Peter Leycester; *Gossip from the Muniment Room* by Lady Newdigate. Lady Newdigate explained at some length that it was most unlikely that Mary and Richard Leveson could have had a couple of bastards - but they did! Leycester accused Leveson of siring two daughters, there is evidence of a son and a daughter, another daughter may have died. Was Mary pregnant, as she was five years later when her husband, William Polewhele, died?
[118] From the church register at Tettenhall in Staffordshire; 9th January 1607 William Fitton was buried; 4th April 1625 *Robert Charnock married Anna Filton alias Levison.*

Richard Barnfield

cousin, John Skrymsher. Further, in the 1598 *Pecunia,* Richard Barnfield dedicated a poem to Master Edward Leigh of Grays Inn, London. It would be useful to establish if Edward was related to Sir Francis Leigh.

There are other connections between the Skrymshers and the Fittons. Richard Barnfield's grandfather, Thomas Skrymsher married Dorothy Gatacre of Gatacre in Shropshire. Many years later Mary Fitton's daughter married a John Gatacre of Gatacre. The Skrymsher family line includes a Talbot, Mary and Anne Fitton's mother, Alice, was a Holcroft. Previously a Holcroft had married a Talbot. There can be little doubt that the Fitton / Newdigate and Barnfield / Skrymsher families knew each other.

Mary Fitton clearly was jilted by William Herbert but, keeping a very open mind, what if hypothetically William also had a brief homosexual flirtation with the passive Richard Barnfield and that *both* Barnfield and Mary left London, albeit for different reasons, at about the same time? This question helps point out that the love poetry of a passive male partner would be very similar to that of a woman's, and certainly it would be difficult to differentiate between them. Pembroke, on his long awaited return to the Palace of Westminster in 1603, had astonished the Court when he had the effrontery, and got away with, kissing the new King on the face[119] (or mouth) – James I (James VI of Scotland, who we know also had pretensions of being a poet) admitted to a homosexual relationship with the Duke of Buckingham a decade later. One can see a certain femininity in the young William Herbert's face. In Sonnet 3 Mary reminds William (who was born in April) of the softness of his face:

> Thou art thy mother's glass, and she in thee
> Calls back the lovely April of her prime;

Mary Fitton and Richard Barnfield are set apart as poets in that;

(a) A Lover's Complaint is the poetry of a jilted woman.

(b) Yet to be explained, the Dedication to the Sonnets hides Mary's name.

(c) there are instances in the Sonnets where a male-male situation does not ring true, especially when Mary appears to be pregnant.

(d) that homoerotic words which Barnfield uses in his early poetry such as bee, honey, mouth, lips, fee, debt, arrow, dart, pipe and purse are almost completely absent from Sonnets 1-126. Conversely the same sonnets contain the very feminine image of flowers, appearing thirteen times, (cf. *Hamlet's* very feminine *Lady of the Flowers,* Ophelia).

The following clumsy, synopsis of *the Authour his work*, has clues in it that suggest it was written by Mary Fitton. It is the *Commendation* by T.T. to read

---

[119] "The Earl of Pembroke, a handsome youth, who is always with the King, and always joking with him, actually kissed his Majesty's face, whereupon the King laughed and gave him a little cough [cuff]." [Ardern Shakespeare]

Richard Barnfield

Cynthia, Barnfield's 1595 book. Mary was about eighteen years old and recently arrived in London. It is not easy reading and our interest is really in the header and the last four lines. which indicate that Mary Fitton and Richard Barnfield knew each other well enough from their pre-London days to be able to collaborate.

T. T. in commendation of the Authour his work.

Whylom that in a shepheards gray coate masked,
(Where masked love the nonage of his skill)
Reares now his Eagle-winged pen, new tasked,
To seale the by-clift Muse sole-pleasing hill:
Dropping sweete Nectar poesie from his quill,
Admires faire CYNTHIA with his iuory pen
Faire CYNTHIA lov'd, fear'd, of Gods and men.
Downe sliding from that cloudes ore-pearing mounteine:
Decking with double grace the neighbour plaines,
Drawes christall dew, from PEGASE foote-sprung fountain,
Whose flower set banks, delights, sweet choice containes:
Nere yet discoverd to the country swaines:
Heere bud those branches, which adorne his turtle,
With love made garlands, of heart-bleeding Mirtle.
Rays'd from the cynders, of the thrice-sact towne:
ILLIONS sooth-telling SYBILLIST appeares,
Eclipsing PHOEBUS[120] love, with scornefull frowne,
Whose tragicke end, affords warme-water tears,
(For pitty-wanting PACOE, none forbeares,
Such period haps, to beauties price ore-priz'd:
Where JANUS-faced love, doth lurke disguiz'd.
Nere waining CYNTHIA yeelds thee triple thankes,
Whose beames unborrowed darke the worlds faire eie,
And as full streames that ever fill their bankes,
So those rare Sonnets, where wits tipe doth lie,
With **Troian Nimph**, doe soare thy fame to skie.
And those, and these, contend thy Muse to raise
(Larke mounting Muse[121]) with more then common praise.

Another ode ends the book but this is preceded by twenty, either homoerotic or female-to-male, sonnets. The Ode starts off in a homoerotic vein, expressing the author's passion for a young, male shepherd, Ganymede. It has this very surprising ending:

But yet (alas) I was deceiu'd,
(Love of reason is bereau'd)
For since then I saw a Lass,
(Lass) that did in beauty pass,

---

[120] The sun
[121] See Sonnet 31

Richard Barnfield

(Pass) faire Ganymede [122]as far
As Phoebus doth the smallest star.
Love commanded me to love;
Fancy bade me not remove
My affection from the swain
Whom I never could obtain:
(For who can obtain that favour,
Which he cannot grant the craver?)
Love at last (though loath) prevailde;
(Love) that so my heart assailde;
Wounding me with her faire eies,
(Ah how Love can subtelize,
And devize a thousand shifts,
How to work men to his drifts)

Her it is, for whom I mourn;
Her, for whom my life I scorn;
Her, for whom I weep all day;
Her, for whom I sigh, and say,
Either She, or else no creature,
Shall enjoy my love: whose feature
Though I never can obtain,
Yet shall my true love remain:
Till (my body turn'd to clay)
My poor soul must pass away,
To the heavens; where (I hope)
It shall find a resting scope:
Then since I loved thee (alone)
Remember me when I am gone.
Scarce had he these last words spoken,
But me thought his heart was broken;
With great grief that did abound,
(Cares and grief the heart confound)

In whose heart (thus riv'd in three)
Eliza written I might see:
In characters of crimson blood,
(Whose meaning well I understood.)
Which, for my heart might not behold,
I hyed me home my sheep to fold.

Meeting this young woman might have been a turning point for Richard Barnfield as his subsequent works were not homoerotic. So who was the unattainable lass whom Richard could not hope to reach? It could have been anyone – or could it? Barnfield has given *Eliza(beth) as the* reason. This was possibly the name of the girl, but more likely he referred to Queen Elizabeth as

---

[122] A male shepherd, cup bearer to the gods, epitomising a youthful male beauty.

the impediment; he saw a warning sign – one did not mess around with a Maid of Honour who was effectively a ward of the Queen. Mary Fitton was beautiful, lively, intelligent and poetic but to Barnfield she would have had the accessibility of a Vestal Virgin.[123] In the next chapter we learn that Mary also appeared to be spoken for by Sir William Knollys.[124]

Here are the clues that connect Mary Fitton and Richard Barnfield. Let us recall the last four lines of the Commendation by T.T. to *Cynthia*.

> So those rare Sonnets, where wits type doth lie,
> With **Troian Nimph,** doe soar thy fame to sky.
> And those, and these, contend thy Muse to raise
> (Lark mounting Muse) with more then common praise.

It is quite clear that the Troian Nimph, whoever she is, has helped Barnfield lift his fame to the sky and certainly *Troian Nimph* is a phonetic anagram of Mary Fitton, Mari Phitonn. One can understand a thought process that likens someone hiding in a Trojan Horse to someone hiding within another poet's book. So now let me explain that T.T. is Mary Fitton's phonetic monogram.

The explanation is simple, **FIT - T- ON.** Draw a capital letter T. Now, *FIT ON* a second T so that the left edge of the second T is touching the middle of the upright of the first T. Here is what I believe is Mary's monogram, one T with another T fitted to it lower down, giving the semblance of an F and T combined. The compositor of the Dedication to the Sonnets would have seen the monogram and assumed it was two T's and typeset accordingly. This is illustrated in the curious ending I have given to Chapter Two.

The Fitton Latin motto in 1570 was FIT ONUS LEVE[125] and apart from FIT-ON, one can also see in reverse LEVE-SUN. The play on the Fitton name that I had expected to see somewhere in Mary's sonnets was *Phaeton*. It did not appear in the Sonnets but I discovered that it had already appeared in 1591 in another Commendatory sonnet, *Phaeton to His friend Florio,* at the start of John Florio's book, *Second Fruits.* The rhyme is abba;abba;cdcd,ee which is different and less mature than the Sonnets' abab;cdcd;efef;gg. Mary Fitton would then have been thirteen years old, and once one has read Shake-Speares Sonnets, one can quickly see that this sonnet has many similar or familiar turns of phrase, but is not as mature.[126]

---

[123] Newdigate p20-21; Mary's father's uncle, Francis Fitton, writes in 1598 that he would like to meet Mary's sister, Anne, at "your father's house in London." An outside possibility exists that Barnfield may have held a position at Mary's father's London home.

[124] Although he was still married he was waiting with confidence for his wife to die!

[125] One meaning could be *make work light.*

[126] Imagine a thirteen-year old Mary Fitton being in the presence of John Florio (1533-1625), asking to read his manuscript, producing the sonnet, and John Florio finding it delightful enough to preface his book. *His* in the header would have been used instead of *Her* to protect Mary's reputation. Had she used *phaeton* in the Sonnets, Mary could have been recognised from this Florio Commendation. Margaret Hannay (op. cit. p74) depicts Florio as having a love-hate relationship with Countess Pembroke and her son, William Herbert. Florio eventually left his poetry to Herbert to be published, but in vain.

Richard Barnfield

Phaeton to His friend Florio

Sweet friend, whose name agrees with thy increase
How fit a rival art thou of the spring!
For when each branch hath left his flourishing,
And green-locked summer's shady pleasures cease
She makes the winter's storms repose in peace
And spends her franchise on each living thing:
The daisies spout, the little birds do sing,
Herbs, gums, and plants do vaunt of their release.
So when that all our English wits lay dead
(Except the laurel that is evergreen)
Thou with thy fruits our barrenness o'erspread
And set thy flowery pleasance to be seen.
Such fruits, such flowerets of morality
Were ne'er before brought out of Italy.

On the balance of probability, TT is Mary Fitton, as is the Troian Nimph and we have firm evidence that Mary and Barnfield are friends. This would almost certainly mean that she read and probably helped enhance Barnfield's twenty sonnets in the book *Cynthia* to attain their high quality. Sonnet XIV is my favourite.

Here; hold this glove (this milk-white cheveril[127] glove)
Not quaintly overwrought with curious knots,
Nor deckt with golden spangs, nor silver spots;
Yet wholesome for thy hand as thou shalt prove.
Ah no: (sweet boy) place this glove near thy heart,
Wear it, and lodge it still within thy breast,
So shalt thou make me (most unhappy,) blest.
So shalt thou rid my pain, and ease my smart:
How can that be (perhaps) thou wilt reply,
A glove is for the hand, not for the heart,
Nor can it well be prov'd by common art,
Nor reasons rule. To this, thus answer I:
If thou from glove do'st take away the g,
Then glove is love: and so I send it thee.

A possible subplot has developed. Leaving University prematurely (perhaps because of his homosexuality), Richard Barnfield, found work in London, possibly at the Court, maybe working for Margaret Vaughan Hawkins, for Sir Edward Fitton, Mary's father, or articled at one of the Inns of Court.[128] In 1594 he published his first book and while completing his second he was swept off his feet by the friendship he developed with Mary Fitton. He knew she was unattainable, either because she was a Maid of Honour, or because she was

---

[127] Cheverel - kid leather - OED 1609.
[128] Greys Inn, for example, where Edward Leigh was involved in law.

spoken for,[129] but being close to her he discovered heterosexuality. We find that his next works did not display any overtly homoerotic verses. For some reason, perhaps a scandal, he left London and in 1599 is recorded as living at Darlaston Hall[130] near Stone in Staffordshire. Mary Fitton eventually settled at Perton in Staffordshire, 25 miles from Stone and in the second half of 1606 Mary's mother [Chapter 5, 5.30] wrote to Mary's sister, *"I take no joy to hear of your sister nor of that boy,"* as if she had heard that Mary and Barnfield had some sort of friendship.[131]

Two sonnets attributed to Barnfield stand way above all his other works in terms of quality. They are both from his 1598 *Pecunia*, in which the author attributes the poems to his *unriper years*, and they were selected to be printed in *The Passionate Pilgrim (poem 8)* of 1599:

To his friend Maister R. L. — In praise of Musique and Poetrie.

If Musique and sweet Poetrie agree,
As they must needes (the Sister and the Brother)
Then must the Love be great, twixt thee and me,
Because thou lou'st the one, and I the other.
Dowland to thee is dear; whose heauenly tuch
Upon the Lute, doeth rauish humaine sense:
Spenser to me; whose deep Conceit is such,
As passing all Conceit, needs no defence.
Thou lou'st to hear the sweet melodious sound,
That Phœbus Lute (the Queen of Musique) makes:
And I in deep Delight am chiefly drownd,
When as himself to singing he betakes.
One God is God of Both (as Poets faigne)
One Knight loves Both, and Both in thee remain.

John Dowland, a composer of songs, (1563-1623) was at Court between 1596-1598 before leaving for Denmark which helps date the poem. Master R.L. is probably Richard Leveson, Mary Fitton's cousin, who was knighted in 1596 and Richard Barnfield's Staffordshire neighbour. The dedication is curious as it is an amorous poem written by a man to a man, but to me the *sister and the brother* parallel suggests that this poem was written by a woman and my candidate has to be Mary Fitton who was close to Barnfield and certainly close to the Court where Dowland performed. A simple typographical "error" would convert *his* into *her*.[132] If one read this poem without knowing the author, its

---

[129] Chapter Five explains.

[130] Darlaston / Dorlaston is 1.5 miles NNW of Stone on the west bank of the Trent only four miles from one of Leveson's homes at Trentham.

[131] *That boy* could also have been a bastard son by Richard Leveson.

[132] Mary Fitton courted a scandal if the dedication had said "her." Barnfield, being a *boy*, was immune.

Richard Barnfield

quality and style would immediately suggest Shakespeare. It was definitely good enough to be selected for the *Passionate Pilgrim*.

The other outstanding "Barnfield" poem, number twenty-one in *The Passionate Pilgrim,* is about the widowed wife of King Pandion and relates how her so-called friends will pander to her in her widowhood;

An Ode [133]

As it fell upon a Day,
In the merrie Month of May,
Sitting in a pleasant shade,
Which a grove of Myrtles made,
Beastes did leap, and Birds did sing,
Trees did grow, and Plants did spring:
Every thing did banish mone,
Save the Nightingale alone.
She (poor Bird) as all forlorn,
Leand her Breast up-till a Thorn;
And there sung the dolefulst Ditty,
That to hear it was great Pity.
Fie, fie, fie; now would the cry
Teru Teru, by and by:
That to hear her so complain,
Scarce I could from Tears refrain:
For her griefes so lively shown,
Made me think upon mine own.
Ah (thought I) thou mournst in vain;
None takes Pity on thy pain:
Senseless Trees, they cannot hear thee;
Ruthless Beares, they wil not cheer thee.
King Pandion, he is dead:
All thy friends are lapt in Lead.
All thy fellow Birds do sing,
Careless of thy sorrowing.
Whilst as fickle Fortune smiled,
Thou and I, were both beguiled.
Every one that flatters thee,
Is no friend in miserie:
Words are easy, like the wind;
Faithful friends are hard to find:
Every man will be thy friend,
Whilst thou hast wherewith to spend:
But if store of Crowns be scant,
No man will supply thy want.
If that one be prodigal,
Bountiful, they will him call:

---

[133] The poem became known also as Philomel.

And with such-like flattering,
Pity but he were a King.
If he be adict to vice,
Quickly him, they will intice.
If to Women he be bent,
They have at Commaundement.
But if Fortune once do frown,
Then farewell his great renown:
They that fawnd on him before,
Use his company no more.
He that is thy friend indeed,
He will help thee in thy need:
If thou sorrow, he will weep;
If thou wake, he cannot sleep:
Thus of every grief, in hart
He, with thee, doeth bear a Part.
These are certain Signs, to know
Faithful friend, from flatt'ring foe.

In this poem *Fie! Fie! Fie!* could / would have been recognised by Elizabethans as something not quite as strong as Shit! Shit! Shit! *Teru* is defined as an "overbearing or brawling woman, or a deity often appearing in morality plays." This ambivalence can change the whole tone of the poem into one of gentle derision. The *"by and by"* is a very Welsh expression, and Margaret Vaughan Hawkins was from Wales.

King Pandion; Pandion is the generic for the sea bird the Osprey; Pandion was also the father of Philomela (Nightingale) in Greek mythology. An Osprey is also known as a fish-hawk; the sense of the poem starts leaning towards Margaret Hawkins, the wealthy widow of the navigator, privateer and great Admiral, Sir John Hawkins, who died at sea in 1595. Perhaps Richard Barnfield had familiarity with the Hawkins' household such that he was confidently able to allude to the widow Margaret in verse. Mary Fitton had much better credentials as firstly, Margaret Hawkins had been a lady of the Queen's bedchamber and secondly, Mary was a cousin of Richard Leveson who would have known Hawkins well as they were both naval men. I believe this poem was written by Mary Fitton and we will see in the next chapter and in the Sonnets that Mary Fitton had more than a few connections with the sea. Mary Wroth in her allegory, *Urania*, certainly has *Antissia* experiencing a number of maritime adventures. Here are the last three lines of Sonnet 66:

> . . .And captive-good attending Captain ill.
> Tired with all these, from these would I be gone,
> Save that to die, I leave my love alone.

A third Barnfield poem, of 164 lines, titled *A Combat betwixt Conscience and Covetousness,* from the 1605 edition of *Pecunia,* is given at Appendix 4. This fits very closely to the relationship between Mary and Pembroke as it may have existed when the poem was published. Its timing is apposite as Pembroke

Richard Barnfield

returned to glory with the start of the new reign in 1603-1604. In a dream, the author imagined a dialogue between the shamed, female Conscience (Mary Fitton fits the bill) and the proud, male Covetousness (Pembroke). The short Dedication talked of a woman exiled the City,[134] and the theme of being exiled is repeated throughout the poem. The first of these two sections could very well refer to Pembroke and the second to Mary.

> The Carle[135] no sooner Conscience had espied,
> But swelling like a Toad, (puft up with pride)
> He straight began against her to invey;
> These were the words, which Covetise did say.
> Conscience (quoth he) how dar'st thou be so bold,
> To claim the place, that I by right do hold?
> Neither by right, nor might, thou canst obtain it:
> By might (thou knowst full well) thou canst not gain it.
> The greatest Princes are my followers,
> The King in Peace, the Captain in the Wars:
> The Courtier, and the simple Countryman:
> The Judge, the Merchant, and the Gentleman:
> The learned Lawyer, and the Politician:
> The skilful Surgeon, and the fine Physician:
> In brief, all sorts of men me entertain,
> And hold me, as their Souls sole Sovereign,
> And in my quarrel, they will fight and die,
> Rather then I should suffer injury.
> And as for title, interest, and right,
> I'll prove its mine by that, as well as might.
> Though Covetousness, were used long before,
> Yet Judas Treason, made my Fame the more;
> When Christ he caused, crucified to be,
> For thirty pence, man sold his mind to me:
> And now adaies, what tenure is more free,
> Then that which purchas'd is, with Gold and fee?

> Conscience.[136]
> Aye me, (distressed Wight[137]) what shall I do?
> Where shall I rest? Or whither shall I go?
> Unto the rich? (woes[138] me) they, do abhor me:
> Unto the poor? (alas) they, care not for me:
> Unto the Old-man? he; hath me forgot:

---

[134] The dedication is; *To his Worshipful good friend, Master John Steventon, of Dothill, in the County of Salop* [Shropshire], *Esquire*.

> Sith Conscience (long since) is exiled the City, O let her in the Country, find some Pity: But if she be exiled, the Country too, O let her find, some favour yet of you.

[135] churl?

[136] Later in the poem, this is Conscience's response.

[137] Wight = person or creature.

[138] Woe is me?

Richard Barnfield

Unto the Young-man? yet he, knows me not:
Unto the Prince? he; can dispense with me:
Unto the Magistrate? that, may not be:
Unto the Court? for it, I am too base:
Unto the Country? there, I have no place:
Unto the City? thence, I am exiled:
Unto the Village? there; I am reviled:
Unto the Bar? the Lawyer there, is bribed?
Unto the War? there, Conscience is derided:
Unto the Temple? there; I am disguised:
Unto the Market? there, I am despised:
Thus both the young and old, the rich and poor,
Against me (silly Creature) shut their door.
Then, sith each one seeks my rebuke and shame,
I'll go again to Heaven (from whence I came.)

What brought Richard Barnfield to be writing about Kings and Princes and a reviled woman exiled from the City? Had Barnfield seen the Sonnets when he and Mary both lived in Staffordshire? Did Richard and Mary collaborate in writing this? Finally, how many women were there in Staffordshire, exiled from Court who had a penchant for brilliant poetry? It is unlikely that there were two such women. The body of evidence, albeit circumstantial after 400 years, connecting Richard Barnfield with Mary Fitton becomes substantial. Within the bounds of statistical probability, we have found Mary Fitton.[139]

If Mary Fitton occasionally published under the name Richard Barnfield, we see she had the ability to write verse of high, if not exceptional quality. This makes it easy to reconcile how a young girl from the country could become a favourite Maid of Honour of a demanding and finicky Queen. It makes it consistent that Mary can be the author of Sonnets 1-126 and of *A Lover's Complaint.*

After leaving London in disgrace and bringing shame on her family, Mary Fitton, it appears, spent time as a guest of John Steventon, she seems to renew an acquaintance with Richard Barnfield, and she definitely had two bastard children by Richard Leveson. In Sonnet 110 we read:

Alas 'tis true, I have gone here and there
And made myself a motley to the view,
Gored mine own thoughts, sold cheap what is most dear,
Made old offences of affections new.

Apart from the reprinting of Pecunia, 1605 saw a number of events that affected Mary Fitton. Richard Leveson died in August, removing a "husband" and a trustworthy source of knowledge of events in London; we will see that

---

[139] In *Urania, Antissia,* upset by *Amphilanthus* rejecting her love enlists *Dolorindus,* who is also estranged from his own country and has been mistakenly disinherited by his father, to murder him. When the plot fails *Dolorindus* allies himself with *Amphilanthus* but eventually marries *Antissia.* [précis from Cavanagh's Cherished Torment. P71; p245.n55].

Richard Barnfield

the influential, sixty-two year old Sir William Knollys turned his back on her and to add insult to injury married the 18 year old Elizabeth Howard[140] and, if this period coincides with Sonnets 95 & 96, Mary fell out with Pembroke.[141]

Reviewing the clues which all happen in a plausible time scale:

Troian Nimph

TT

Connections between the families of Fitton, Leveson, Leigh, Barnfield, Skrymsher, Holcroft and Talbot.

The sentiments written in a *Combat betwixt Conscience and Covetousness.*

The proximity of the protagonists in Staffordshire, Warwickshire and Cheshire.

The naval connections between two Admirals. The poem to Master R.L.

The young woman whom Barnfield meets and collaborates with in London.

In Mary Wroth's *Urania,* echoes of *Antissia,* (Mary Fitton) reconciling with and marrying the estranged, and wrongfully disinherited *Dolorindus.* [142]

If William Shakespeare of Stratford-upon-Avon could be linked to any one of the plays in the first Folio with so many clues it would be ample evidence that he wrote drama, but there is no such evidence.

Before reading Mary Fitton's Sonnets, the next chapter gives more biography about her. The information mainly derives from an 1897 book, *Gossip from a Muniment-room* compiled by Lady Newdigate-Newdegate who transcribed contemporary letters from, and to the Fittons, including letters to Anne Newdigate, Mary's sister. Her research also identified the names of Mary's two husbands, Captain Richard Polewhele and John Lougher, the will of the first husband, and Mary's will and its references to her children. We will find that Mary Fitton was meditative, excitable and moody.

Afterthoughts

In the play, *As you Like It,* there are two characters called Jacques. One is simply Jacques; the other is Jacques de Boyes. Jacques de Boyes has such a minor role at the very end of the play that there is no time for the character to

---

[140] Elizabeth Howard became the proud mother of two sons after her marriage to Knollys, and when Knollys died she married the boys' father. She was a distant cousin of Leveson's wife.

[141] Early in 1606 Mary's father dies but there appears to be no echo of this in the Sonnets.

[142] Richard Barnfield possibly. There is an interesting line of investigation deriving from Francis Beaumont's letter [5.32] which shows that the widowed Mary Fitton had remarried before 1612.

Richard Barnfield

be developed, but his name is the very essence of a homosexual pun. The melancholy Jacques, on the other hand, does have a role to play and one easily can read a certain campness into the part. Was the character based on Richard Barnfield? Did Richard Barnfield introduce Thomas Lodge's *Rosalynde*, with its Ganymede and Corydon (Corin), to William Herbert and Mary Fitton, or to William Shakespeare the actor and director? Poem 18 from *The Passionate Pilgrim*, (Appendix 2), could easily fit into the play; it is a lament by a shepherd, Corydon, on losing a lover after a slight tiff. *As You Like It* also has a character, Orlando, with whom Rosalind (disguised as a young man) is in love. Orlando, is also madly in love with Rosalind (but he does not recognise her in disguise) and nails to the trees in the forest his very inferior love poems, only for Rosalind to make great fun of him, and amuse the audience, by reading them out aloud. We have the real parallel in that we know that Mary Fitton improved what she considered were Richard Barnfield's inferior verses.

CHAPTER FIVE

MARY FITTON

Mary Fitton's married sister, Anne Newdigate (1575-1618), lived her adult life at Arbury Hall near Nuneaton in Warwickshire.[143] In 1897 Lady Anne Emily Newdigate-Newdegate (Lady Newdigate), wife of the five-time-great-grandson of Anne and John Newdigate, discovered unknown letters in the Arbury muniments room. After considerable research she wrote biographies of Anne and Mary in a book called *Gossip from a Muniment-room.* The book, with its embossed cover of lilies and four-leaf pansies[144] was dedicated to her husband.

The origin of the theory that Mary Fitton was the *Dark Lady of the Sonnets* derives erroneously from certain people reading this book. Their theory is also firmly refuted in the second edition. Two portraits of Mary [PLATES 1 & 2] can be seen in the dining room of Arbury Hall which is opened to the public at Bank Holiday weekends [PLATE 8]. One shows her at the age of fourteen standing alongside her older sister, Anne. The other has her, as a young woman, in a very elaborate court gown decorated with an unusual motif of, what look like, caterpillars and moths.[145] In the paintings her dark, slightly reddish-brown hair is lighter than that of her sister's and her eyes are a slate blue. Visually, she is not a *Dark Lady* as described in Sonnets 128-154.

It was early twentieth-century researchers that made Mary Fitton into a strumpet, promoting her for a while as the mistress of William Shakespeare. We will see in this chapter how Mary appeared to play loose and fast with her guardian, the pompous Sir William Knollys, a much older, married man who was Comptroller of the Queen's household. Sir William was not an innocent; he was infatuated with, or genuinely loved Mary and the ridiculous Knollys-Fitton Court saga is parodied in *Twelfth Night* (Malvolio-Olivia). We will read of Mary being demonstrably over-familiar with the Queen, and her running like a man through the London streets to meet William Herbert. Contemporary letters relate of William Herbert's admission to the paternity of the child that died in infancy, of the scandal at his refusal to marry her, and their both being dismissed from Court. Her mother bemoans the shame and

---

[143] Arbury has the distinction of another famous female author who used a man's name. Mary Ann Evans, 1819-80, was born and, for twenty years, lived at Arbury Farm. She wrote under the name George Eliot. The same trees, rivers and fields that inspired her had once inspired Mary Fitton, although the hall that Mary Fitton knew was rebuilt in its current exquisite style.

[144] A pansy was the Emblem of the Fittons [PLATE 4]; the Lily was the emblem of the Newdigates. Leaded windows, in the form of pansies, help decorate Arbury's delightful architecture.

[145] Thomas Moffet, Mary Sidney Herbert's physician, dedicated a light-hearted poem, *Silkworms and their Flies*, to the Countess. Perhaps there is a connection.

Mary Fitton

humiliation that Mary has brought on the Fitton name. Mary is also rumoured to have had two daughters out of wedlock, at least eight pregnancies by four men, and we will find she was twice widowed. Finally, recent history has discovered that at least one famous playwright parodied her in such an unambiguous and salacious way that an infuriated Mary would have wanted her revenge. Unfortunately the playwright died the same year as his play was published.

I had thought that Mary Sidney Wroth, William's first cousin, was in the unique position to have written Sonnets 1-126 but, when reading this footnote to page 36 of Lady Newdigate's book, I realised that Mary Fitton was a possible candidate:[146]

> [5.1] A writer in Literature of Nov. 4th, 1897, gives us an interesting sonnet addressed to *Mistress Mary Fitten by the author*[147] *of a quaint and rare volume printed in 1599, and entitled:*
>
> *A Woman's Woorth Defended against all the Men in the World, proving them to be more perfect, excellent, and absolute in all virtuous Actions than any Man of what qualitie soever. Written by one that hath heard much, seene much, but knows a great deal more.*
>
> This testimonie of my true hart's zeale,
> Faire and (for euer honord) vertuous maide:
> To your kind fauor humbly dooth appeale
> That in construction nothing be mis-saide.
> Those fierie spirits of high temperd wit,
> That drink the dewe of Heaven continually:
> They could have graced you with termes more fit,
> Then [148]can my lowlie, poore, weake ingenie.
> Let not my love (yet) nightly pass respect,[149]
> Devoted onely to your excellence:
> Winke woorthy Virgin at my lines defect,
> Let will extenuate what ere offence.
> It is no bountie that is giuen from store,
> Who giues his hart, what gifts can he giue more?

---

[146] For ease of cross reference, the body of this chapter has numbered sections. Lady Newdigate's text is indented.

[147] The book was actually translated from French by Anthony Gibson; publisher J Wolfe, 12o. [copy in the British Library] so it appears that the Sonnet was hand-written into the book.

[148] fit-then

[149] We shall read that Knollys passed by her bedroom every night. Is it reasonable to read the word *Willy* in the initial letters - **w**eake **i**ngenie. **L**et not my **l**ove (**y**et) nightly pass respect and does *pass respect* mean stand to *attention?*

Mary Fitton

Clues in the text suggest that the writer was Sir William Knollys, her guardian and then a member of the Privy Council. Knollys recognised something special in Mary Fitton that made her very attractive to him; sex, intellect, property, perhaps all three – but not a leg up on the social ladder, he was already the better connected. From his letters we find that he wanted, and certainly expected, Mary Fitton to one day be his wife. However when in 1605 his wife did die he turned his back on Mary and at the age of 58 managed to obtain the eighteen-year-old Elizabeth Howard,[150] daughter of Thomas, 1st. Lord Suffolk, as his bride. Having read this sonnet and its dedication I had to look again at the evidence concerning this woman in whom he saw having, *"those fierie spirits of high temperd wit...."*.

This chapter is filled mostly by abstracts from *Gossip from a Muniment-Room*. One needs a little patience in reading them; a lot is being said or can be implied. If you happen to know the stylised way in which Malvolio speaks in *Twelfth Night* you will hear him again in Sir William Knollys' letters. Nearly all the letters were undated. The playwright must have known Knollys' speech and his foibles very well.

The narrator in the text that follows is Lady Newdigate, although I do interrupt, occasionally. Her research is excellent, especially considering she did not have the tools or mobility we have now.

＊ ＊ ＊ ＊ ＊

[5.2] It was about 1595 that Mary Fitton, being seventeen years old, began her Court life. Sir Edward Fitton, in his natural anxiety for his young daughter's[151] welfare in her new and trying position, made interest on her-behalf with a personage of importance at the Court, who was now Comptroller of the Household and, later on, Treasurer. This was an old friend, Sir William Knollys, son of Sir Francis Knollys, and first cousin once removed to the Queen on her mother's side. At this time Knollys was upwards of fifty years old, and had been some time married to Dorothy[152], daughter and co-heiress of Lord Bray, and widow of Edmund Brydges, Lord Chandos, who had been left her husband's sole executrix and the possessor of much wealth for her life. In his will Lord Chandos grants her this life interest, *as his most faithful and loving wife, for her obedience truth and faithful love towards him.* Though Dorothy was a valuable prize as regards her wealth, she must have been considerably older than her second husband, and we have reason to believe he chafed at the chain that prevented his marriage with a younger and fairer spouse.

---

[150] A remote cousin of Margaret Howard, Sir Richard Leveson's wife.

[151] His elder daughter, Anne was betrothed, aged twelve, five years before she went to live with her husband, John Newdigate at Arbury. Sir Edward Fitton seems to have supported the Newdigates for the years before the marriage was consummated.

[152] Lady Chandos was a godparent to Mary Sidney Herbert.

Mary Fitton

[5.3] The earliest letter we find from Sir William Knollys is addressed:

To my verye lovyng frend Sr Edward Fytton, Knight.
Sr Edward, I am sorry your disease should so trouble you, as it deprives me of your company whilst you remain in London, but I will by no means that you trouble yourself with going abroad, but since you must undertake so great a journey, be careful to make yourself strong until you go. I wish I were at liberty to accompany you to Arbury & so to Drayton[153]. I will not fail to fulfil your desire in playing the Good Shepherd & will to my power defend the innocent lamb from the wolfish cruelty & fox-like subtlety of the tame beasts of this place, which when they seem to take bread at a man's hand will bite before they bark; all their songs be Syren-like, and their kisses after Judas fashion, but from such beasts deliver me and my friends. I will with my counsel advise your fair daughter, with my true affection love her and with my sword defend her if need be. Her innocency will deserve it and her virtue will challenge it at my hands, and I will be as careful of her well doing as if I were her true father.
Touching yourself I will say only this, that your love to me is not unrequited & that whensoever any occasion shall be offered wherein I may stand you in stead, I will never fail to use my uttermost power. In the mean time with my best salutations to yourself and my Lady, wishing you both health & happiness,

I remayne ever
Your assured lovyng ffrend
W. KNOLLYS.

[5.4] Thus Mary Fitton was launched on her Court life under powerful protection, but the "innocent lamb" soon turned out to be an arrant coquette and Sir William's professions of fatherly affection rapidly grew warmer and blossomed into ardent love, which he confides in a series of letters to her sister Anne. Sometimes he veils his sentiments in the language of parable, but more often they are expressed in the frankest terms, apparently with no compunctions in regard to the existing Lady Knollys.

Mrs Newdigate, [writes Knollys]
Your kind letter to your dear sister I have seen, wherein I find that though you be nearly joined by the law of nature, yet are you more surely united in the bond of love which exceedeth all bands and bringeth with it in the end a blessing

---

[153] Drayton Basset, his brother Henry's country place in Warwickshire.

Mary Fitton

where it is truly continued. Your thanks I accept as a recompence sufficient for my lines, but your excuse of not presuming to write again I nothing allow, seeming thereby to make my white staff an argument of your sloth, if I may so say, but to you & yours I desire neither to be head nor foot, but in that equal proportion where friendship is like to continue surest & longest & what is dear to you is dearest to me. Wherefore once again I will bid you the base, hoping you will not always keep the goal in silence. Some reasons methinks might breed a better sympathy between us, for I imagine we both having too much do yet want, though in divers respects our summer is turned to winter, the one by the airy element, the other by the earthly. The fairest flowers of our gardens be blasted, yours in the bud by some unwholesome easterly wind,[154] mine in the leaf by the hoar frost and the difference is that because the wind may change your hopes may revive & by reason of the continual frosts my looking for any fruit of my garden is in vain, unless the old tree [his wife!] be cut down & a new graft of a good kind planted.

But I leave to parable and in plain English wish you what you most desire. As for me my hopes being desperate & fortune ever frowning, were it not that by the sunshine of some pleasing thoughts I were somewhat relieved I should die both in hope & heart. Yet hope is the only food I live by & patience is my pillow to rest upon, both which I wish you to make your companions as remedies against all diseases of the mind. If I have been too long blame the matter which leadeth me along, if too bold with you let my desire to provoke you to a lyterall quarrel be my excuse, & if too open impute it to my trust. But it is time to leave troubling you any longer & forgetting myself.

Wherefore wishing you all health & happiness both of body and mind I desire to be esteemed in the number of your best friends, both for the love I bear to your father & all his & for your own worthiness, remaining ever this 20th of May, Your assured ffrend

W. KNOLLYS.

[5.5] It seems difficult to find any excuse for this writer's open avowal of impatience at the impediment that obstructed the desired end to his courtship of the attractive Maid of Honour. Neither is it easy to understand how Anne, the excellent Anne of whom nothing but good is known, could by her sympathy permit these frank avowals of Sir William's love for her sister. He even seemed so sure of her approval

---

[154] One would assume that Anne have kept her sister, Mary Fitton, informed of these letters and this line looks very like Sonnet 18.2, "rough winds do shake the darling buds of Maie."

and co-operation as to ask for her prayers on his behalf in a subsequent
letter. Here we find the disadvantage of a one-sided correspondence.
There may have been extenuating circumstances of which we know
nothing. Otherwise we can only be thankful we no longer live in the age
of *good Queen Bess* but in the more outwardly decorous days of our
Sovereign Lady, Queen Victoria.

   The letters which follow are given verbatim, for were they to be
curtailed, or any sentences omitted, their historical interest and value
would be injured. They have been considered of sufficient importance
to have been preserved for nearly three hundred years in the muniment
room at Arbury, though never yet made known, even to the immediate
members of the family. It is also necessary to remember that letters of
this period were written with infinite pains and much consideration,
and consequently have a value far superior to the hasty scrawls of
today. From their style and superscription they appear to have been
invariably sent by hand, and months often intervened between their
dates. We must now let Sir William continue the tale of his tantalising
courtship. In his next letter he refers to Anne's hopes of becoming a
mother, her previous expectations having been disappointed, as we
may gather from his former remarks:

> Honorable Lady,
>   The more you go about to disable your own worthiness the
> more do you make it shine in yourself & by that means bring
> me farther indebted to so great a kindness. The least good
> thought of your well wishing mind is a recompence sufficient
> for my small power to afford you what you are worthy of, but
> such as they are command and think that your Dearest Dear
> doth not wish you better than I do. As God hath blessed you
> with increase so blessed be you ever & freed from all
> discontents, & though myself can not but be now upon the
> stage & play his part who is cloyed with too much & yet ready
> to starve for hunger, my eyes see what I can not attain to, my
> ears hear what I do scant believe, & my thoughts are carried
> with contrary conceits, my hopes are mixt with despair & my
> desires starved with expectation, but were my enjoying
> assured, I could willingly endure purgatory for a season to
> purchase my heaven at the last. But the short warning, the
> distemperature of my head by reason of the toothache & your
> sister's going to bed without bidding me goodnight will join in
> one to be a means that for this time I will only trouble you
> with these few lines scribbled in haste, and wishing you all
> happiness, a good delivery of your burden and your sister in
> the same case justifiable, I leave you to God's good protection,
> myself to your dearest sister's true love and her to a constant

resolution to love him only who cannot but ever love her best
& thus with my best salutations I will ever remain
    Your most assured ffrend
    I would fayne saye brother
    W. KNOLLYS.

[5.6] In the next letter Knollys becomes still more outspoken:

    Honorable sister (I cannot choose but call you so because I
desire nothing more than to have it so).
    Your fair written letter & more fairly indited I have
received & read more than once or twice seeking to find there
which so much you endeavour to put me in hope of. It is true
that winter's cold is the murderer of all good fruits in which
climate I dwell & do account it as a purgatory allotted to me
for my many offences committed against the Highest, the
rather because I am more observant & devoted unto his
creature than to himself, from which to be delivered since
there is no means but the devout prayers & orasions of my
good friends. Let me entreat your fair self to pierce the
heavens with your earnest & best prayers to the effecter &
worker of all things for my delivery & that once I may be so
happy as to feel the pleasing comfort of a delightful summer,
which I doubt not will yield me the deserved fruit of my
constant desires, which as yet no sooner bud by the heat of the
morning sun, but they are blasted by an untimely frost, so as
in the midst of my best comforts I see nothing but dark
despair. I could complain of fortune which led me blindly into
this barren desert where I am ready to starve for want of my
desired food & of myself that would suffer my reason to be
betrayed by my will in following so blind a guide. But to all
my wounds I will apply your plaster which is patience, a
virtue I must needs confess, but having in a sort lost her force
because it is forced. Continue, I earnestly entreat you, your
prayer for my delivery, and your best means for my
obtaining that without the which I am not myself, having
already given my best part to whose I am more than mine
own. But I must cry silence lest I speak too loud, committing
this secret only to your self to whom as I wish all happiness
and your own heart's desire, so will I ever remain
    Your most affectionat brother
    W. KNOWLESSE then I would.

[5.7] Anne's first child, a daughter, was born in [May] 1598. The
godparents or *gossips* chosen for the baby were Lady Fitton, the
grandmother; Anne's greatest friend, Elizabeth Lady Grey and Sir

Mary Fitton

William Knollys. Immediately after this happy event Sir Edward Fitton writes as follows:

> Good Nan,
>   God in heaven bless thee and my daughter and continue thy health and life as my dearest friend and thereby comfort, next thy poor mother whose love and kindness to me and her children I fear will shorten her days, but she shall never want that comfort that I can afford her. . . . God bless your little one and grant thee as much comfort as ever mother had of child, but I am sorry that yourself will needs nurse her. . . . Thus longing sore to see thee . . farewell this xvii of May 1598
>   Thy treuest friend
> Ed. FfYTTON.

[5.8] And again in another letter dated the 3rd of July 1598:

> Nan Newdigate,
>   I am to think myself much beholden to you as a father can be to a daughter. Your mother will needs send Frelan and I send nobody but my own heart which ever shall be with you wheresoever my body is. I will see thee so soon as I can and that is soon as I can, and until then I will love thee. and ever remain more thine than my own.
>   Ed. FYTTON.

[5.9] This latter date may have been that of the christening, for Lady Fitton writes on the same day:

> My good Nan,
>   I pray God bless you and my little daughter. I long to hear exceedingly how you both do. I had sent before this but that I hoped some other would have sent that do not. ... I have sent you a nurse's reward xli[155] to buy you a kirtle for my daughter. I will provide somewhat when she is bigger to remember me by. I long to hear how all things about your new Charge goeth, for I persuade myself that my son Newdigate will not go back with his word. I pray God send you well to do with it. And we can do you any good let us know it and it shall be done. If you hear anything of your sister I pray let know, for I never heard from her since.
>   God bless you and yours and send us all merry to meet.
>   Gawsworth this third of July
>   Your lovyng Mother A. ffyTTON.
>   Commend me kindly to your husband.
>   To my good daughter Mrs Anne Newdygat at Erbery.

---

[155] Xli x=10 li = £ i.e. £10 (£2,500 in modern values - some kirtle, a gown or outer petticoat).

Mary Fitton

[5.10] Sir William Knollys accepts the post of *Gossip* to Anne's little daughter in the next letter, and at the same time he tenders advice on a subject that is not usually considered one of the duties of godparents.

To my verye Lovyng ffrend Mrs Anne Newdygate.

How desirous I am in person to perform the office of a godfather mine own heart knoweth & you should have seen if I were within mine own power, but such is my bondage to this place as I have neither liberty to please myself nor satisfy my good friends' expectation, amongst which I must account you in the foremost rank, as well for your own worthiness as for being so nearly united both in nature & love to those which I honour much & who may more command me than all the world besides. But my thoughts of that party I will leave to be discovered not by this base means of pen & paper but by myself. Accept I pray you of my lawful excuse for not coming myself, assuring you that I will be ever ready to perform any friendly duty to you. I have entreated my brother Blunt[156] to supply my place in making your little one a Christian soul & give it what name it shall please you. Imagine what name I love best and that do I nominate but refer the choice to yourself, and if I might be as happy to be a father, as a godfather, I would think myself exceeding rich, but that will never be until one of your own tribe be a party player. I should like nothing that you play the nurse if you were my wife. I must confess it argueth great love, but it breedeth much trouble to yourself & it would more grieve you if sucking your own milk it should miscarry, children being subject to many casualties. But you may tell me I am more curious in this point than I need, but I speak it in friendly council not meaning either to contrary your own will or dissuade you from your resolution if by a reasonable persuasion yourself think not good to alter your purpose. Thus without further compliments, wishing you a happy mother of many children & your own heart's desire, with my best salutations I commend you to God & will ever remain

Your assured poore ffrend & gossepp
W. KNOLLYS.

[5.11] The suggestion of the writer in regard to the naming of his goddaughter was carried out. She was christened Mary; but Sir William's advice on a more domestic matter was not as effective. Anne was too devoted a mother to abandon any duty towards her child. Henceforth this correspondent always addresses her as his *Gossip*.

---

[156] Sir Christopher Blount - brother-in-law, married to his sister Lettice Knollys.

Mary Fitton

Fair Gossip,

the conveniency of this bearer and the desire I have not to be behind with you in any kindness is cause that I may not leave you unsaluted. The many testimonies you have made of your worthy respect of me bind me to be thankful by all the means I may, and you shall ever be assured I will not fail to perform the part of a true friend whensoever you shall have cause to try me. I am sorry I cannot assure my coming to Arbury being under the command of a greater power but if it be possible for me to break loose but a little I will, God willing, see Drayton and take Arbury in my way. Until then I recommend you to your best delights & thus wishing you as much happiness as your heart can think with my best salutations to yourself & my blessing to your little one I remain ever

Your verye assured ffrend

W. KNOLLYS.

[5.12] Amongst all Anne's numerous correspondents we only find one letter from her sister Mary [PLATE 6]. This is written in a scrawling hand[157], is more than usually ill-spelt, and contains nothing of interest. It is given here because it shows the affectionate terms existing between the two sisters:

To my dearest syster Mrs. An Newdigate.[158]

Sinc distanc bares me from so great hapenes as I can seldom hear from you, which when I do is so welcom as I esteme nothing more worthie, and for your love which I dout not of shall be equaled in ful mesure, but lest my lines to tedius weare, and time that limets all things bares me of wordes, which eles could never ses[159] *to tel howe dear you ar, and with what zele I desire your retorne, than can wish nothing more then your hartes desire, and wil ever contineu; your afectina sister. . .*[160]

Mary phytton

---

[157] I disagree! This is an artist's hand from the way she signs the letter M. Lady Newdigate had corrected the original spelling, but this is the original.

[158] This line is on the reverse (outside) of the letter.

[159] cease

[160] Only this one letter, but what style! I find it breathtaking. The *return* she mentions could be the return of Anne's birthday, 6th October. Note how she spells her surname. In looking through the *Muniment-Room* letters one occasionally finds a comment to the effect, "nothing of interest, kept for sentimental reasons." I think this was one such letter and all her other letters were destroyed. Her handwriting is in the Roman, Italic, style. *Twelfth Night Act 3.iv,* Malvolio on finding a dropped letter says, "I think we do know the sweet Roman hand."

Mary Fitton

[5.13] Sir William Knollys at this time had other troubles to distract him in addition to his hapless love affair. He writes his next hurried letter when much disturbed by the disgrace of his nephew, the valiant but reckless Earl of Essex.

Fair Gossip,
I must crave pardon for my so long silence, not grown by a negligent forgetfulness of so good a friend, but forced by a distraction I have had concerning the Noble Earl of Essex[161], which hath made me careless to satisfy myself or my friends. I leave to you to imagine the discomforts I take hereof when your sister is fain to blame me for my melancholy & small respect of her, who when I am myself is the only comfort of my heart. She is now well & hath not been troubled with the mother[162] of a long time. I would God I might as lawfully make her a mother as you are. I would be near both at Arbury to shun the many griefs which this place affordeth & she should enjoy the company of the most loving & kind sister that ever I knew. My heart is so full of sorrow at this time for my lord of Essex being dangerously sick before his restraint, as I am scant myself. Receive therefore I pray you these ragged lines from a broken head as a remembrance of [a] most faithful friend who will ever be ready to do all good offices wherein I may stead you. Thus leaving for this time abruptly with my best wishes of your best desires, I commend you to God & will ever remain
Your assured lovyng gossepp & ffrend
W. KNOLLYS.
God bless my fair daughter & kiss it I pray you kindly for me.

[5.14] In the next letter Mary Fitton appears still to be encouraging her elderly lover with hopes that she would be willing to wait for him until he was free to marry her.

Fair gossip,
Your uncle's sudden departure and my coming – by chance – to London when he was ready to take his journey is cause you must look for no compliments at this time, only you shall know that true affection is as well expressed in few words as in many & I assure myself your wisdom doth not measure love by lines. So as having saluted you with my best commendations & assured you that I will be ever ready to perform toward you all the good offices of a true friend: the best news I can send you is that your sister is in good health & going to the Court within 2 or 3 days,[163] though I think she could be better pleased to be with her best sister upon some conditions. Her greatest fear is that while the grass groweth the horse may starve & she thinketh a bird in the bush is worth 2

---

[161] This was probably about the end of 1598 / early 1599 after Essex's return from Ireland.
[162] Hysterical passion; so called as being imagined peculiar to women. (Johnson's Folio Dictionary, 1755.) Mary appeared to have moods.
[163] It reads as if Mary has not yet been at Court, or has been away from Court for a while.

in the hand. But both she and I must have patience & that will
bring peace at the last. Thus in some haste with my best
salutations to your self, and my kindest blessing to my daughter
I wish you your heart's desire & will remain ever
Your ffaythffull ffrend & gossepp
W. KNOLLYS.

[5.15] This is the last letter in which the writer and Mary seem to have
been on the best of terms. A cloud intervenes, which will be explained in
due course:

Honorable gossip,
Your few lines but very pithy and significant were very
welcome to me & I think I shall be forced in as brief manner to
return you mine by reason of this bearer's hasty departure, but
with them a very thankful & brother-like acceptance of your kind
remembrance. It was against my will I saw you not this summer. I
had purposed it but being restrained of my liberty by necessary
state occasions I was disposed of otherwise.
It is true that winter's approach hindered my journey to
Arbury and so unhappy I am as I never find summer, but being
fain to feed upon the dead stalk I live in doubt ever to enjoy the
sweet fruit of my summer's harvest. My ground is covered with
the bramble & the brier which until it be grubbed & cut up there
is no hope of good. It may be you country wits may give council in
such a case. Advise me I pray you in this extremity and if I may
once bring it to a fruitful soil, I doubt not but you shall be
partaker of my longed for husbandry. This bearer hasteth away &
I will find some other time to send to you, so as for this time
wishing you your heart's desire I remain ever
Your most assured ffrend
W. KNOLLYS.

[5.16] And again:

Fair Gossip,
having so convenient a messenger though my warning be but
short I may not suffer him to pass by you without some
salutations which in regard of the humour I am put into though
they can be but melancholy yet to one to whom I have been so
much beholden as your fair self I will ever be thankful & just.
Methinks it is pity that 2 bodies & one mind, so firmly united as
your sister's & yours, should not endure so much distance of
place, but that you are both bound – the one by her Majesty's
service, the other by a commanding Husband – & yet I that am at
the next door[164] do think myself now farther from the place I most
desire than in the beginning of my journey. Such is the variety of
this world & the uncertainty of this time I must live in frost &
snow subject to blasts & all ill winds & shall I fear never be so
happy as to possess the fair flower of the summer's garden. I hope

---

[164] His bedroom is next to a room used by the Maids of Honour.

Mary Fitton

you dwell under a better climate where the sun sometimes comforteth though the soil be subject to fogs & mists. Make a virtue of necessity & since your lot fell not to dwell in the land of promise where all things were given that were desired, work your own contentment out of your own worthiness & be ever happier than your unfortunate gossip who will be ever ready to do you respectable service remaining ever
> Your affectionate ffrend & gossepp
> W. KNOLLYS.

[5.17] Anne's *unfortunate gossepp* seems to have been, when at Court, not only figuratively but literally next door to the abode of the Maids of Honour. Sir Nicholas L'Estrange relates the following anecdote:

> The Lord Knollys (as he became at James I's coronation) in Queen Elizabeth's time had his lodging at Court, where some of the Ladies and Maids of Honour used to frisk and hey about in the next room, to his extreme disquiet a nights, though he often warned them of it. At last he gets one to bolt their own back door when they were all in one night at their revels, strips off his shirt, and so with a pair of spectacles on his nose and Aretine [165] in his hand comes marching in at a postern door of his own chamber, reading very gravely, full upon the faces of them. Now let the reader judge what a sad spectacle and pitiful fright these poor creatures endured for he faced them and often traversed the room in this posture above an hour.

[5.18] In the 1600 William Kempe, the Clown in Shakspeare's Company, dedicated his *Nine daies wonder* "to Mistris Anne Fitton, Mayde of Honour to most sacred Mayde Royal Queene Elizabeth."[166] The name Anne is plainly a misnomer for Mary, and shows how slight was Kempe's knowledge of the Mayde of Honour, though doubtless he selected her as his patroness not only on account of her natural gifts but

---

[165] The Italian Pietro Aretino, 1492-1556, wrote true pornography. Here, downloaded from an extract on the Internet, is an illustration of what these *poor creatures* had to suffer that night:

"No, I wouldn't say he consumed it, because placing his paintbrush, which he first moistened with spit, in her tiny colour cup, he made her twist and turn as women do in the birth throes or the mother's malady. And to be doubly sure that his nail would be driven more tightly into her slit, he motioned to his back and his favorite punk pulled his breeches down to his heels and applied his clyster to the reverend's visibilium, while all the time the General himself kept his eyes fixed on the two other young louts, who, having settled the sisters neatly and comfortably on the bed, were now pounding the sauce in the mortar to the great despair of the last little sister. Poor thing, she was so squint-eyed and swarthy that she had been spurned by all. So, she filled the glass tool with water heated to wash the messer's hands, sat on a pillow on the floor, pushed the soles of her feet against the cell wall, and then came straight down on that great crozier, burying in her body as a sword is thrust into a scabbard."

[166] In *As You Like It* Rosalind says in Act 3.2; *"I was seven of the nine days out of the wonder. . . . I was never so berhymed since Pythagoras' time that I was an Irish rat, which I can hardly remember."* [Mary Fitton probably spent some of her earliest years in Ireland and was probably born in Dublin.]

Mary Fitton

in order to ingratiate himself with one so high in favour with Queen Elizabeth.[167] The book gives an account of a journey which Kempe had performed morris-dancing from London to Norwich. In his dedication Kempe says:

> To shew my duty to your honourable self, whose favours (among other bountiful friends) make me (despite this sad world) judge my heart Cork and my heels feathers, so that methinks I could fly to Rome (at least hop to Rome as the old Proverb is) with a Mortar on my head. But in a word, your poor servant offers the truth of his progress and profit to your honourable view; receive it I beseech you, such as it is, rude and plain; for I know your pure judgment looks as soon to see beauty in a Blackamoor, or hear smooth speech from a Stammerer, as to find any thing but blunt mirth in a Morris dancer, especially such a one as Will Kemp, that hath spent his life in mad Jigs and merry jests.

[5.19] It was in June[168] of this same year (1600) that there was a remarkable festivity at Blackfriars. William Herbert was present, as was also a lady with whom we shall be still further concerned in the sequel. The occasion of this festivity was the marriage of Lord Herbert (son of the Earl of Worcester) with a lady of the Court, Mrs. Anne Russell. The Queen herself was there and having come to Blackfriars by water, she was carried from the water side in a lectica borne by six knights.[169] The bride was conducted to church by the nobleman with whom we are now more particularly concerned, William Herbert (son of Lord Pembroke), and Lord Cobham. The Queen supped and passed the night at Lord Cobham's.

Rowland Whyte, to Sir Robert Sidney, letter dated 14th June 1600 says:

> There is to be a memorable masque of eight ladies. They have a strange dance newly invented; their attire is this: each hath a skirt of cloth of silver, a rich waistcoat wrought with silks & gold & silver, a mantle of carnation taffeta cast under the arm, and their hair loose about their shoulders curiously knotted and interlaced. These are the Masquers: My Lady Dorothy [Hastings], Mrs Fitton, Mrs Carey, Mrs Onslow, M^rs

---

[167] An alternative is that Will Kempe knew Mary Fitton *very* well if he, William Herbert and Mary Fitton worked together to create *As You Like It*. Using her sister's name would avert suspicion from Mary and at the same time give her recognition.

[168] 16th June 1600, Anne Russell, a Maid of Honour, married Henry Somerset, 5th Earl of Worcester, at St. Martin's Church, Ludgate. Lord Herbert, his elder brother, had died a couple of years earlier. Blanche Somerset (next paragraph) was the groom's sister.

[169] The wedding is thought to be depicted by the Sherborne Castle [PLATE-4] painting, "Queen Elizabeth in Procession," It has been suggested that eight Maids of Honour are being led by Mary Fitton in white and Sir William Knollys is thought to be holding the Chamberlain's white staff. However, the lady in white equally looks like Anne Russell, the bride, and *Knollys* appears to be a garter knight conflicting with his garter creation in 1615.

Mary Fitton

Southwell, Mrs Bess Russell, Mrs Darcy and my Lady Blanche Somerset. These eight dance to the music Apollo brings, &. there is a fine speech that makes mention of a ninth, much to her Honour & Praise.[170]

And again, in another letter written shortly afterwards, he says:

> After supper the masque came in as I writ in my last; and delicate it was to see 8 ladies so prettily and richly attired. Mrs Fitton led, & after they had done all their own ceremonies, these 8 lady masquers chose 8 ladies more to dance the measures. Mrs Fitton went to the Queen & wooed her to dance; her Majesty asked what she was; " Affection," she said. "Affection!" said the Queen; "Affection is false." Yet her Majesty rose and danced . .[171]

[5.20] In the next January William Herbert became Earl of Pembroke on the death of his father. The goings on at the Court at this time seem to have been notorious:

> One Mrs Martin who dwelt at the Chopping Knife near Ludgate told me that she hath seen priests marry gentlewomen at the Court, in that time when that Mrs Fitton was in great favour, and one of her Majesty's maids of honour, and during the time that the Earl of Pembroke favoured her she would put off her head tire and tuck up her clothes and take a large white cloak and march as though she had been a man to meet the said Earl out of the Court.

[5.21] It must have been about this time that Sir William Knollys writes to Anne in evident distress about Mary's conduct:

> Honorable gossip,
>   So much have I been ever beholden to you in your true respectable good opinion of me as I should greatly blame myself & be thought unworthy if I should suffer your letters to return unanswered, not having other means to manifest how much I account myself indebted to you for many kindnesses, especially in your well wishing to me in a matter which most

---

[170] Sir Roland also wrote to Sir Robert Sidney that on Friday, 30th May 1600 at Baynards Castle, Mr William led the dance with Mrs. Mary.

[171] It is interesting to recall, from *Hamlet*, Ophelia's talking to her father about Hamlet. The use of *affection* reflects what the Queen said to Mary Fitton.

| Ophelia | He hath, my lord, of late made many tenders Of his affection to me. |
| Polonius | Affection! Puh! - you speak like a green girl Unsifted in such perilous circumstance. |

The night of the Masque would fit almost perfectly to the conception of William and Mary's child. One can imagine how excited Mary was that night, she must have been hyper.

imported me, which I think will be clean extinguished, though I leave nothing on my part to be done for the continuance thereof. But since I know this discourse will nothing please you, let me assure you that no friend you have shall be more ready to do all the offices of a true friend than myself wishing the party I spoke of before so worthy & fair a mind as my gossip hath. But since wishes can not prevail I will hope the best & pray that God will rectify if anything be amiss, accounting myself the unfortunate man alike to find that which I had laid up in my heart to be my comfort should become my greatest discomfort. But why do I trouble you with these things, let me live in your good opinion & I will ever deserve it, & thus wishing you all contentment & your heart's desire
> I will ever remain
> Your ffaythffull ffrend
> W. KNOLLYS.

[On 5th January 1601, on the eve of Twelfth Night, William Herbert wrote anxiously from Wilton to Sir Robert Cecil giving his excuses for not attending the Twelfth Night celebrations in London. His first consideration was shortage of time, but he and his parents, who were also on the list of invitees, would have remained at Wilton as his father Earl Pembroke was terminally ill and died just two weeks later. That following day the play *Twelfth Night* was premiered in a gala performance in Whitehall in honour of Don Virginio Orsini, the Italian Duke of Bracciano. It would appear from a line in the play, (Act 1, iii: *Are they to take dust like Mistress Mall's picture?*) that the scandal with Mary Fitton was already known, or breaking. William Herbert, therefore, had at least two reasons why he did not want to come, a third if the words *utterly* and *fit* to in the paragraph below have any significance;

> *I was sent unto by a very friend of mine to come post to the Court, and not to fail of being there to wait on Tuesday at dinner, if I would not utterly lose the Queen's favour: a sentence of little more comfort than hanging: and yet if I had made all the haste I could, I should hardly have been there by the time, receiving the letters but this Monday morning about 8 o'clock; and if I could perchance have been there by the time, I leave to your judgment how fit to wait that day.*[172]]

[5.22] Mary Fitton seems to have been launched on a mad career that could only end in disgrace. In a letter of January 26th of this year (1601) from Sir John Stanhope to Sir G. Carew we find this paragraph:

> Of the persecution is like to befall the poor maid's chamber in Court, and of Fitton's afflictions, and lastly her commitment to my Lady Hawkyns,[173] of the discouragement thereby of the

---

[172] Leslie Hotson's book, *"The First Night of Twelfth Night."* HMC Cecil Papers 11.3.
[173] Here is the link between Richard Barnfield's Pecunia, Mary Fitton & Lady Margaret Hawkins. See Chapter Four.

rest, though it be now out of your element to think of, yet I doubt not but that some friend doth more particularly advertise you.

Next month, on February 5th, in the postscript of a letter written from the Court by Sir Robert Cecil to Sir George Carew it is recorded:

> We have no news but that there is a misfortune befallen Mistress Fitton, for she is proved with child, and the Earl of Pembroke being examined confesseth a fact but utterly renounceth all marriage. I fear they will both dwell in the Tower awhile, for the Queen hath vowed to send them thither.[174]

Then we come to a letter from Tobie Matthew to Dudley Carleton on March 25th, which contains the following passage:

> The Earl of Pembroke is committed to the Fleet;[175] his cause is delivered of a boy who is dead.

[5.23] Thus Mary Fitton's short but brilliant career at Court came to an untimely end in dire disgrace. The Maid of Honour especially favoured by the Queen and adored by the Comptroller of the Household only seems to have escaped imprisonment in the Tower by *commitment to my Lady Hawkyns* for her confinement.

It is not surprising that her parents were greatly distressed at this shameful catastrophe, though they still apparently hoped that Pembroke could be induced to marry their daughter. Sir Edward Fitton writes to Anne from London[176] soon afterwards:

> Sweet Nan,
> I am very sorry that you are not well and so is your good Gossip also who hath him commended to you heartily. I pray you let hear from you as I do. I am in some hope of your Sister's enlargement[177] shortly, but what will be the end with the Earl I cannot tell. So soon as [I] can you shall hear. I have

---

[174] In 1598 Earl Southampton had angered the Queen by impregnating her Maid of Honour, the twenty-nine year old Elizabeth Vernon. He was forced to marry. The following year Southampton was involved with the Earl Marshall, Robert Devereux, 2nd Earl Essex, in what looked like traitorous dealings with the Irish. On 8th February 1601, a few days after commissioning the playing of *Henry II*, they tried but failed to instigate a rebellion in London. Essex was hanged and Southampton incarcerated until James I came to the throne in 1603.

One would assume that William Herbert would have been able to buy preferential treatment when in prison and it is worth noting that his London home, Baynards Castle, was about four minutes' walk away, near today's Blackfriars Bridge. Margaret Hawkins, in whose care Mary Fitton was placed, lived about a mile to the east, on Mincing Lane in St. Dunstan's Parish near to the Tower of London.

[175] The Fleet Prison

[176] On 22nd April 1601.

[177] enlargement = release from being confined.

Mary Fitton

delivered your letter to my Lady Derby and so praying you if this bearer cannot otherwise do, that you help to hire him a horse to Lichfield to my host at the George: and so with my very hearty commendations I bid you farewell this xxijth of Aprill 1601.

       Yr loving father & friende
       Ed ffYTTON.

[5.24] There is a letter from Sir Edward Fitton to Sir R. Cecil in Lord Salisbury's collection on this matter. It is dated May 16, 1601, and shows that some pressure had been exercised to induce Lord Pembroke to consent to a marriage, but without effect:

I can say nothing of the Earl, but my daughter is confident in her chance before God and wisheth my Lord and she might but meet before in different scenes. But for myself I expect no good from him that in all this time hath not shewed any kindness. I count my daughter as good a gentlewoman as my Lord is though the dignity of honour (be greater only in him) which hath beguiled her I fear, except my lord's honesty be the greater "vertuoes."

This letter is written from Stanner[178], where Sir Edward was obliged to stop on his road to Cheshire, his daughter being with him, and too weak to travel farther. Thus he had obtained her "enlargement" from my Lady Hawkyns' keeping, and was carrying her homewards, but apparently in secrecy.

[5.25] Francis Fitton [from London] writes to his great-niece, Anne Newdigate, eight days later, on the 24th of May 1601:

Mine own sweet niece,

I thank you much for your last of the 14th of this instant (lately by me received) and so likewise for many other before, because I honor you and love you as any the dearest friends you have. I supp⌐ ⸳ ⸱ your father by his stolen journey into Cheshire (unknown to me) hath acquainted you with something concerning your sister's estate. How true I know not for I find halting with me in their courses for her. God grant all be for the best but for ought I know & can see I see nothing better nor cause of better hope than before & I wish all things for her good so well as you desire which is all I can do, and so good niece farewell ten thousand times, from my lodginge the signe of the Black Boye, a Chandler's house neare the weste end of the Savoye in the Strand this 24th of Maye 1601.

       Your lovinge uncle & assured poore frind,
       fRANCYS fYTON.

---

[178] Is this Stanmore in Middlesex, about 12 miles from London?

Mary Fitton

A L Rowse; *The Elizabethan Renaissance: The Life of the Society;* pp 51-53, wrote, "On release from his confinement the unregenerate Pembroke was rusticated; whereupon he wrote to Cecil;

> *I have not yet been a day in the country, and I am as weary of it as if I had been prisoner there seven year. I see I shall never turn good Justice of the Peace. Therefore I pray, if the Queen determine to continue my banishment and prefer sweet Sir Edward [Fitton] before me, that you will assist me with your best means to go into some other land, that the change of the climate may purge me of melancholy; for else I shall never be fit for any civil society. . . . . if the Queen continue her displeasure a little longer, undoubtedly I shall turn clown, for Justice of Peace I can by no means frame unto, and one of the two a man that lives in the country must needs be.*

Finally he obtained leave to travel abroad, but, after the Queen's death, married the earl of Shrewsbury's rich, but misshapen daughter:[179] with whom he lived unhappily and by whom he had no children. Edward Hyde, Lord Clarendon wrote of the Pembroke marriage that it was, *'most unhappy, for he paid too dear for his wife's fortunes by taking her person into the bargain.'*

In *Philip's Phoenix,* Margaret P Hannay wrote that Pembroke tried to obtain from the Queen the patent of the Forest of Dean for Sir Edward Fitton and, when unsuccessful, in September 1601 complained, *thereby destroying that poor reputation that I was desirous to preserve ..... I am disgraced.* As Hannay nicely pointed out, Pembroke could not see the impropriety of asking the Queen to pay for his own irresponsibility.

In a draft agreement, dated 29th May 1601, William, Earl of Pembroke, offered to buy from Sir Robert Sidney, for fifteen hundred pounds a "jewell called the ffether of diomonds" worth, today, between £250,000 and £500,000. Was this to be a present for Mary Fitton?

In Sex in Elizabethan England, Alan Haynes wrote that William Herbert, *remained phlegmatic while imprisoned, writing verse and refusing to marry his mistress.*

* * * * *

[5.26] The next letter from Sir William Knollys must have been written after Mary had left the Court and gone to her faithful sister Anne. In spite of all that had occurred, the infatuated man seems still a victim to her charms:

> Fair Gossip,
>   sweet & pleasant was the blossom of my love, so comfortable & cordial to my heart as I had therein placed all my delight, I must confess the harvest was overlong expected yet had I left nothing undone in manuring the same but that it might have brought

---

[179] I have not found a contemporary note confirming that Mary was small or misshapen.

forth both wholesome & pleasing fruit. But the man of sin[180] having in the night sowed tares amongst the good corn both the true husbandman was beguiled and the good ground abused. How much more unhappy am I who though with all the care & industry I can use to bring this soil to her former goodness, yet is it impossible for me to prevail & God knows I would refuse no penance to redeem what is lost. I write not this to grieve her whom I have so much loved nor your good self, for there can be no greater punishment to me than to be a cause of either your sadness to whom I wish so well without comparison. I know your sister is apt to be melancholy[181] & you can apprehend her grief more deeply than I wish. But you are not alone, neither can either of you be so often remembered with sad thoughts as I am for that which I can not remedy & yet can never cease to grieve at. Be you yet a comforter & I will not be wanting to add anything lying in my power to increase both your contentments, & if you were nearer that sometime I might play a part, I would not doubt but to pacify though not thoroughly to purge that humour of melancholy.

Thus leaving you both to God's protection with my best salutations & blessing to my pretty daughter I remain ever
Your assured ffrend
W. KNOLLYS.

[5.27] There are only two more of Sir William's letters to be given. The next refers to the proposed marriage of his niece Letitia Knollys, the daughter and co-heiress of Henry Knollys and Margaret Cave, the latter being first cousin to John Newdigate's mother, Martha Cave:

Fair gossip,
having occasion to send this bearer to Drayton I should fall in good manners & might justly be accounted ungrateful if with some few lines I did not yield you my best thanks for your many kindnesses which I will ever be ready to requite to the uttermost of my power. Whether yet you be delivered or not of your pretty burden I know not but in both I wish you as much joy & comfort as your self can desire. I pray you tell Mr Newdigate that Her Majesty understanding of the match between Mr Paget and my niece doth so well like thereof as she doth not only commend him but all those which wrought a deliverance of my Niece from her bondage & it were too long to write how exceedingly she alloweth of the match. But he shall not need to speak too much hereof until my Nephew Paget hath been here and is disposed to publish it. Whether your sister be with you or no I know not, but if she be, add something to your love of her for my sake who would desire nothing more of God: than that she were as capable of my love

---

[180] William Herbert, by now Lord Pembroke.
[181] This is the second time Knollys refers to Mary having periods of depression.

Mary Fitton

as I have ever meant it, & what will become of it God only
knoweth. Let it suffice that my first love shall ever bind me to
love her, yourself and all that love her, & thus praying God to
send you health & happiness. I remain ever
> Your trulye affectionate gossepp
> W. KNOLLYS.
> Burn my letters if you please.[182]

[5.28] We now come to Sir William Knollys' last letter and give it here,
although the date is in advance of the period to which we must return
later. It could not have been written until after July 1603, as it is
addressed "To my very lovyng ffrend & gossepp my La: Newdigate,"
and John Newdigate was not knighted until the above date:

> Fair & worthy Gossip,
>   your father being the messenger I may not but answer both
> your lines with this simple pen & your kindness with
> whatsoever a true honest heart may afford, desirous still to
> cherish all the branches of that root into the which my
> unchangeable love was so firmly engrafted. What it was your
> self & the world did know, but what it is my heart only is
> sensible of, yet may I boldly say no earthly creature is
> Mistress of my Love, nor is like to be, as not willing to trust a
> woman with that which was so truly given & so undeservedly
> rejected. Where to find it I know not, unless it be either hidden
> in myself or laid up by some who suffer it to rust in some out
> room of their careless thoughts. But were I not tied to a white
> staff in court & had liberty I would like a knight adventurer
> never rest until I found better entertainment for so good a
> guest. But what spirit guides my pen, or whither do I wander?
> You may guess at my meaning, she is not far from you that
> may decipher this riddle & I may boldly say that Mary did
> not choose the better part, yet let her I pray you know that no
> man can wish her more happiness & contentment than I do
> which I will be ready to manifest upon any offered occasion &
> though her commendations to me in your last letter were very
> ordinary yet let me be remembered to you both in the best
> manner I can as one who can not separate his thoughts from
> the remembrance of former bands. No more at this time, but
> wishing you & my godson[183] health & happiness I remain ever
> > Your ffaythffull ffrend & gossepp
> > W. KNOLLYS.
> Excuse me I pray you for not writing to your unkind sister
> whose so long silence maketh me think she hath forgotten me
> & herself, I having deserved more than a few lines, but I am
> pleased since she will have it so.

---

[182] She didn't burn them!
[183] Anne's second child, Richard, born before 1602.

[5.29] In spite of this last touching appeal, Mary does not seem to have been inclined to respond to her old friend's protestations of affection. Consequently, when, in 1605, Dorothy, Lady Knollys, died, and Lord Knollys (as he was created at the coronation of James I.) became released from the ties he had borne so impatiently, it was not Mary Fitton who succeeded to the vacant place. Two months after Lady Knollys' decease her husband married Lady Elizabeth Howard, daughter of Thomas, Earl of Suffolk – she being nineteen and her bridegroom sixty-one.

In 1614 Lord Knollys was appointed Master of the Wards, and within a short time installed Knight of the Garter. In 1616 he was created Viscount Wallingford, and advanced in 1626 by King Charles I to the Earldom of Banbury. He died in 1632, at the advanced age of eighty-eight.

> July 1603; [from her Father]
> Good Nan,
> God bless you and your sister as my own life, peruse this document and then send it to your mother I pray you ... Your best Gossip & honourable friend commandeth me to tell you he wisheth you both as much heart's ease as to himself & every day saith he shall not be well until he see you both.

[5.30] Lady Fitton[184] alludes to Sir Fulke Greville's death in the letter next given. It is addressed "to my best and dearest daughter the Ladie Newdygat at Erburie":

> My own sweet Nan,
> I pray God to bless you and all yours. I am sorry for the death of good Sir Fulke Greville, your good friend and mine; your loss is great as can be of a friend, he was a very old man, it was marvel he lived so long: no doubt but your husband and you shall find his son a very honorable gentleman, and one that will be glad of both your friendships ... Your brother doth enter into physic to-morrow for the pain in his nose. God send it well, Mr Neithsmyth doth doubt but cure him afore Christmas, if please God. I take no joy to hear of your sister nor of that boy. If it had pleased God when I did bear her, that she and I had been buried it had saved me from a great deal of sorrow and grief, and her from shame and such shame as never had Cheshire woman, worse now than ever.[185] Write no more to me of her. Thank my pretty Jack for his token. I will wear it for his sake, and send him another afore it be long.

---

[184] Sir Fulke Greville being dead, means that this was written soon after 26th May 1606.

[185] The story is told that Mary Fitton's father, Sir Edward, had been anticipating entertaining the Queen at Gawsworth. As a result of the disgrace he had to cut short a huge project to improve his estate and that Mary was banned from the family home and had to stay at the Rectory from where her ghost is occasionally reported seen wandering around the estate.

Mary Fitton

Commend me to Moll, Dick and little pretty Letti. God bless them all.
Let me be kindly remembered to your husband. Praying God to send us all well to meet I end, and will ever remain to you A kynde mother.
A. ffyTTON.
I would wish you to send to your sister this enclosed to see. I have left them unsealed, you may read them and seal them. Good Nan fail not, It standeth much.

Poor mother! what must she not have suffered to write thus about her erring daughter! Stern as she is in the first part, her mother's heart relents in the postscript, whilst Anne, as ever, seems tender and charitable towards this sister's frailty. Notice should be taken of " the boy" referred to in this letter in connection with Mary's disgrace. In the following year she married a certain William Polewhele, about whom there seem to have been different opinions in the family. She is known to have had a son by him, and possibly this was the boy born before her marriage. This son was living in September 1609, the date of William Polewhele's will.

[Lady Newdigate is possibly wrong in her interpretation of "that boy" being the child born out of wedlock; by May 1606 Mary had two children by Richard Leveson, William and Anna.[186] A greater possibility is that *that boy* was Richard Barnfield as explained in the previous chapter, but there is still an outside possibility that he could have been William Herbert aged twenty at the time of the affair and twenty-six at the time of the letter. The shame and scandal are unlikely to have been about an illegitimate child that died at birth but more likely that the Cheshire Fitton's name and dowry were not good enough for the Pembroke family – the family not only felt rejected by the Pembrokes, but also had to suffer the great humiliation of their daughter having been abruptly expelled from Court by the Queen.

There is not one malevolent comment about Mary in the Newdigate letters. After Mary married William Polewhele her sister Anne went to visit her in her married home at Perton in Staffordshire – they seem to have been on very good terms. Here is a 1607 letter from the sisters' mother.]

[5.31] What Dick[187] hath written I know not, but this he told me was his answer, that Sir John Newdigate were best to come and answer it himself. It should seem some other had affirmed it; he would not do your brother that kindness as to send for the Information given against your husband that he might see it, but fell into railing against you for speaking

---

[186] I do not discount Leveson being the putative father while William Herbert, or someone else for that matter, was the biological father.

[187] Mary's brother, Lady Fitton's son.

against the marriage of your sister to Polewhele[188]; it was out of your humor and that he was worthy her. My Lady Frances [189]said she was the vilest[190] woman under the sun. To conclude they did use Dick so unkindly as he hath no great heartburning to go there since Christmas. I had the kindest messages from them that could be and that they would come see me. But Polewhele is a very kave [sic; knave?] and taketh the disgrace of his wife and all her friends to make the world think him worthy of her and that she deserved no better.

[5.32] At various times Richard Leveson writes to Anne Newdigate:

- commend my service to your sister.

- commend me to your sister if she be there [1603].

- [after July 1603][191] You and your sister must shortly visit my lodge.

- [Nov. 1604] Sweet Nan, I have sent you by this bearer an odd Ruff of a new fashion when your sister left it for you and withal a poor remnant of my own which I found in the corner of a trunk and do entreat you to accept on good part.

Sweet wife: [27th Jan 1605]
    In this short space of my arrival in these parts I understand not so much touching your affairs as I desire to know and therefore you must not look for such satisfaction from me now as I hope to send you by my next. But falling aboard some of your friends near Chancery Lane I have now brought them to

---

[188] C.G.O Bridgeman when cataloguing the Arbury portraits found that Captain Polewhele served with Sir Richard Leveson in 1603. Sir Richard captained the *Repulse* and Captain Polewhele the *Lyon's Whelpe*. In *Cymbeline*, (1609) there is a letter containing a reference to a *Lion's Whelp*;
    "as a lion's whelp shall, to himself unknown, without seeking find, and be embraced by a piece of tender air; and when from a stately cedar shall be lopped branches which, being dead many years, shall after revive, be jointed to the old stock, and freshly grow; then shall Posthumus end his miseries, Britain be fortunate and flourish in peace and plenty."
    A Soothsayer interprets the letter at the end of the play;
    Thou, Leonatus, art the lion's whelp; the fit and apt construction of thy name, being Leo-natus, doth import so much. [To Cymbeline] The piece of tender air, thy virtuous daughter, which we call *mollis aer* and *mollis aer* - we term it mulier [To Posthumus] which mulier I divine is this most constant wife, who even now, answering the letter of the oracle, unknown to you, unsought, were clipped about with this most tender air.
    Mollis is Latin for gentle, *aer* is lower-atmosphere, and *mulier* for wife or woman. Does one hear a phonetic *Mal is here*? The play talks of Britain but is set in Wales with an emphasis on Milford Haven on the Pembrokeshire Coast.
[189] Lady Frances Stanley, daughter of Ferdinando, Earl Derby, and wife of Sir John Egerton.
[190] See Sonnet S71
[191] The guest book at Arbury records the visit in August 1603 of Mary Fitton, with her gentlewoman, manservant and footman.

be of our side albeit they were strongly against us. (They do only take it to be my project and no other private humour,) and we are all resolved to run one course (viz to sound the pleasure of the great one, how this great God send him us shall be disposed) that thereby your friends may speedily resolve for you, either to entertain the project or to have the honour of refusing it: in the mean Time your own aptness and sufficiency shall be so infused to the Q. as I dare assure you no other will leap over your head: I met yesterday with one of the K's physicians my familiar friend and thinking to extract something from him by way of discourse, at last he told me that there were divers Gentlewomen's names put in to a Bill for this employment, and that the K's physicians were to examine and give their opinions of their aptness for that charge as by tasting of their Milk, etc.. This is probable, but rather than my wife shall be drawn in by this kind of election I'll walk on foot to Arbury to keep her at home. To be short I will use all my best faculties in handling of the business, wherein I'll either join reputation with hope of preferment or I'll do nothing. But already I can assure you that you have had very good offices done for you which shall be continued with my best help and so sweet Nan, farewell,

Yours, Yours

RICHARD LEVESON: This 27th of Jan: 1604 [1604-5]

For want of paper I will write nothing of Mr. Marwood, but you have been too liberal of my purse. Good Nan, send my uncle's business letter away with speed.

1603   her great-uncle Francis Fitton to Anne Newdigate:

- I pray to be remembered very kindly to my niece, your sister.

1607 Feb. Francis Fitton to John Newdigate

- you are very much beholden to my cousin Polewhele for his diligent care and friendly diligence in labouring about your cause...... In his will he then makes a bequest of his best horse to Mr William Polewhele who married my niece Mistress Marie Fitton.

1611   Francis Beaumont[192] to Anne Newdigate: Anne, now a widow whom he was attempting to court.

- Salute I pray you in my name your Sister, whom the less I know and the more friendly she accepteth it, the more I am beholden unto her. When you see my Counsellor, your only sister, command I pray you unto her moine affectionate love,

---

[192] The father of the playwright of the same name. The son lived from c1584-1616

Mary Fitton

but not my quintessential, for that is become a confined recusant, having disavowed sacrifice unto all living temples, save only unto the living temple of the fairest and dearest deserving Cynthia.

- I must entreat you when you see my counsellor to commend my heartiest love unto her and tell her that though she be a married wife,[193] yet I will take leave to love her for ever while I carry within me a heart that can love. If her husband will give me this liberty (which is in mine own power to take myself) he shall love my wife (when I have her) as much as pleaseth him, and for his kindness I will love him far the letter. Though I love not you, yet for your sake I love all your generation.

A Mr. C. G. O. Bridgeman discovered that William Polewhele made his will on 19th Sep. 1609 and it was proved on 23rd June 1610. He is described as being of Perton, county Stafford. His executors are his wife, Mary Polewhele, Sir Walter Leveson and Sir Richard Titchborne. He devises his lands to Mary until his son, William, reaches the age of twenty-one. He divides *the parsonage of Brownsover als Rugby county Warwick, one third to his wife, one third to his son William and one third to such child as my wife is now with child of.* The child was called Mary,[194] survived to marry John Gatacre of Gatacre, but died early leaving a daughter, Anne. Mary Polewhele is mentioned in her sister's will of 1610; her sister died in 1618. Mary was again a widow by 1636 when she took out letters of administration to her second husband's, John Lougher's, estate. Arthur Marlowe (*op. cit.*) found that the death of (Captain) John Lougher was recorded at Chester and he was interred at Gawsworth on 8th January 1635-6.

[5.33] Mary Lougher's will is dated December 19. 1640, and was proved in the Prerogative Court of the Archbishop of Canterbury on July 5, 1647: it was proved a second time, before the Probate Court established by Cromwell, on September 22,1653. The executors appointed by the will were her son, William Polewhele, and her daughter Elizabeth Lougher,

---

[193] It is this letter that shows that Mary Fitton remarried for a second time between 1610 and 1612. In *Urania* Mary Wroth tells of *Antissia* marrying *Dolorindus*, who had conspired with her to kill *Amphilanthus*. Was *Dolorindus* William Polewhele, or was he Mary Fitton's second husband, John Lougher, or was it figurative? Although Mary Fitton was acting as a counsellor to Francis Beaumont, Arthur Marlowe (op cit, p48) says that she was also advising another suitor, Matthew Saunders of Shangton, Leicestershire.

[194] Mary Fitton appears to have had the following eight pregnancies. (1) infant by William Herbert; (2) William, by Richard Leveson, who died after a few years; (3) Anne, by Leveson, who married Robert Charnock (4) William, by William Polewhele, who survived into adulthood, married and had children. (5) Frances, by William Polewhele, who died after a week. (6) Mary? by William Polewhele, born after his death who one assumes married John Gatacre and died early, probably in childbirth. (7) Elizabeth, by John Lougher, who died before probate was granted after her mother's death; (8) John by John Lougher who married Mary Wrottesley at Darlaston on 25th January 1633 but died in 1637. Mary Wrottesley Lougher remarried Edward Williams; [Arthur Marlowe- *Shakespeare, digging for the truth*].

Mary Fitton

but probate was granted to William Polewhele alone, as surviving executor.

She bequeaths the lease of Perton to her son William Polewhele; the lease of Rinkeston or Rinteston and Kilkelly, in Pembrokeshire, to her daughter Elizabeth Lougher.[195] She makes bequests to her "little grandchild Ann Gattachree"[196] to her son-in-law John Gattachree, his wife and three children. She mentions her son-in-law, Robert Chernnock, and gives directions for her burial at Goulsworth, co. Chester.

Thus she apparently continued to flourish like a green bay-tree until 1647 the date of her death, when she must have been sixty-nine years old.[197]

The impression one gets of Mary Fitton from the Newdigate book is that she was considered a genteel and respected woman who has been unfortunate to have her head turned and become pregnant by a high ranking man who would not marry her – and she suffered the consequences. Filling in some of the gaps, one sees that she also had a mind of her own and today would be considered an *independent woman*.

We know that the Queen would not suffer fools to be around her, in fact, she selected vivacious and intelligent young women for her Court and amusement. At the Worcester's wedding [5.19] Mary Fitton was clearly the leader of the pack. The Queen responded to her like a loving mother[198]. Knollys desperately wanted her[199]; even knowing that she is moody [5.13]. He sincerely believed she was virtuous – but, being married, he could not have her. William Herbert, the courtier and poet, did have her but then was seen to discard her. Her parents still loved her, her father travelled to London to rescue her from incarceration

---

[195] Kilgetty 3.5 miles north of Tenby in South Wales and Rinaston near Ambleston, eight miles N.N.E. of Haverfordwest. These leases are Mary's gift; not those of her dead husband. The relationship between Mary Fitton, John and Elizabeth Lougher may not be straightforward. Could Elizabeth be a bastard child, stepdaughter or daughter-in-law, or did the child take the name of her stepfather? Arthur Marlowe notes that Elizabeth died at Tenby having given birth to a daughter, Lettice Lougher, who married a Thomas Dainton on October 27th 1635. Marlowe says (op. Cit. p42) that Mary Fitton had affairs with both the Earls of Essex and Southampton; that Southampton gave her two thousand acres of land in Tenby and that after a year his wife called a halt to the affair which had become an acute embarrassment to her and her family. I do not discount these statements but have not yet seen any evidence of support, other than Mary Fitton did bequeath land in Tenby to her daughter.

[196] Gatacre or Gateacre; £200 is left to Anne Gatacre out of £1,000 owed by Robert Charnock, her son-in-law, who had married Mary Fitton's daughter, Anne (Fitton) Leveson, at Pensford Church, Staffordshire in 1626.

[197] Arthur Marlowe [op cit.] found that Mary Fitton's burial was recorded in the Tettenhall Church Register on 19th September 1641 and the register entry is confirmed at Lichfield. She would have been sixty-three years old.

[198] The fiery character of Olivia in *Twelfth Night* would appear to be modelled on Mary Fitton whose character was seen to be similar to the Queen's when a young woman.

[199] As seen in the way Malvolio is parodied and teased in *Twelfth Night*.

Mary Fitton

[5.25]; her mother, naturally, was deeply shamed by what has happened but still did not lose contact [5.30]. Mary's marriage to William Polewhele was found acceptable and he received gifts from the family [5.32]. Widowed, she remarried, mothered her children and left bequests for her grandchildren.

Before she married William Polewhele she did have a full relationship with Richard Leveson. Having read the Leveson letters addressed to Mary's sister, Anne (Nan), it would appear that the intended recipient was really Mary, whom he addresses as *wife*. The letter at 5.32 is an example of the correspondence, and indicates that one of the two sisters had experienced a stillbirth. This may have been an attempt by Leveson to get Mary back into favour by nursing the Queen's child.

Clearly there was a very passionate side to Mary Fitton which we will find reflected in her sonnets and which was also echoed by her allegorical character, *Antissia*, in Mary Wroth's *Urania*. Mary Fitton's and, for that matter, Mary Wroth's[200] love for William Herbert became passions that, I believe, never really left either of them. Mary Fitton, however, appears to have been something of a tomboy, with a mind of her own, who flaunted the accepted mores of the period by travelling around as an independent woman, entering into relationships with men and making her own decisions. From her poetry one finds she was at times passionate, at times driven by a dementia, and throughout was frightfully astute with all her observations, testing the use of the English language to its limits, and sometimes beyond. Remarkably, she had conceit or a vision that her poetry would last the tribulations of time – and, thankfully, she was right; it did.

Two rhetorical questions to end the chapter. Did she write only the one letter to her sister? If not, did all the others end up in the fire?

Addendum

In *Gossip from the Muniment Room* are published some of the 1612 letters of a Francis Beaumont to Mary Fitton's widowed sister, Anne Newdigate. A (Matthew?) Saunders was wooing Anne and, when he was rejected, the elder Francis Beaumont tried his luck but Anne immediately and firmly squashed any ideas he had. Mary Fitton, herself widowed in 1610, had remarried by the time of these letters, and acted in this matter both as the counsellor for Beaumont and, it appears, Saunders.

The playwrights Francis Beaumont and John Fletcher[201] wrote a the comedy called *The Scornful Lady* which was *acted (with great applause) by the children of Her Majesty's*[202] *Revels in the Blackfriars*, and published in 1616. This was the same year Beaumont died on 3rd March at the age of thirty-two. Francis

---

[200] Sir Robert Wroth had been a hunting companion of the King. His death in 1615 made Mary Wroth a widow leaving her with a child who died aged two. Mary caused a minor scandal by living with Pembroke and their two illegitimate children at Baynards Castle in London. Pembroke's wife remained in Wiltshire at one of the Pembroke houses.

[201] John Fletcher collaborated in some of the later Shakespeare plays.

[202] Queen Anne, King James' wife.

Mary Fitton

was the son of the same Francis Beaumont who with (Matthew) Saunders was the suitor to Anne Newdigate.

The characters in the play greatly resemble these four people although the actual relationships in the comedy are different. The parallels are:

Anne Newdigate   (*The Lady*)
Mary Fitton   (*Martha*, the *Lady's* sister[203]
        and also *Abigal,* the *Lady's* waiting-gentlewoman)
Francis Beaumont   (*Elder-Loveless*, an elder brother)
(Matthew) Saunders   (*Younger-Loveless,* his prodigal, younger brother).

Three other characters make up four couples;

a *Rich Widow,*
Harry Welford (Matthew Saunders lived in Welford)
Sir Roger, the *Lady's* curate.

Elder-Loveless and *Welford* are competing suitors of the recently widowed *Lady*. Ultimately, *Young-Loveless* marries the *Rich Widow; Elder-Loveless* marries the *Lady; Welford* marries *Martha* and *Sir Roger* marries *Abigal*.

The younger Francis Beaumont was a youth of sixteen at the time of the Fitton-Pembroke scandal, so when his play was written, over a decade later, his knowledge of Mary Fitton would have been from gossip and the apocryphal tales that had circulated. In *The Scornful Lady,* he and his co-writer, John Fletcher, have Young-Loveless describe *Abigal,* the Lady's waiting-gentlewoman as follows;

ELDER-LOVELESS   Why, she knows not you.

YOUNG-LOVELESS   No, but she offered me once to know her: to this day she loves a youth of eighteen; she heard a tale how Cupid struck her in love with a great Lord in the Tilt-yard, but he never saw her; yet she in kindness would needs wear a willow-garland at his wedding[204]. She loved all the players in the last Queen's time once over: She was struck when they acted Lovers, and forsook some when they played Murthers. She has nine Spur-royals, and the servants say she hoards old gold; and she herself pronounces angrily, that the farmer's eldest son, or her mistress husband's clerk shall be, that marries her, shall make her a jointure of fourscore pounds a year; she tells tales of the serving-men.

Is Abigal not Mary Fitton? In 1610, when William Polewhele died he left Mary Fitton one third part of the Parsonage of Brownsover near Rugby in Warwickshire. The rents of the Parsonage were part of the 1567 endowment of

---

[203]Martha has very few lines in the play.
[204] Willow denotes mourning. In Othello IV iii, Desdemona says: *My mother had a maid called Barbara, she was in love and he she loved proved mad and did forsake her: she had a song of willow, an old thing 'twas, but expressed her fortune, and she died singing it.*

Mary Fitton

Lawrence Sheriff which created Rugby School; but they were not fully obtained until 1653 - the very same year that probate was granted on Mary Fitton's will. *In the play, Abigal* married the *Lady's Curate* which might parallel the fact that William Polewhele owned a parsonage. This probably connects with a William Polewhele who was a minister in that area during the eighteenth century.

Martha, Lady's sister, (Mary Fitton) marries *Welford,* (Matthew? Saunders). In real-life this did not happen, but Mary and Saunders seem to have been friends and the play suggests that she offered herself to him. If Mary Fitton felt she had been libelled by the play she was never able to get her revenge. Francis Beaumont died that same year.

In 2002 Stephanie Nolen, a writer for the *Globe and Mail* of Canada, wrote a book called *Shakespeare's Face.* It is the story of a painting dated 1603 of a young man which has been handed down through generations, the story being that this was a portrait of William Shakespeare painted by an actor from Worcester. A copy of the picture has been placed in PLATE 7 alongside that of the First Folio Shakespeare for comparison. The name of the family is Sanders but some serious research would be needed to find if there was any link between the Saunders family of Leicestershire whom Mary Fitton knew, and the Sanders family of Worcestershire.[205]

It would make a wonderful story if, when Mary Fitton married John Lougher, he did not like having a portrait of William Herbert in the house so she gave it to Matthew Saunders for safekeeping and, when Saunders asked whose was the portrait, she told him, off the cuff, *William Shakespeare!*

Talking about portraits – if we take another look at the Arbury House portrait of Mary Fitton [PLATE 1], one can see over Mary's heart what looks like a piece of jewellery, the shape of a miniature. The dress and the jewellery are very much a statement of the times and having seen the miniatures of William Herbert and Richard Leveson in their gilt cases [PLATES 3 & 5] one begins to wonder if underneath the dark shape there was a portrait, and if so, of whom. Knowing Mary's history there could have been yet another man.

---

[205] Mary Fitton's brother's wife, Anne Barrett, came from Tenby. Her cousin was a Jenet Barrett who was married to one Erasmus Saunders. Jenet's mother was a Lougher.

CHAPTER SIX

THE LEAP YEAR SONNETS, 1 – 17

It was probably on the night of 16th. June 1600 that Mistress Mary Fitton, in the company of the twenty-year-old Lord William Herbert, *daff'd her white stole of chastity*. This was the night of the Earl of Worcester's wedding [PLATE-4] which the Queen had attended with all its royal pomp and ceremony [5.19]. A few years later, Mary Fitton, in her forty-seven-stanza poem, *A Lover's Complaint*, recollects the courtship that led up to that night. So, before enjoying Mary Fitton's sonnets which she started writing in the January[206] following the seduction, here are the last seven stanzas of *A Lover's Complaint*. The complete poem is given at Appendix 1.

In stanza-40 the woman says she believed the young man, (William Herbert), when he promised to marry her and so she let his gushing tears wash away her residual resistance. In the last stanza she admits that, despite the lesson she has learnt about perfidious men, she would allow it to happen all over again.

> 40 Now all these hearts that do on mine depend,
>   Feeling it break, with bleeding groans they pine;
>   And supplicant their sighs to you extend,
>   To leave the battery that you make 'gainst mine,
>   Lending soft audience to my sweet design,
>   And credent[207] soul to that strong-bonded oath
>   That shall prefer and undertake my troth.'
>
> 41 This said, his watery eyes he did dismount,
>   Whose sights till then were levell'd on my face;
>   Each cheek a river running from a fount
>   With brinish current downward flow'd apace:
>   O, how the channel to the stream gave grace!
>   Who glazed with crystal gate the glowing roses
>   That flame through water which their hue encloses.
>
> 42 O father, what a hell of witchcraft lies
>   In the small orb of one particular tear!
>   But with the inundation of the eyes
>   What rocky heart to water will not wear?
>   What breast so cold that is not warmed here?
>   O cleft effect! cold modesty, hot wrath,
>   Both fire from hence and chill extincture[208] hath.

---

[206] A winter month.
[207] believing
[208] A word that Mary Fitton has invented.

43 For, lo, his passion, but an art of craft,
　Even there resolved my reason into tears;
　There my white stole of chastity I daff'd,
　Shook off my sober guards and civil fears;
　Appear to him, as he to me appears,
　All melting,[209] though our drops this difference bore,
　His poison'd me, and mine did him restore.

44 In him a plenitude of subtle matter,
　Applied to cautels, all strange forms receives,
　Of burning blushes, or of weeping water,
　Or swooning paleness; and he takes and leaves,
　In either's aptness, as it best deceives,
　To blush at speeches rank to weep at woes,
　Or to turn white and swoon at tragic shows.

45 That not a heart which in his level came
　Could 'scape the hail of his all-hurting aim,
　Showing fair nature is both kind and tame;
　And, veil'd in them, did win whom he would maim:
　Against the thing he sought he would exclaim;
　When he most burn'd in heart-wish'd luxury,
　He preach'd pure maid, and praised cold chastity.

46 Thus merely with the garment of a Grace[210]
　The naked and concealed fiend he cover'd;
　That th' unexperient gave the tempter place,
　Which like a cherubin above them hover'd.
　Who, young and simple, would not be so lover'd?
　Ay me! I fell; and yet do question make
　What I should do again for such a sake.

47 O, that infected moisture of his eye,
　O, that false fire which in his cheek so glow'd,
　O, that forced thunder from his heart did fly,
　O, that sad breath his spongy lungs bestow'd,
　O, all that borrow'd motion seeming owed,
　Would yet again betray the fore-betray'd,
　And new pervert a reconciled maid!

Imagine that, amongst the tokens of his love, William Herbert gave Mary Fitton a timepiece, a mirror (glass), a picture of himself and a copybook in which to write her verses. The time was propitious; his aged father was a seriously ill, he himself was just a few months from his coming-of-age; he was

---

[209] This suggests they both experienced orgasm and he gave her a venereal infection (which may have resulted in the loss of her baby at birth).

[210] grace = penis

under constant pressure to marry[211], and Mary Fitton, who could only bring to him what to him was a relatively small dowry, was pregnant with his child.

While Mary was writing her first seventeen sonnets, she was perhaps also anticipating William's twenty-first birthday, on 8th April 1601, when he would set forth in adult life. She composed into her copybook this unusual dedication, which many people have tried to fully comprehend. Capital letters were used throughout and full stops were placed between words. There is a space after W.H. on line-three.[212]

TO.THE.ONLIE.BEGETTER.OF.
THESE.INSVING.SONNETS.
M^r.W.H. ALL.HAPPINESSE.
AND.THAT.ETERNITIE.
PROMISED.
BY.
OVR.EVER-LIVING.POET.
WISHETH.
THE.WELL-WISHING.
ADVENTVRER.IN.
SETTING.
FORTH.
T. T. [213]

If one counts the number of characters in each line including the full-stops and uses the 17th letter of the alphabet to be A, 18th B etc., each line produces a letter. The letters are i f f c s m e r a x p n which can be rearranged to form *marx ff's prince*. If the line *adventvrer.in.* had one more letter it would produce a y instead of an x. I believe either (a) the typesetter lost a letter or (b) Mary made a mistake of one letter in composing this riddle or (c) she made a deliberate mistake but allowing an x to look like a y. The extra letter would change Marx Ff's Prince into **Mary Ff's Prince**. There are a number of other possibilities such as *A X FR MF's PRINCE* or MARE FF's PRINC, X. The correlation is just

---

[211] There was a threat that if his father died before he was twenty-one, William Herbert would become a Ward of Court. This meant that his property would revert to the Crown until whoever was ascribed the wardship reached a satisfactory settlement as to the Release of the wardship, which may have involved William's having to marry. While his father was terminally ill, his mother virtually grovelled to the Queen to avoid this happening should her husband die. When he did there were just twelve weeks to William's coming of age.

[212] This is how the printer's compositor of the typeface interpreted what he saw in manuscript.

[213] The monogram TT has been explained at the end of Chapter Four. Initials TT, which people had here assumed was Thomas Thorpe, the publisher of the Sonnets, also appeared in the commendation to Barnfield's *Cynthia,* and elsewhere in a commendation to John Trussell's *First Rape of Fair Helen.* Again, in the six-line dedication to Lord Derby, the first letters of the lines were OITTST which may have a significance. Lord Derby acceded in April 1594 and married Elizabeth de Vere two months later. William Herbert's brother, Philip, married Susan de Vere in 1604. William Herbert rejected a third sister, Brigit.

Pembroke may have used Mary Sidney Wroth's friendship with Ben Jonson to have the Sonnets published; Jonson used Thomas Thorpe to publish his plays.

too close to be a coincidence, and we have Mary Fitton's letter as evidence of the vagaries of her spelling.

For the person publishing the Sonnets it would be most important that he owned the copyright or intellectual property, so when the dedication was to the "only begetter of these ensuing sonnets" it is very difficult to conceive any third party ever being in a position to claim ownership later; either William Herbert owned the sonnets or he inspired them, or he wrote them, or a bit of each.

Sonnets 1-17 are a gift to William Herbert from someone who loves him, urging and giving him reasons why he should marry. Sonnets 127-154 are from William's own pen. Sonnets 18-126 are given to him by the woman who loves him and who has expressed her love and her emotions in fourteen line epistles to him. So, on all three counts, the dedication, even in hindsight, is either truthful or not dishonest. One final note: the year then ended on 24th March a few days after the vernal equinox. Up until then the year was 1600. The year 1600 was a leap year when woman could show the initiative to ask their men to marry them as do all three women in *Twelfth Night;* Marie asks Sir Toby Belch, Viola asks Sebastian, and Olivia asks Count Orsino. The last of these sonnets was written before 25th March and Valentine's Day, 14th February, suggests itself although by then William Herbert was then in prison. The sonnet sequence starts in a winter month of 1601.[214]

Sonnet 1: Mary, six months' pregnant, is confined with Lady Margaret, widow of Admiral Hawkins. William is refusing to marry her.

From fairest creatures we desire increase,
That thereby beauty's rose might never die,
But as the riper should by time decease,
His tender heir might bear his memory;
But thou, contracted to thine own bright eyes,
Feed'st thy light's flame with self-substantial fuel,
Making a famine where abundance lies,
Thyself thy foe, to thy sweet self too cruel.
Thou that art now the world's fresh ornament [215]
And only herald to the gaudy spring,[216]
Within thine own bud buriest thy content,
And, tender churl, mak'st waste in niggarding.
Pity the world, or else this glutton be,
To eat the world's due, by the grave[217] and thee.

---

[214] The first months of Mary's pregnancy coincided with the registration on 4th August 1600 of Shakespeare's *As You Like It* where the heroine is the exuberant and tomboyish *Rosalind*. The play is based on the 1590 romance *Rosalynde* by Thomas Lodge (1558-1625).

[215] He succeeded his father on 19th January. Sonnet 77 indicates that the Sonnets were compiled in one book.

[216] The start of the sonnet sequence is in Winter.

[217] Mourning his father.

The Leap Year Sonnets, 1 – 17

2 Mary points out the advantages of having a successor.

When forty winters shall besiege thy brow,[218]
And dig deep trenches in thy beauty's field,
Thy youth's proud livery, so gazed on now,
Will be a tattered weed of small worth held.
Then being asked where all thy beauty lies,
Where all the treasure of thy lusty days,
To say within thine own deep-sunken eyes
Were an all-eating shame and thriftless praise.
How much more praise deserved thy beauty's use
If thou couldst answer *'This fair child of mine
Shall sum my count,[219] and make my old excuse'*
Proving his beauty by succession thine.
This were to be new made when thou art old,
And see thy blood warm when thou feel'st it cold.

3 She tells him his child will be beautiful . .

Look in thy glass and tell the face thou viewest
Now is the time that face should form another,
Whose fresh repair if now thou not renewest,
Thou dost beguile the world, unbless some mother.
For where is she so fair whose uneared womb
Disdains the tillage of thy husbandry? [220]
Or who is he so fond will be the tomb
Of his self-love to stop posterity?
Thou art thy mother's glass,[221] and she in thee
Calls back the lovely April of her prime; [222]
So thou through windows of thine age shalt see,
Despite of wrinkles, this thy golden time;
But if thou live remembered not to be,
Die single, and thine image dies with thee.

4 . . and that William should not waste his talents.

Unthrifty loveliness, why dost thou spend
Upon thyself thy beauty's legacy?
Nature's bequest gives nothing but doth lend,
And being frank she lends to those are free;
Then, beauteous niggard, why dost thou abuse

---

[218] When he is twice his present age.
[219] Shall succeed me as my heir.
[220] You can have any woman you like.
[221] You are the image of your mother (Mary Herbert nee Sidney). (Is there an implication that he looks nothing like his father?). Barnfield's mother died before Mary was born and Barnfield born in June, which eliminates Barnfield as being the object of Mary's love.
[222] Calls = recalls; William was born 8th April 1580.

The Leap Year Sonnets, 1 – 17

The bounteous largess given thee to give? [223]
Profitless usurer, why dost thou use
So great a sum of sums, yet canst not live?
For having traffic with thy self alone,
Thou of thyself thy sweet self dost deceive;
Then how when nature calls thee to be gone,
What acceptable audit canst thou leave?
Thy unused beauty must be tombed with thee,
Which used, lives th' executor to be.

5 She projects what will happen as he grows old . .

Those hours that with gentle work did frame
The lovely gaze where every eye doth dwell
Will play the tyrants to the very same,
And that unfair which fairly doth excel;
For never-resting Time leads summer on
To hideous winter, and confounds him there,
Sap checked with frost, and lusty leaves quite gone,
Beauty o' and bareness everywhere.
Then, were not summer's distillation left
A liquid prisoner pent in walls of glass, [224]
Beauty's effect with beauty were bereft,
Nor it nor no remembrance what it was;
But flowers distilled, though they with winter meet,
Leese but their show, their substance still lives sweet.

6 . . his need to have progeny . .

Then let not winter's ragged hand deface [225]
In thee thy summer ere thou be distilled;
Make sweet some vial; treasure thou some place
With beauty's treasure ere it be self-killed.
That use is not forbidden usury
Which happies those that pay the willing loan;
That's for thyself to breed another thee,
Or ten times happier be it ten for one.
Ten times thyself were happier than thou art,
If ten of thine ten times refigured thee;
Then what could Death do if thou shouldst depart,
Leaving thee living in posterity?
Be not self-willed, for thou art much too fair
To be Death's conquest and make worms thine heir.[226]

---

[223] Both immensely wealthy and gifted
[224] Is William still in the Fleet Prison? Or a reminder that he has been in the Fleet.
[225] One senses he is in prison and it is autumn.
[226] She fears he will die in prison and has suggested it is better to pay the price to be released.

7 . . as life becomes meaningless without an heir.

Lo, in the orient when the gracious light
Lifts up his burning head, each under eye
Doth homage to his new-appearing sight,
Serving with looks his sacred majesty;
And having climbed the steep-up heavenly hill,
Resembling strong youth in his middle age,
Yet mortal looks adore his beauty still,
Attending on his golden pilgrimage;
But when from highmost pitch, with weary car,
Like feeble age he reeleth from the day,
The eyes, 'fore duteous, now converted are
From his low tract, and look another way;
So thou, thyself outgoing in thy noon,
Unlooked on diest unless thou get a son.

8 She appeals to him through his love for music . .

Music to hear, why hear'st thou music sadly?
Sweets with sweets war not, joy delights in joy;
Why lov'st thou that which thou receiv'st not gladly,
Or else receiv'st with pleasure thine annoy?
If the true concord of well-tuned sounds,
By unions married, do offend thine ear,
They do but sweetly chide thee, who confounds
In singleness the parts that thou shouldst bear.
Mark how one string, sweet husband to another,
Strikes each in each by mutual ordering;
Resembling sire, and child, and happy mother,
Who all in one one pleasing note do sing;
Whose speechless song, being many, seeming one,
Sings this to thee: *'Thou single wilt prove none.'*

9 . . asking if he loves her so much that he fears making her a widow?

Is it for fear to wet a widow's eye
That thou consum'st thyself in single life?
Ah, if thou issueless shalt hap to die,
The world will wail thee like a makeless wife;
The world will be thy widow, and still weep
That thou no form of thee hast left behind,
When every private widow well may keep,
By children's eyes, her husband's shape in mind.
Look what an unthrift in the world doth spend
Shifts but his place, for still the world enjoys it;
But beauty's waste hath in the world an end,
And kept unused, the user so destroys it.

No love toward others in that bosom sits
That on himself such murd'rous shame commits.

10 She challenges him, *Deny that you love me. Why do you hate yourself?*

For shame deny that thou bear'st love to any,
Who for thy self art so unprovident.
Grant, if thou wilt, thou are beloved of many,
But that thou none lov'st is most evident;
For thou art so possessed with murd'rous[227] hate
That 'gainst thyself thou stick'st not to conspire,
Seeking that beauteous roof to ruinate,
Which to repair should by thy chief desire.
O change thy thought, that I may change my mind
Shall hate be fairer lodged than gentle love?
Be as thy presence is, gracious and kind,
Or to thyself at least kind-hearted prove;
Make thee another self for love of me,
That beauty still may live in thine or thee.

11 His child is growing within her.

As fast as thou shalt wane, so fast thou grow'st
In one of thine from that which thou departest;
And that fresh blood which youngly thou bestow'st
Thou mayst call thine when thou from youth convertest.[228]
Herein lives wisdom, beauty, and increase;
Without this, folly, age, and cold decay.
If all were minded so, the times should cease,
And threescore year would make the world away.
Let those whom Nature hath not made for store,
Harsh, featureless, and rude, barrenly perish.
Look whom she best endowed she gave thee more;
Which bounteous gift thou shouldst in bounty cherish;
She carved thee for her seal, and meant thereby
Thou shouldst print more, not let that copy die.

12 So why allow everything to go to waste?

When I do count the clock that tells the time,
And see the brave day sunk in hideous night;
When I behold the violet past prime,

---

[227] Sonnets 9.14 & 10.5 both use the word murderous. The tone of this line negates a theory that William Herbert's mother commissioned William Shakespeare to write these seventeen sonnets for her son's seventeenth birthday.

[228] One can read in this that she is carrying his child and it is due at about the time he reaches the age of 21. Line 4 removes any ambiguity of the first three lines.

And sable curls all silvered o'er with white;
When lofty trees I see barren of leaves,
Which erst from heat did canopy the herd,
And summer's green all girded up in sheaves
Borne on the bier with white and bristly beard;
Then of thy beauty do I question make
That thou among the wastes of time must go,
Since sweets and beauties do themselves forsake,
And die as fast as they see others grow;
And nothing 'gainst Time's scythe can make defence
Save breed to brave[229] him, when he takes thee hence.

13 – 14 Is he really prepared to let his lineage come to nothing?

O that you were yourself! But, love, you are
No longer yours than you yourself here live.
Against this coming end you should prepare,
And your sweet semblance to some other give.
So should that beauty which you hold in lease
Find no determination; then you were
Yourself again after your self's decease,
When your sweet issue your sweet form should bear.
Who lets so fair a house fall to decay,
Which husbandry in honour might uphold
Against the stormy gusts of winter' day,
And barren rage of death's eternal cold?
O, none but unthrifts! Dear my love, you know
You had a father,[230] let your son say so.

14

Not from the stars do I my judgement pluck,
And yet methinks I have astronomy;[231]
But not to tell of good or evil luck,
Of plagues, of dearths, or seasons' quality;
Nor can I fortune to brief minutes tell,
Pointing to each his thunder, rain, and wind,
Or say with princes if it shall go well
By oft predict that I in heaven find;
But from thine eyes my knowledge I derive,
And, constant stars, in them I read such art
As truth and beauty shall together thrive
If from thyself to store thou wouldst convert;
Or else of thee this I prognosticate:
Thy end is truth's and beauty's doom and date.

---

[229] defy
[230] *Had*, not *have* a father - post 19 January 1601.
[231] The Sidneys were known to be very interested in astronomy.

15 She offers him a successor, recreating him.

When I consider everything that grows
Holds in perfection but a little moment,
That this huge stage presenteth nought but shows
Whereon the stars in secret influence comment;
When I perceive that men as plants increase,
Cheered and checked even by the selfsame sky,
Vaunt in their youthful sap, at height decrease,
And wear their brave state out of memory;
Then the conceit of this inconstant stay
Sets you most rich in youth before my sight,
Where wasteful Time debateth with Decay
To change your day of youth to sullied night;
And all in war with Time for love of you,
As he takes from you, I engraft you new.[232]

16 Asking why does he withdraw into a man's world?

But wherefore do not you a mightier way
Make war upon this bloody tyrant Time,
And fortify yourself in your decay
With means more blessed than my barren rhyme?
Now stand you on the top of happy hours,
And many maiden gardens, yet unset,
With virtuous wish would bear your living flowers,
Much liker than your painted counterfeit.
So should the lines of life that life repair
Which this, Time's pencil or my pupil pen,
Neither in inward worth nor outward fair
Can make you live yourself in eyes of men.
To give away yourself keeps your self still,
And you must live drawn by your own sweet skill.

17 Mary makes a last attempt to persuade him.

Who will believe my verse in time to come
If it were filled with your most high deserts?
Though yet, heaven knows, it is but as a tomb[233]
Which hides your life and shows not half your parts.
If I could write the beauty of your eyes,
And in fresh numbers[234] number all your graces,
The age to come would say *'This poet lies;*
Such heavenly touches ne'er touched earthly faces.'

---

[232] She is replacing what Time is taking from him.

[233] Onomatopoeic *womb?*

[234] A number is a verse or poem.

The Leap Year Sonnets, 1 – 17

So should my papers, yellowed with their age,
Be scorned,[235] like old men of less truth than tongue,
And your true rights be termed a poet's rage
And stretched metre of an antique song.
But were some child of yours alive that time,
You should live twice in it, and in my rhyme.

By 25th March 1601 it was known that a son, the love-child of Mary Fitton and William Herbert, had died soon after birth [5.22]. With the infant's last breath expired the pressure on William to marry, although the Queen remained very unhappy with them. Sonnet 17 ends the *"Dearest William, you need to marry and have children"* sequence and forms a natural breakpoint, but Mary continued to write over a hundred more sonnets, creating a diary of her emotions that covered her next four or five years.

What of William Herbert? We learnt in the last chapter [5.23] that he had been sent to the Fleet Prison by the Queen, and it was probably while he was there that his father died at Wilton. The next chapter shows parallels between the William Herbert / Mary Fitton story, and the relationship depicted between *Ophelia* and *Hamlet, Prince of Denmark.*

---

[235] Almost what happened, ignored rather than scorned. Nobody has ever considered Mary Fitton as a writer of the Sonnets. I recall at Grammar School asking the English master what the Sonnets were. He replied that they were love poems by William Shakespeare, but he chose not to say any more, although his hesitation told me he wanted to. Only in the last few months have I understood that the poems were and are considered to be homoerotic, and his reticence is only now explained. Many generations of school children must have experienced the same bewilderment. Anyone with any literary pretensions can immediately see that here is some beautiful poetry, if only one could understand how it fitted together.

PLATE 1

MARY FITTON
Original at Arbury Hall, Warwickshire.
Printed by kind permission of Viscount Daventry

PLATE 2

Mary Fitton (right) and her married sister, Anne Newdigate, aged 15 and 18.
Mary holds three types of flowers, one of which is a pansy.
Original at Arbury Hall. By Kind Permission of Viscount Daventry.

From the tombstone of Sir Edward Fitton; effigies of his wife, Agnes and two
of four children, Mary and Edward . Gawsworth Parish Church, Cheshire.

PLATE 3

Left: Sir Philip Sidney, brother of (right) Robert Sidney, 1st Earl Leicester, (father of Mary Sidney Wroth). Centre, sister, Mary Sidney Herbert, Countess Pembroke (by Hilliard); Courtesy of the National Portrait Gallery, London.
Porpentine & Sidney Arms Courtesy of Lord d'Lisle, Penshurst Place, Kent.
Sidney; Pheon Blazon;   Pembroke; Lions Blazon

PLATE 4

The Procession of Queen Elizabeth of 16th June 1600. By kind permission of Mr J K Wingfield Digby, Sherborne Castle, Dorset. Second from the left, with white hair, is Charles Howard. The man with the white staff is thought to be Sir William Knollys. The face of the man between them appears to be Sir Richard Leveson, Howard's son-in-law [see PLATE-5], however Knollys and Leveson appear to be garter-knights. The Lady in White may be Mary Fitton leading the Maids of Honour, or the bride, Anne Russell; the two looked very similar.

Agnes Fitton with her daughter, Mary Fitton, and son Edward, c1586.
Painting at Gawsworth Hall, Cheshire, in the possession of Mr Timothy Richards whose permission to reproduce is greatly appreciated.
[detail right] Above the helmet on the crest is a **pansy**.

PLATE 5

Top: William Herbert, 3rd. Earl of Pembroke; by permission of the Folger Shakespeare Library, Washington D.C.; Sir Richard Leveson: reproduced by kind permission of the trustees of the Wallace Collection, London. Lady Margaret Hawkins: reproduced by kind permission of the Lady Hawkins School, Kington, Herefordshire.

PLATE 6

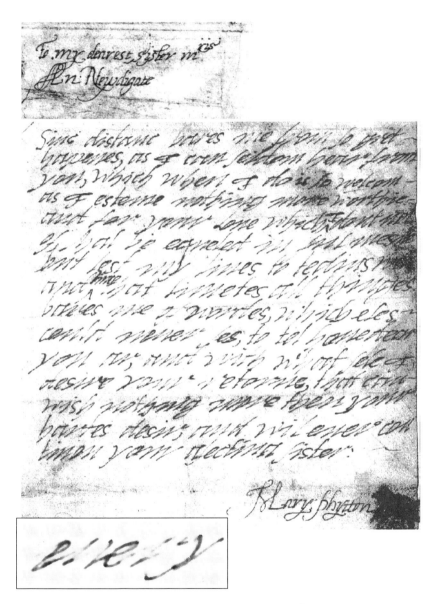

Mary Fitton's undated letter to her sister, M^{ris} An Newdigate; in Roman (italic) handwriting; signed Mary Phytton. The panel is a composite of ever (from n-ever) to which a "y" has been added to make the word *every* , as in Sonnet 76;
That every word doth almost tell my name.

PLATE 7

SHAKE-SPEARES

SONNETS.

Neuer before Imprinted.

AT LONDON
By *G. Eld* for *T. T.* and are
to be folde by *William Afhley.*
1609.

Mr. WILLIAM
SHAKESPEARES
COMEDIES,
HISTORIES, &
TRAGEDIES.
Published according to the True Originall Copies.

LONDON
Printed by Ifaac Iaggard, and Ed. Blount. 1623.

TO.THE.ONLIE.BEGETTER.OF.
THESE.INSVING.SONNETS.
Mr.W. H. ALL.HAPPINESSE.
AND.THAT.ETERNITIE.
PROMISED.

BY.

OVR.EVER-LIVING.POET.

WISHETH.

THE.WELL-WISHING.
ADVENTVRER.IN.
SETTING.
FORTH.

T. T.

William Shakespeare by Martin Droeshout and Miniature of William Herbert;
both by kind Permission of the Folger Shakespeare Library.

(right top) The Sanders Portrait of 1603, by kind permission of Mr. Lloyd Sullivan.

Title Page to the Sonnets, and the Dedication.

PLATE 8

Gawsworth Hall, Cheshire, the home of the Fittons

Gawsworth Church

Arbury Hall, Warwickshire, the home of the Newdigates

CHAPTER SEVEN

HAMLET, PRINCE OF DENMARK

Perhaps only when one has recently lost a parent one can understand the ongoing dialogue that continues to play on one's mind. Let me ask you to recall the ghost of Hamlet's father. Remember?

Outside it was pouring. My father had died a few weeks earlier and a shortage of shirts forced me to catch up on laundry. I was beginning to despise a thick, white, cotton shirt. While ironing I always watch a video, and that day I was revisiting the play, *Hamlet, Prince of Denmark*. Suddenly my mind alerted me that two words I had just heard, *"Affection, puh!,"* I has read elsewhere in a different context. In the time it took to blink, a link had flashed across my mind connecting Mary Fitton with the play. The link, of course, needed to be investigated but my conclusion is that elements of the real-life story of William Herbert and Mary Fitton were translated by William Herbert into the dramatic relationship between Prince Hamlet and Ophelia.

Imagine the mental condition, at the start of 1601, of the precocious, vain and highly intelligent William Herbert. He had been thrown out of Court by an angry and powerful monarch and was locked up in the Fleet Prison. Pressure was being put on him to marry. His girlfriend whom he loved, but would not marry, was pregnant, and her father and her brother were creating problems for him. To add to all this, on 19th January 1601 William's ailing father died and William now became the 3rd. Earl of Pembroke. He was still three months from being twenty-one so there was a threat that he would become a Ward of Court which his mother was trying hard to prevent.[236] Underage and in prison, all his powers were subject to the Queen's will, or whim. With all this happening, and knowing he was not going to be able to say goodbye to his father, would it not be surprising that the twenty-year old William Herbert's brain was in turmoil? This would have been a time for a huge emotional outpouring from a man who was sensitive and melancholy. Going through his mind was a cocktail of love, shame, sex, marriage, birth, death, health, freedom, reputation, honour, family, estate, and present and future wealth.[237]

There was a six week's hiatus between the death of William Herbert's father in January 1601 and his burial. It would appear that William was still in prison in London as his father's body was interred at Salisbury Cathedral. One historian notes that William spent his time in prison writing verses.[238] [239] I

---

[236] Hannay op. Cit. p163
[237] Hamlet makes great play on it not being two months since his father died which could position the writing of the play in March 1601.
[238] Haynes, op. cit. p49.
[239] Another Earl in prison at that time was Henry Wriothesley, 2nd. Earl Southampton who had been involved, with the Earl of Essex, in the failed rebellion on 8th February 1601. The two

Hamlet, Prince of Denmark

posit that he actually was working on the play, *Hamlet, Prince of Denmark*, but think it was William's mother, Countess Pembroke, perhaps with her brother, Robert Sidney, who originated or commissioned the play in the late 1580's, possibly in collaboration with the playwright Thomas Kyd.[240] I believe it was her son who in 1601, in prison, dramatically improved the play using the drama of his situation with Mary Fitton as the basis of the offhand, uncertain relationship between Hamlet and Ophelia; although he wrongly assessed that the emotional woman he had jilted and shamed would commit suicide. William Herbert, however, did not write the original play, aged nine in 1589, he would have been too young. What he did do was convert a crude, unsuccessful play into a great psychological drama, therapeutically writing his way through his torments, introducing to the play the tensions of the love affair, the emotions of having lost his father, and the feeling of hopelessness that we all, at times, can experience; whether to be or not to be – there's the point.

So, for Hamlet read William, and for Ophelia read Mary. Yet Hell hath no fury like a woman scorned and, in the play, Hamlet, or the writer, has to handle his words to the jilted Ophelia with great care. There are constant hints to Mary, through the guise of Ophelia, that, despite his apparent mad state, he loved her, that he still loves her, but in her own self interest he must release her from their emotional ties.

The play's story is that Prince Hamlet finds out from his father's ghost that he was poisoned by his uncle who quickly married his mother, the widowed Queen. Hamlet acts the idiot to protect himself from being killed and escapes to England. He returns as an adult to seek vengeance. During the play Hamlet rejects Ophelia, a young woman he loved, and she becomes distracted and drowns herself. The play ends tragically with all the protagonists dead, poisoned or slain, except Ophelia's brother, Laertes, who assumes the crown.

The development of the play Hamlet, Prince of Denmark, can be traced back to the Saxo Grammaticus's Historiae Danicae.[241] The prince, Amleth, acts madly when he fears for his own life after his uncle killed his father to obtain the throne. To find out if Amleth is shamming, the uncle attempts to trick Amleth into having sex with an attractive woman, but the plot is discovered to them by a friend. The two enjoy sex in secret and then lie to the King. There is no love affair as such, the woman does not appear elsewhere in the story and she certainly does not go mad. A French translation by François de Belleforest was first published in Histoires Tragiques in 1570. The first English translation of Belleforest, published anonymously in 1608, has a slight embellishment stating that the woman loves him more than she loves herself.[242]

Shakespeare poems of 1593 and 1594 were dedicated to Henry Wriothesley who had paid handsomely for a performance of Shakespeare's Henry II a few days before the attempt to seize control of London.

[240] Like the Countess Pembroke, Kyd was also a translator from French.

[241] Saxo Grammaticus wrote his History of the Danes between 1206 and 1218.

[242] Did Thomas Kyd, William Herbert or Countess Pembroke make the translation and when?

Hamlet, Prince of Denmark

The play Hamlet has parallels with Thomas Kyd's earlier *The Spanish Tragedy*, having a wailing ghost and a vengeance for the murder of a father. In 1589 the poet, Thomas Nashe, in his introduction to Robert Greene's *Menaphon* writes, *"he will afford you whole Hamlets, I should say handfuls of tragical speeches."* The diary of the owner of the Rose Theatre, Philip Henslowe, records a performance of a play called *Hamlet*, on 11th June 1594, in a short season shared by the Lord Admiral's Men[243] and the Lord Chamberlain's Men[244]. This early play has no surviving script and was nicknamed Ur-Hamlet[245].

It was not until 26th July 1602 that a play was registered with the name *Hamlet*. A printer named James Roberts placed an entry in the Stationers' Register for *A booke called the Revenge of Hamlett Prince Denmarke as yt was latelie Acted by the Lord Chamberleyne his servantes.* The first known printed edition, *The Tragicall Historie of HAMLET Prince of Denmarke By William Shake-speare (now known as Q1 –the Bad Hamlet)*, was dated 1603 and printed by Nicholas Ling and John Trundell. It is 2,200 lines long compared with the 3,800 lines of Q2 of 1604. So, Ur-Hamlet existed from about 1589; the Bad Hamlet, Q1, was registered and printed in 1602; the first good Hamlet (Q2) was printed in 1604. In Q2, Act 3.1 Laertes[246] explains succinctly to Ophelia (Mary) why Hamlet (William) would not marry her;[247]

> Perhaps he loves you now,
> And now no soil nor cautel[248] doth besmirch
> The virtue of his will; but you must fear,
> His greatness weighed, his will is not his own,
> For he himself is subject to his birth;
> He may not, as unvalued persons do,
> Carve for himself, for on his choice depends
> The sanity and health of the whole state;
> And therefore must his choice be circumscribed
> Unto the voice and yielding of that body
> Whereof he is the head. Then if he says he loves you,
> It fits your wisdom so far to believe it
> As he in his particular act and place
> May give his saying deed; which is no further
> Than the main voice of Denmark goes withal.[249]

---

[243] The Lord Admiral was Charles Howard, Richard Leveson's father-in-law.

[244] Aemelia Lanier, the Lord Chamberlain's (Henry Carey) mistress, probably watched this play. Charles Howard was married to Henry Carey's sister.

[245] Ur; German for earliest. It was German scholars that first realised there was a lost version.

[246] Mary Fitton had a brother, Edward. Ophelia's brother is Laertes, their father is called Polonius (Corambis in Q1, possibly meaning two-faced) and in the play he is Lord Chamberlain to the King. The Lord Chamberlain then was George Carey, Lord Hunsdon, whose sister Lady Margaret Hoby, was a friend of Mary's sister. A Mistress Carey was one of the eight Masquers with Mary Fitton at the 1600 wedding [Chapter 5.19].

[247] The Scottish queen tells Amleth, "the wise man must reckon the lustre of her birth and not of her beauty."

[248] Trickery; the word appears in exactly the same context in *A Lover's Complaint*, stanza 44.

[249] This speech appears in Q2 but not Q1.

Hamlet, Prince of Denmark

I started my investigation by reading Q1, the Bad Hamlet and immediately I could picture William Herbert as Hamlet. However basic research quickly showed that the story and the drama had been around for at least ten years. It certainly would not be credible for William Herbert to be writing the most complex, psychological, Shakespeare play when he was ten! But then I noticed these two, highlighted, Q1 references to Sir Philip Sidney, the Countess' brother, William's Herbert's late uncle.

Ghost   Nay pitty me not, but to my vnfolding
           Lend thy listning eare, but that I am forbid
           To tell the secrets of my prison house
           I would a tale vnfold, whose lightest word
           Would harrow vp thy soule, freeze thy yong blood,
           Make thy two eyes like stars start from their spheres,
           Thy knotted and combined locks to part,
           And each particular haire to stand on end
           Like quils vpon the fretfull Porpentine,
           But this same blazon must not be, to eares[250] of flesh and blood
           Hamlet, if euer thou didst thy deere father loue.
           [Q1 text, at 1.5 in Folio]

Ophelia Great God of heauen, what a quicke change is this?
           The Courtier, Scholler, Souldier, all in him,
           All dasht and splinterd thence, O woe is me,
           To a seene what I haue seene, see what I see.
           [Q1 text, at 3.1 in Folio]

The first quotation refers to the Sidney family coat of arms with a porcupine as its crest [PLATE 3]. The second quotation exactly describes Sir Philip Sidney's death.[251] *"O woe is me, to a seen what I have seen, see what I see,"* are words that Philip's younger brother, Robert, who was by his side when he died, would have articulated.

In the context of the play, Hamlet was a royal prince about to continue his studies. Aged about seventeen he could neither be considered an established soldier nor a courtier (he was a royal prince), and hardly a scholar. Sir Philip Sidney, William Herbert's dead uncle, was exactly those things. In 1586, aged 31, Philip along with his younger brother, Robert, took part in a skirmish against the Spanish at Zutphen in Holland. He was wounded by a musket shot that shattered his thighbone and died of the wound twenty-two days later.[252] A huge crowd of Londoners witnessed the 700-strong funeral progression, having the highest regard for a man who was known and universally popular as a

---

[250] heirs?

[251] In Henry VI part II Act 3.1 is written, *"his thighs with darts were almost like a sharp quilled porpentine."*

[252] On the right hand wall of the Front Hall at Wilton House is a painting of the fatally wounded Sir Philip Sidney at the battle of Zutphen. He is being offered water, but points to a soldier and is supposed to have said, "his need is greater than mine." Amazingly (for me) before one can see this painting, everyone who enters the House through the Hall has first to look up to a life-size statue of none other than our Mr. William Shakespeare.

Courtier, Scholler, and *Souldier.*[253] In the contemporary illustration of the Procession, two heralds of the College of Arms carry Philip Sidney's helmet crested by a porcupine (porpentine) and his shield with its single down-pointing arrowhead (pheon). On this strong evidence the date of origination of the play gravitates, therefore, towards 1586-90 when such things would have been current.

This evidence suggests that the originators of Hamlet, Prince of Denmark could have been the Countess Pembroke and her brother, Robert Sidney, a consequence of that terrible year when they lost their parents and favourite brother. Their father's death was swift and unexpected. Did Mary think he had been poisoned?[254] Could Mary or Robert have had an afterlife experience, imagining their father on the ramparts of Ludlow Castle where they had spent childhood years when Henry Sidney was Lord President of Wales? Did either of them extend the story of Amleth to include a ghost - using Elsinore Castle, so much like Ludlow Castle, as the backcloth? [255]

We may never know what *Hamlet* was circulating during the 1590's. This root play appears to have been performed occasionally but to little acclaim and some scorn. Then, following the death of his father or perhaps during his ailing father's last illness, Countess Pembroke's very distressed son decided to improve it.[256] The departure from the modest, linear, historical story-line of Amleth by the introduction of the tragic love story of Hamlet and Ophelia hugely increases the psychological factor, adding new, highly-charged dimensions. The complexity of the love story could not have derived from just a few lines in Saxo Gramaticus or Belleforest - these passions had to have been experienced.

So, was it the Countess, who had already translated from French the stories of Anthony and Cleopatra, or was it Thomas Kyd who read Belleforest's[257] story of Amleth that around 1590 created Ur-Hamlet, the precursor of Q1?[258] In prison in 1601 William would have had to rely only on memory or used a rough script but, once released, he could have asked any one of a number of playwrights to improve his revised text.[259] The crude Q1 (the Bad Hamlet) was

---

[253] In *Walsingham* by Alan Haynes, he suggests that the huge procession on 16th February 1587 was arranged by Francis Walsingham, Philip Sidney's father-in-law, to *bury the news* of Mary Queen of Scots' execution on 8th February.

[254] Having purged himself, he travelled down the river Severn from Bewdley to Worcester where he caught a chill and soon died. (5th May 1586) (Hannay, op. Cit. p55)

[255] Countess Pembroke's father did not have a brother. It is worth visiting Ludlow Castle to climb the ramparts and look into Wales. (The road up to the castle is quite steep!)

[256] When Mary Fitton calls William *Mary's Prince* in the *Dedication* to the Sonnets it would appear that the revision of the Play might have been already under way.

[257] Belleforest appears to be a cartographer 1530-1583 who produced maps in England.

[258] It is just about plausible that Thomas Kyd (1558-1594) should write both the *Spanish Tragedy* and *Ur-Hamlet*. The play *Hamlet* omits *Amleth's* years and loves in England and Scotland.

[259] Two of the three speeches from Q2, not printed in the 1623 Folio, impugn Hamlet's mother and could, therefore, have been considered criticism of the late Countess Pembroke.
It is difficult to understand why, after his years in England, Hamlet's return coincides with

Hamlet, Prince of Denmark

registered in 1602, confirming ownership pending the polished version, Q2, of 1604.

I think William Herbert worked on the play to help pass the time. He had been six-years-old when his poet-uncle and England's hero died and it must have been a very impressionable event in his life. Perhaps it was a project he had already set his mind to, or maybe it was a catharsis giving him an opportunity to understand and write of his own despair, his estimate of the value of life and contemplate an exit by suicide. *To be or not to be, that is the question* - a soliloquy unparalleled in English literature – which does not derive either directly or indirectly from Amleth. William, from his recent experience, wove Hamlet's love for Ophelia into the story, the futility of their marrying and imagined that his callous rejection of her would cause her to go insane and to commit suicide. Perhaps, at some point, Mary Fitton had threatened she would end her own life.

Here are four extracts from Q1 (The *Bad Hamlet*). The scene numbers relate to the modern play.

2.1 Ophelia's describing Hamlet's sorry state to her father;
3.1 Hamlet's famous soliloquy, "To be or not to be..."
3.1 Hamlet's dialogue with Ophelia "get thee to a nunnery..."
4.5 Ophelia, the lady of the flower's final mad scene.

2.1 Ophelia describes to her father a meeting with Hamlet. The extract is to show how William Herbert thought Mary Fitton saw him.[260]

> O young Prince Hamlet, the only flower of Denmark,
> He is bereft of all the wealth he had,
> The jewel that ador'nd his feature most
> Is filcht and stolen away, his wit's bereft him,
> He found me walking in the gallery all alone,
> There comes he to me, with a distracted look,
> His garters lagging down, his shoes untide,[261]
> And fixt his eyes so steadfast on my face,
> As if they had vow'd, this is their latest object.
> Small while he stood, but gripes me by the wrist,
> And there he holds my pulse till with a sigh
> He doth unclasp his hold, and parts away

Ophelia's burial as, in the play, Ophelia appears to drown herself just after Hamlet left for England. If the author wanted to be faithful to Amleth and have a sojourn in England and Scotland, it would have worked better if Ophelia's descent into madness and suicide happened *after* she heard that Hamlet has returned to Denmark with a bride. There is a suggestion that the actor who played Marcellus wrote Q1. It would have been quite possible for William Herbert to have taken that role.

[260] Perhaps she was able to visit him in the Fleet Prison.

[261] Compare this with Rosalind in As You Like It Act 3.2, describing the symptoms of a man in love: Then, your hose should be ungartered, your bonnet unbanded, your sleeve unbuttoned, your shoe untied, and everything about you demonstrating a careless desolation.

Silent, as is the mid time of the night:
And as he went, his eye was still on me,
For thus his head over his shoulder looked,
He seemed to find the way without his eyes:
For out of doors he went without their help,
And so did leave me.

3.1 Disturbed, Hamlet (William Herbert) considers the value of living.

To be, or not to be, I there's the point,
To Die, to sleep, is that all? I all:
No, to sleep, to dream, I mary there it goes,
For in that dream of death, when we awake,
And borne before an everlasting judge,
From whence no passenger ever retur'nd,
The undiscovered country, at whose sight
The happy smile, and the accursed damn'd.
But for this, the joyful hope of this,
Who'd bear the scorns and flattery of the world,
Scorned by the right rich, the rich cursed of the poor?
The widow being oppressed, the orphan wrong'd,
The taste of hunger, or a tirants raigne,
And thousand more calamities besides,
To grunt and sweat under this weary life,
When that he may his full Quietus make,
With a bare bodkin, who would this indure,
But for a hope of something after death?
Which pusles the brain and doth confound the sense,
Which makes us rather beare those evilles we have,
Than fly to others that we know not of.
I that, O this conscience makes cowards of us all,
Lady in thy orizons[262], be all my sins remembred.

Q2 has the longer, much more refined speech that is so familiar. Here, we can compare the last lines, noting that in Q2 Hamlet calls Ophelia a *nymph.*[263]

Soft you now, The fair Ophelia! Nymph, in thy orisons
Be all my sins remembered.

3.1 Immediately following is the scene with Ophelia which displays Hamlet's (William's) view about the value of marriage. His offensive attitude may be the response to being repeatedly asked to marry, as in sonnets 1-17.

---

[262] prayers

[263] Is this an abreviated reference to Mary Phitton, when she appears to have performed as an nymph in the 1600 wedding masque?

Ophelia   My Lord, I have sought opportunitie, which now I have, to
redeliver to your worthy hands, a small remembrance, such
tokens which I have received of you.

Hamlet   Are you faire?

Ophelia   My Lord.

Hamlet   Are you honest?

Ophelia   What means my Lord?

Hamlet   That if you be faire and honest[264]
Your beauty should admit no discourse to your honesty.

Ophelia   My Lord, can beauty have better priviledge than with
honesty?

Hamlet   Yea may it; for Beauty may transform
Honesty, from what she was into a bawd:
Then Honesty can transform Beauty:
This was sometimes a Paradox,
But now the time gives it scope.
I never gave you nothing.

Ophelia   My Lord, you know right will you did,
And with them such earnest vows of love,
As would have moov'd the stoniest breast alive,
But now too true I find,
Rich gifts wax poor, when givers grow unkind.

Hamlet   I never loved you.

Ophelia   You made me believe you did.

Hamlet   O thou shouldst not a believed me!
Go to a Nunnery go, why shouldst thou
Be a breeder of sinners? I am my self indifferent honest,
But I could accuse my self of such crimes
It had been better my mother had ne're borne me,
O I am very prowde, ambitious, disdainful,
With more sins at my beck, then I have thoughts
To put them in, what should such fellows as I
Do, crawling between heaven and earth?
To a Nunnery go, we are arrant knaves all,
Believe none of us, to a Nunnery go.

Ophelia   O heavens secure him!

Hamlet   Where's thy father?

Ophelia   At home my lord.

Hamlet   For God's sake let the doors be shut on him,
He ay play the fool now where but in his
Own house: to a Nunnery go.

Ophelia   Help him, good God.

Hamlet   If thou dost marry, I'll give thee
This plague to thy dowry:

---

[264] See Sonnet 105 for fair, honest and true.

> Be thou as chaste as ice, as pure as snow,
> Thou shalt not scape calumny, to a Nunnery go.

Ophelia   Alas, what change is this?

Hamlet   But if thou wilt needs marry, marry a fool,
> For wisemen know well enough,
> What monsters you make of them, to a Nunnery go.

Ophelia   Pray God restore him.

Hamlet   Nay, I have heard of your paintings too,
> God hath given you one face,
> And you make your selves another,
> You sigh, and you amble, and you nickname Gods creatures,
> Making your wantonness, your ignorance,
> A pox, t'is scurvy, I'll no more of it,
> It hath made me mad: I'll no more marriages,
> All that are married but one, shall live,
> The rest shall keep as they are, to a Nunnery go,
> To a Nunnery go.   exit.

Ophelia   Great God of heaven, what a quick change is this?
> To a scene what I have seen, see what I see.

4.5   From her *Flowers* scene; Ophelia has become distracted before we hear of her drowning herself. Was this William explaining what he fears might happen to Mary Fitton? Had Mary threatened him? Ophelia enters the Court and her brother Laertes greets her with, "How now Ofelia?"

Ophelia   Well God a mercy, I a bin gathering of flower:
> Here, here is rew for you,
> You may call it hearb a grace a Sundayes,
> Heere's some for me too: you must wear your rew
> With a difference, there's a dazie.
> Here Love, there's rosemary for you
> For remembrance: I pray Love remember,
> And there's pansy for thoughts.[265]

---

[265] The Pansy, genus *viola*, is the Fitton emblem; a violet is also a *viola* and appears three times in the Sonnets. This is the unique occurrence of Pansy in Shakespeare's plays. Pansy from the French word pensée means *thought* (also known as heartease & love-in-idleness). In the double portrait of Mary and Anne Fitton, aged 15 and 18, Mary has three different flowers in her hand one of which is a pansy. In sonnets 1-126 allusions to flowers appear many times, as in Sonnet 99;

> The forward **violet** thus did I chide: "Sweet thief, whence didst thou steal thy sweet that smells,
> If not from my love's breath? The purple pride which on thy soft cheek for complexion dwells
> In my love's veins thou hast too grossly dyed" The **lily** I condemned for thy hand,
> And buds of **marjoram** had stol'n thy hair; The **roses** fearfully on thorns did stand,
> Our blushing shame, another white despair; A third, nor red nor white, had stol'n of both,
> And to his robb'ry had annexed thy breath; But, for his theft, in pride of all his growth
> A vengeful canker eat him up to death. More **flowers** I noted, yet I none could see
> But sweet or colour it had stol'n from thee.

Laertes	A document in madness, thoughts, remembrance:
	O God, O God!
Ophelia	There is fennel for you, I would a giu'n you
	Some violets, but they all withered, when
	My father died: alas, they say the owl was
	A Bakers daughter[266], we see what we are,
	But can not tell what we shall be.
	For bonny sweet Robin is all my joy.
Laertes	Thoughts and afflictions, torments worse than hell.
Ophelia	Nay Love, I pray you make no words of this now:
	I pray now, you shall sing a down,
	And you a down a, t'is a the Kings daughter
	And the false steward, and if any body
	Ask you of any thing, say you this.
	To morrow is saint Valentines day,[267]
	All in the morning betime,
	And a maid at your window,
	To be your Valentine:
	The young man rose, and dan'd his clothes,
	And dupt the chamber door,
	Let in the maid, that out a maid
	Never departed more.
	Nay I pray mark now,
	By gisse and by saint Charitie,
	Away, and fie for shame:
	Young men will do't when they come to't
	By cock they are to blame.
	Quoth she, before you tumbled me,
	You promised me to wed.
	So would I a done, by yonder Sun,
	If thou hadst not come to my bed.
	So God be with you all, God bwy Ladies.
	God bwy you Love.

In *Q2* the words are altered slightly. Ophelia says, "There's rose**mary**, that's for remembrance – pray you, love, remember – and there is **pansies**, that's for thoughts." Her brother, Laertes, responds, "A document in madness, thoughts and remembrance **fitted**." Mary / Pansy / Fitted.[268]

It is quite clear that the *A Lover's Complaint* and Sonnets 1-17 complement the Hamlet / Ophelia story. We have William (Hamlet) explaining to Mary (Ophelia) through Ophelia and her brother, Laertes, the nature of his love for her and why matters of (e)state take precedence. We have her telling the world that they *tumbled* but only after he had promised to marry her, just as in *A*

---

[266] Was the Baker's daughter the owl-like Anne Clifford, whose mother was a Baker?

[267] Did the lovers meet on 14th February or the day in 1601 when this line is being written?

[268] If Mary Fitton was expected to watch the play, she would have read hope in these words.

Hamlet, Prince of Denmark

Lover's Complaint, stanza 40: *And credent soul to that strong-bonded oath that shall prefer and undertake my troth.* I think one can safely conclude that here, in *Hamlet, Prince of Denmark,* we have identified Mary Fitton's prince.

This Chapter started with an iron, a shirt, pouring rain, a video and two words, "Affection! Puh!" In Q2: Act 1, iii Ophelia talks to her father of Hamlet;

Ophelia	He hath, my lord, of late made many tenders Of his affection to me.
Polonius	Affection! Puh! – you speak like a green girl Unsifted in such perilous circumstance.

The use of *affection* closely reflects what the Queen said to Mary Fitton at the wedding celebrations in June 1600 [Chapter 5.19]:

> *Mrs Fitton went to the Queen & wooed her to dance; her Majesty asked what she was; "Affection," she said. "Affection!" said the Queen; "Affection is false." Yet her Majesty rose and danced.*

Is it a coincidence that the plays attributed to Shakespeare started to appear immediately after Countess Pembroke came out of mourning? I think not.[269] Could the *Shakespeare* plays have been created as follows? A member of the Sidney – Herbert family with its history of patronage of the literary arts and its enjoyment of theatre, would discover a story, its characters and create a rough-cut text of a play. Wordsmiths like Kyd, Chapman, Spenser, Daniel, Fletcher, Middleton or even Marlowe, would then cobble and hone to bring out the drama. The final touches, to obtain the critical timing and pace of the play, would be done by a director-actor, probably William Shakespeare.[270]

---

[269] The Shakespeare First Folio did not include two plays, *Pericles,* and *The Two Noble Kinsmen.* The latter is thought to have been written with John Fletcher (1579-1625). Logic suggested that since this was a late play, and if William Herbert had a hand in it, there may be some autobiography written into it. This is discussed in Appendix 5.

[270] A lost letter (Hannay; op. cit. p122) records that (in December 1603) Countess Pembroke induced the King to come to Wilton, from nearby Salisbury, about four miles away, to see a performance of *As You Like It,* saying, "we have the man Shakespeare with us." I doubt whether the King rushed over to meet a playwright but he may have made the journey if he knew he was going to be entertained by a great actor. In Calvin Hoffman's *The Man who was Shakespeare,* Hoffman points out that although the play was Registered on 4th August 1600, a caveat, "A book to be stayed," was placed upon it. The play not appear in print until the first Folio in 1623.

CHAPTER EIGHT

SONNETS FROM AFAR, 18 – 126

With the death of their infant son in March 1601, Mary Fitton would have lost much of the emotional hold she had felt she had over William Herbert. On 24th of that month the Leap Year ended and, by the start of May, the two lovers were physically apart. Mary was still in London with Lady Margaret Hawkins where she had been detained for her confinement. William appears to have been at Wilton, although occasionally he may have stayed at Baynards Castle, the Pembroke's London home. Mary continued to express herself through the medium of sonnets but the theme of Sonnets 1-17, that William should marry her, came to an abrupt end. A flow of cleverly constructed sonnets followed which tried to impress on him her loving feelings. They start with the most famous of all lines, from which comes the title of this book:

> Shall I compare thee to a summer's day?
> Thou art more lively and more temperate.
> Rough winds do shake the darling buds of Maie,

Sonnets 18-126 are those of a passionate, sometimes demented woman, longing for her lover, going through a whole spectrum of moods and, at times, being pregnant. Occasionally one senses that there was an ongoing dialogue between the two lovers as she responds to the news she somehow obtains about him. They actually meet very briefly, as recorded in Sonnet 34. Equally, it would seem from reading Sonnet 112, he gave the impression he ignored her.

If March 24th 1601 was the latest date at which Mary Fitton completed composing Sonnets 1-17, then the earliest date at she would have started to write Sonnets, 18-126 would have been around 25th March when William was just a mile away in the Fleet Prison; this was before her father came in May to take her away from Lady Hawkins' custody, and back to Cheshire.

An analysis of Sonnets 18-126 indicates that Mary Fitton wrote spasmodically over perhaps four or five years, and just a few sonnets at a time. In Sonnets 18-25 Mary continued to woo William while she was still in London; 26-32 describe the shock of leaving London having lived for five years at the epicentre of Court excitement, 33-34 relate the emotions of a fleeting meeting; 35-39 show how she reconciled herself to their being apart before 44-42, when she became jealous because of his infidelity causing great sadness 43-45, and a feeling of isolation 46-49.

She crossed the country[271] in Sonnets 50-52 and, very lonely, she consoled herself by reflecting on his external beauty, 53-55. When William Herbert showed jealousy, Sonnets 56-61 find her trying to impress on him that he had a life of his own. He had cause to be jealous when at Sonnet 59 she appears to

---

[271] I think to the South Wales Coast where she also writes *A Lover's Complaint.*

miscarry. Again, 62-65, she became frightened of losing him and felt suicidal writing in 66-68 that she did not like the man she is with. In 69-70 there was some issue about a slander.

Sonnets 71-81 show that she was again pregnant fearing in 71-76 that she might die. Before the birth she talked to him about vanity, 78-79 and at 80-81 she talked about the baby. But now, 82-87 they cooled towards each other and fell out. In Sonnets 88-93 Mary tried to release him from their emotional bond but she continued to love him. Still zealous about his activity she warned him he is taking advantage of his elevated, social position, and that Time will catch up with him. A year passed, another pregnancy, and 97-99 they became friends again. Out of nostalgia, she tried to start composing again, 100-103, but lacked the great passion, although she continued to praise him, 104-106.

Pregnant again, she knew that Time 107-108 was taking its toll, and in 109-112 admitted to him that there had been other men and she herself was the cause of her own poor reputation. Despite this, he was everywhere in her mind's eye 113-116 and her love for him was just as intense. Sonnet 115 hints that she again is pregnant. Here she begged for forgiveness saying, 117-121, she had paid heavily for her worldly experience. The result was that, 122-126, she handed over the copybook with its Sonnets to Pembroke, adding her final thoughts in the last five sonnets. As final gestures, she embedded her name in Sonnet 123 and did not complete Sonnet 126 where and when she finally released him – and the Story Ends There.

Sonnets 18-126
18 After their baby died, Mary's approach to William changes. He says he will not marry her and she starts to use charm.

Shall I compare thee to a summer's day?
Thou art more lively and more temperate.
Rough winds do shake the darling buds of Maie,[272]
And summer's lease hath all too short a date.
Sometime too hot the eye of heaven shines,
And often is his gold complexion dimmed; .
And every fair from fair sometime declines,
By chance or nature's changing course untrimmed;
But thy eternal summer shall not fade,
Nor lose possession of that fair thou ow'st,
Nor shall Death brag thou wander'st in his shade,
When in eternal lines to time thou grow'st,
So long as men can breathe or eyes can see,
So long lives this, and this gives life to thee.[273]

---

[272] c.f. *King Lear* Act 3.4; *"through the sharp hawthorn blows the cold wind."* Lines two and three are comparisons - you are temperate - I am buffeted. Nashe writes: *"Their breasts they embuske up on a hie and their round roseate buds unmodestly lay forth."* Here *buds* means *nipples*. If simply a rustic scene, then why *darling*, an adjective that describes a creature. Was *Maie* William Herbert's pet name for Mary? Did he awaken her sensuality by touching her darling nipples?

[273] So far, for 400 years!

19 She asks Time not to allow William to grow old.

Devouring Time, blunt thou the lion's paws,[274]
And make the earth devour her own sweet brood;
Pluck the keen teeth from the fierce tiger's jaws,
And burn the long-lived phoenix in her blood;
Make glad and sorry seasons as thou fleet'st
And do whate'er thou wilt, swift-footed Time,
To the wide world and all her fading sweets;
But I forbid thee one most heinous crime:
O, carve not with thy hours my love's fair brow,
Nor draw no lines there with thine antique pen;
Him in thy course untainted do allow
For beauty's pattern to succeeding men.
Yet do thy worst, old Time; despite thy wrong
My love shall in my verse ever live young.

20 [275] Mary tells him she is his to love . . .

A woman's face with Nature's own hand painted
Hast thou the master-mistress[276] of my passion,
A woman's gentle heart but not acquainted
With shifting change as is false women's fashion,
An eye more bright than theirs, less false in rolling,
Gilding the object whereupon it gazeth;
A maiden hue all Hues in his controlling,
Which steals men's eyes and women's souls amazeth.
And for a woman wert thou first created,
Till Nature as she wrought thee fell a-doting
And by addition me of thee defeated
By adding one thing to my purpose nothing.
But since she pricked thee out for women's pleasure,
Mine by thy love and thy love's use their treasure.

21 . . and praises him except for his stubbornness.

So is it not with me as with that Muse,
Stirred by a painted beauty to his verse,
Who heaven itself for ornament doth use,
And every fair with his fair doth rehearse,
Making a couplement of proud compare
With sun and moon, with earth and seas, rich gems

---

[274] The Herbert blazon has three lions on it. The Phoenix, line-4 would be Countess Pembroke.

[275] Noting in him an effeminate face and feminine attitudes perhaps reflecting the association with Richard Barnfield.

[276] *Thou has the master of my passion* is self explanatory - he controls her passion. The corollary is *Thou has the mistress of my passion* he is subjected to her passion. If one looks at the Orlando-Rosalind relationship in *As You Like It*, although Orlando is a strong wrestler, Rosalind is the stronger, more forceful character. In *Twelfth Night* Act 5.1.314, Orsino says to Viola, *"You shall from this time be your master's mistress."*

With April's first-born[277] flowers, and all things rare
That heaven's air in this huge rondure hems.
O, let me true in love but truly write,
And then, believe me, my love is as fair
As any mother's child, though not so bright
As those gold candles fixed in heaven's air.
Let them say more that like of hearsay well;
I will not praise that purpose not to sell.[278]

22 You promised me your heart, she reminds him . .

My glass shall not persuade me I am old
So long as youth and thou are of one date;
But when in thee Time's furrows I behold,
Then look I death my days should expiate.
For all that beauty that doth cover thee
Is but the seemly rayment[279] of my heart,
Which in thy breast doth live, as thine in me;
How can I then be elder than thou art?[280]
O, therefore, love, be of thyself so wary
As I not for myself, but for thee will,[281]
Bearing thy heart, which I will keep so chary
As tender nurse her babe from faring ill.
Presume not on thy heart when mine is slain;
Thou gav'st me thine, not to give back again.

23 . . but begins do lose some of her self-confidence . .

As an unperfect actor on the stage,
Who with his fear is put besides his part,
Or some fierce thing replete with too much rage,
Whose strength's abundance weakens his own heart;
So I, for fear of trust, forget to say
The perfect ceremony of love's rite,
And in mine own love's strength seem to decay,
O'er-charged with burden of mine own love's might.
O, let my looks be then the eloquence
And dumb presagers of my speaking breast,
Who plead for love and look for recompense
More than that tongue that more hath more expressed.
O, learn to read what silent love hath writ;
To hear with eyes belongs to love's fine wit.

---

[277] William was the first born, and born on 8th April. There was a colon and the end of line-six.

[278] Not to sell himself for a large dowry.

[279] Q has rayment, achaic clothing; the word contains *Mary*.

[280] Mary is two years older.

[281] For thee, Will...., his name, but **bearing thy heart** provides the letters for **Herbert again** which could derive from **heart & breast** earlier.

24 . . living her life through him. .

Mine eye hath played the painter, and hath steeld
Thy beauty's form in table of my heart;
My body is the frame wherein 'tis held,
And perspective it is best painter's art;
For through the painter must you see his skill
To find where your true image pictured lies,
Which in my bosom's shop is hanging still,[282]
That hath his windows glazed with thine eyes.
Now see what good turns eyes for eyes have done:
Mine eyes have drawn thy shape, and thine for me
Are windows to my breast, wherethrough the sun
Delights to peep, to gaze therein on thee.
Yet eyes this cunning want to grace their art:
They draw but what they see, know not the heart.[283]

25 . . although life is ethereal.

Let those who are in favour with their stars
Of public honour and proud titles boast,
Whilst I, whom fortune of such triumph bars,[284]
Unlooked for joy in that I honour most.
Great princes' favourites their fair leaves spread
But as the marigold at the sun's eye,
And in themselves their pride lies buried,
For at a frown they in their glory die.
The painful warrior famoused for might,
After a thousand victories once foiled,
Is from the book of honour razed quite,
And all the rest forgot for which he toiled.
Then happy I that love and am beloved
Where I may not remove nor be removed.[285]

26 Mary sends a last message before she leaves London for Cheshire.

Lord of my love, to whom in vassalage
Thy merit hath my duty strongly knit,
To thee I send this written embassage,
To witness duty, not to show my wit;
Duty so great, which wit so poor as mine
May make seem bare in wanting words to show it,

---

[282] Shop = store. The sonnet has both bosom and breast and his picture hangs there.

[283] These two lines are full of sexual puns if one reads them that way.

[284] Mary would like to have the reflected glory of Pembroke's public honour and title but she is barred.

[285] Mary feels she is still loved by William. The last line indicates she was still under house arrest at Margaret Hawkins'. Her father obtained her release in May 1601.

But that I hope some good conceit of thine
In thy soul's thought, all naked, will bestow it;
Till whatsoever star that guides my moving[286]
Points on me graciously with fair aspect,
And puts apparel on my tattered loving
To show me worthy of thy sweet respect.
Then may I dare to boast how I do love thee;
Till then, not show my head where thou mayst prove me.

*About the middle of May 1601, Sir Edward Fitton obtained the release of
Mary and took his daughter back to his home at Gawsworth in Cheshire,*
[chapter 5.25]. The next five sonnets express her being alone, her emotional
and physical tiredness, restlessness and anxiety.

27 Mary writes during a long journey.

Weary with toil I haste me to my bed,
The dear repose for limbs with travel tired;
But then begins a journey in my head
To work my mind when body's work's expired;
For then my thoughts, from far where I abide,
Intend a zealous pilgrimage[287] to thee,
And keep my drooping eyelids open wide,
Looking on darkness which the blind do see;
Save that my soul's imaginary sight
Presents thy shadow to my sightless view,
Which like a jewel hung in ghastly night
Makes black night beauteous and her old face new.
Lo, thus by day my limbs, by night my mind,
For thee and for myself no quiet find.

28 – 33 Now she grieves for William

How can I then return in happy plight
That am debarred the benefit of rest,
When day's oppression is not eased by night,
But day by night and night by day oppressed,
And each (though enemies to either's reign)
Do in consent shake hands to torture me,
The one by toil, the other to complain
How far I toil, still farther off from thee?
I tell the day to please him thou art bright,
And dost him grace when clouds do blot the heaven;
So flatter I the swart-complexioned night,
When sparkling stars twire not, thou gild'st the even.
But day doth daily draw my sorrows longer,
And night doth nightly make grief's length seem stronger.

---

[286] She appears about to leave London after five years.
[287] A play on *Passionate Pilgrim*?

29 She arrives at her destination, desolate, disgraced and tearful.

When in disgrace with Fortune and men's eyes
I all alone beweep my outcast state,
And trouble deaf heaven with my bootless cries,
And look upon myself and curse my fate,
Wishing me like to one more rich in hope,
Featured like him, like him with friends possessed,
Desiring this man's art, and that man's scope,
With what I most enjoy contented least;
Yet in these thoughts myself almost despising,
Haply I think on thee, and then my state,
Like to the lark at break of day arising[288]
From sullen earth, sings hymns at heaven's gate;
For thy sweet love remembered such wealth brings
That then I scorn to change my state with kings'.[289]

30 She grieves for him and friends that are now dead to her.

When to the sessions of sweet silent thought
I summon up remembrance of things past,
I sigh the lack of many a thing I sought,
And with old woes new wail my dear time's waste;
Then can I drown an eye, unused to flow,
For precious friends hid in death's dateless night,
And weep afresh love's long since cancelled woe,
And moan th'expense of many a vanished sight;
Then can I grieve at grievances foregone,
And heavily from woe to woe tell o'er
The sad account of fore-bemoaned moan,
Which I new pay as if not paid before.
But if the while I think on thee, dear friend,
All losses are restored, and sorrows end.

31 All Mary's loving memories are vested in him.

Thy bosom is endeared with all hearts
Which I by lacking have supposed dead;
And there reigns love and all love's loving parts,
And all those friends which I thought buried.
How many a holy and obsequious tear
Hath dear religious love stol'n from mine eye,
As interest of the dead, which now appear
But things removed that hidden in thee lie!
Thou art the grave where buried love doth live,
Hung with the trophies of my lovers gone,

---

[288] Lark arising; cf. Lark mounting, T.T.'s commendation to Barnfield's Cynthia. Chapter 4.
[289] L13-14 The memory of Williams's love makes her happy; she hated being at Court.

Who all their parts of me to thee did give:
That due of many now is thine alone.
Their images I loved I view in thee,
And thou, all they, hast all the all of me.

32 Mary's mode changes from depressive to objective as she tells him her words will be an eternal testament of her love.

If thou survive my well-contented day
When that churl Death my bones with dust shall cover,
And shalt by fortune once more resurvey
These poor rude lines of thy deceased lover,
Compare them with the bett'ring of the time
And though they be outstripped by every pen,
Reserve them for my love, not for their rhyme,
Exceeded by the height of happier men.
O then vouchsafe me but this loving thought:
'Had my friend's Muse grown with his growing age,
A dearer birth than this his love had brought
To march in ranks of better equipage;
But since he died, and poets better prove,
Theirs for their style I'll read, his for his love.'

33 She has spent an hour with him . .

Full many a glorious morning have I seen
Flatter the mountain tops[290] with sovereign eye,
Kissing with golden face the meadows green,
Gilding pale streams with heavenly alchemy,
Anon permit the basest clouds to ride
With ugly rack on his celestial face,
And from the forlorn world his visage hide,
Stealing unseen to west with this disgrace.
Even so my sun one early morn did shine
With all triumphant splendour on my brow;
But out, alack! he was but one hour mine:[291]
The region cloud hath masked him from me now.
Yet him for this my love so whit disdaineth;
Suns of the world may stain when heaven's sun staineth.

34 . . when they get caught in rain.

Why didst thou promise such a beauteous day
And make me travel forth without my cloak,
To let base clouds o'ertake me in my way,
Hiding thy brav'ry in their rotten smoke?

---

[290] Was she in Wales?

[291] This and the next sonnet suggest that Mary and William arranged to meet, Mary got caught in the rain and they only had an hour to themselves.

'Tis not enough that through the cloud thou break
To dry the rain on my storm-beaten face,
For no man well of such a salve can speak
That heals the wound and cures not the disgrace.[292]
Nor can thy shame give physic to my grief;
Though thou repent, yet I have still the loss;
Th' offender's sorrow lends but weak relief
To him that bears the strong offence's cross.
Ah, but those tears are pearl which thy love sheeds,[293]
And they are rich, and ransom all ill deeds.

35 She forgives him for what he has done to her but admits she must take some of the blame.

No more be grieved at that which thou hast done:
Roses have thorns, and silver fountains mud;
Clouds and eclipses[294] stain both moon and sun,
And loathsome canker lives in sweetest bud.
All men make faults, and even I in this,
Authorising thy trespass with compare,
Myself corrupting, salving thy amiss,
Excusing thy sins more than thy sins are;
For to thy sensual fault I bring in sense,
Thy adverse party is thy advocate,
And 'gainst myself a lawful plea commence;
Such civil war is in my love and hate
That I an accessory needs must be
To that sweet thief which sourly robs from me.

36 An acceptance that they, despite loving each other, must be apart and ignore each other if they meet in public.

Let me confess that we two must be twain,
Although our undivided loves are one;
So shall those blots that do with me remain,
Without thy help, by me be borne alone.
In our two loves there is but one respect,
Though in our lives a separable spite,
Which, though it alter not love's sole effect,
Yet doth it steal sweet hours from love's delight.
I may not evermore acknowledge thee,
Lest my bewailed guilt should do thee shame;

---

[292] Their lost child and the disgrace at Court.

[293] Sheds; previously in the line, a tear in a piece of wood is called a shake, i.e. shakes and pearl without l is pear.

[294] There were two solar eclipses in 1603 and two eclipses of the moon in 1605; on 3rd April and 27th September; there may, however, be no chronological connection. Line two can be read as relating to the vulva.

Nor thou with public kindness honour me,
Unless thou take that honour from thy name.
But do not so; I love thee in such sort
As, thou being mine, mine is thy good report.

37 She will live her life vicariously through him.

As a decrepit father takes delight
To see his active child do deeds of youth,
So I, made lame[295] by Fortune's dearest spite,
Take all my comfort of thy worth[296] and truth.
For whether beauty, birth, or wealth, or wit,
Or any of these all, or all, or more,
Entitled in thy parts do crowned sit,
I make my love engrafted to this store.
So then I am not lame, poor, nor despised,
Whilst that this shadow doth such substance give
That I in thy abundance am sufficed,
And by a part of all thy glory live.
Look what is best, that best I wish in thee;
This wish I have, then ten times happy me.

38 She tells him that he inspires her.

How can my Muse want subject to invent
While thou dost breathe, that pour'st into my verse[297]
Thine own sweet argument, too excellent
For every vulgar paper to rehearse?
O, give thyself the thanks if aught in me
Worthy perusal stand against thy sight;
For who's so dumb that cannot write to thee,
When thou thyself dost give invention light?
Be thou the tenth Muse[298], ten times more in worth
Than those old nine which rhymers invocate;
And he that calls on thee, let him bring forth

---

[295] I don't think she is physically lame although Sonnet 89 also implies lameness.

[296] I sense Mary plays on *worth* and *Wroth*. In the first 36 sonnets *worth* appears on a frequency one in 12. After Sonnet 36 the frequency is one in seven. Mary Wroth calls Mary Fitton *Antissia* meaning *opponent*. Was the feeling was mutual? Mary Fitton had cause to be jealous - William Herbert loaned part of the money for his cousin's dowry to marry Robert Wroth. Mary and Robert Wroth were very soon estranged after their wedding on 24th September 1604. Mary Wroth's father, Robert Sidney, bumped into Robert, his son-in-law, on 10th October in London and wrote to Lady Sidney, " I find by him somewhat that does discontent him; but the particulars I could not get out from him: only that he protests that he cannot take any exceptions to his wife, nor her carriage towards him. It were very soon for any unkindness to begin..." In Sonnet 83 *worth* appears three times. Ben Jonson, a friend of Mary Wroth's, also parodied Sir Robert Wroth's name by frequently using the word *worth*.

[297] They seem to collaborate on their work.

[298] In Greek mythology there were nine muses, the daughters of Zeus.

Eternal numbers[299] to outlive long date.
If my slight Muse do please these curious days,
The pain be mine, but thine shall be the praise.

39 Though they are apart, he has set her mind at rest.

O, how thy worth with manners may I sing,
When thou art all the better part of me?
What can mine own praise to mine own self bring,
And what is't but mine own when I praise thee?
Even for this let us divided live,
And our dear love lose name of single one,
That by this separation I may give
That due to thee which thou deserv'st alone.
O absence, what a torment wouldst thou prove
Were it not thy sour leisure gave sweet leave
To entertain the time with thoughts of love,
Which time and thoughts so sweetly doth deceive[300]
And that thou teachest how to make one twain,
By praising him here who doth hence remain[301].

40 Jealous, she is desperately in love with him.

Take all my loves, my love, yea, take them all;
What hast thou then more than thou hadst before?
No love, my love, that thou mayst true love call;
All mine was thine before thou hadst this more.
Then if for my love thou my love receivest,
I cannot blame thee, for my love thou usest;
But yet be blamed, if thou thyself deceivest
By wilful taste of what thyself refusest.
I do forgive thy robb'ry gentle thief,
Although thou steal thee all my poverty;
And yet love knows it is a greater grief
To bear love's wrong than hate's known injury.
Lascivious grace[302], in whom all ill well shows,
Kill me with spites, yet we must not be foes.

---

[299] a verse or poem. They did, indeed, become eternal!
[300] Although they are apart their collaboration on their work allows them to come together, and to communicate with each other. If they were sending scripts to each other, then it would be easy to slip in a love letter in iambic pentameter without being discovered.
[301] Praise for Richard Leveson who was away at sea?
[302] Lascivious nobleman; he seems to be having a series of small flings.

41 She comments on his infidelities and on a woman's power to seduce a man.[303]

Those pretty wrongs that liberty commits
When I am sometime absent from thy heart,
Thy beauty and thy years full well befits,
For still temptation follows where thou art.
Gentle thou art, and therefore to be won;
Beauteous thou art, therefore to be assailed.
And when a woman woos, what woman's son
Will sourly leave her till he have prevailed?
Ay me, but yet thou mightst my seat forbear,
And chide thy beauty and thy straying youth,
Who lead thee in their riot even there
Where thou art forced to break a twofold truth:
Hers, by thy beauty tempting her to thee,
Thine, by thy beauty being false to me.

42 Mary reconciles that William is now coupled with her closest friend.[304]

That thou hast her it is not all my grief,
And yet it may be said I loved her dearly;
That she hath thee is of my wailing chief,
A loss in love that touches me more nearly.
Loving offenders, thus I will excuse ye:
Thou dost love her because thou know'st I love her,
And for my sake even so doth she abuse me,
Suff'ring my friend for my sake to approve her.
If I lose thee, my loss is my love's gain,
And, losing her, my friend hath found that loss;
Both find each other, and I lose both twain,
And both for my sake lay on me this cross.
But here's the joy: my friend and I are one;
Sweet flattery, then she loves but me alone.

43 Nights become days when she sees him in her dreams.[305]

When most I wink, then do mine eyes best see,
For all the day they view things unrespected;
But when I sleep, in dreams they look on thee,
And, darkly bright, are bright in dark directed.

---

[303] Later she apologies for her own infidelities.

[304] It would be interesting to know the name of the friend of Mary's that Pembroke was involved with. Another Maid of Honour was unlikely before the death of Queen Elizabeth. His cousin Mary Sidney is a strong possibility but *Lay on me this cross* looks like a cryptic clue for E-M-LYA. It would be interesting to know how Mary kept up with Court gossip.

[305] These three sonnets run together.

Then thou, whose shadow shadows doth make bright,
How would thy shadow's form form happy show
To the clear day with thy much clearer light,
When to unseeing eyes thy shade shines so!
How would, I say, mine eyes be blessed made
By looking on thee in the living day,
When in dead night thy fair imperfect shade
Through heavy sleep on sightless eyes doth stay!
All days are nights to see till I see thee,
And nights bright days when dreams do show thee

44 Mary philosophises about the distance between them.

If the dull substance of my flesh were thought,
Injurious distance should not stop my way;
For then, despite of space, I would be brought,
From limits far remote, where thou dost stay.
No matter then although my foot did stand
Upon the farthest earth removed from thee,
For nimble thought can jump both sea and land
As soon as think the place where he would be.
But ah, thought kills me that I am not thought,
To leap large lengths of miles when thou art gone,
But that, so much of earth and water wrought,
I must attend time's leisure with my moan,
Receiving nought by elements so slow
But heavy tears, badges of either's woe.

45 Messages between them are terse and brief.

The other two, slight air and purging fire,
Are both with thee wherever I abide;
The first my thought, the other my desire,
These present-absent with swift motion slide;
For when these quicker elements are gone
In tender embassy of love to thee,
My life, being made of four, with two alone
Sinks down to death, oppressed with melancholy;
Until life's composition be recured
By those swift messengers[306] returned from thee,
Who even but now come back again assured
Of thy fair health, recounting it to me.
This told, I joy; but then, no longer glad,
I send them back again, and straight grow sad.

---

[306] They are still in contact. A messenger brings news from William and she quickly turns the messenger round and sends him back. It seems William has been ill.

46 – 47 A conflict between her emotions and what she knows to be reality.

Mine eye and heart are at a mortal war
How to divide the conquest of thy sight:
Mine eye my heart thy picture's sight would bar,
My heart mine eye the freedom of that right.
My heart doth plead that thou in him dost lie,
(A closet never pierced with crystal eyes)
But the defendant doth that plea deny,
And says in him thy fair appearance lies.
To side this title is impanelled
A quest of thoughts, all tenants to the heart;
And by their verdict is determined
The clear eyes moiety and the dear hearts part.
As thus: mine eye's due is thy outward part,
And my heart's right thy inward love of heart.

47 She treasures a portrait of him . .

Betwixt mine eye and heart a league is took.
And each doth good turns now unto the other:
When that mine eye is famished for a look,
Or heart, in love, with sighs himself doth smother,
With my love's picture then my eye doth feast,
And to the painted banquet bids my heart.
Another time mine eye is my heart's guest,
And in his thoughts of love doth share a part.
So, either by thy picture or my love,
Thyself, away, are present still with me;
For thou not farther than my thoughts canst move,
And I am still with them, and they with thee;
Or if they sleep, thy picture in my sight
Awakes my heart, to heart's and eye's delight.

48 – 49 . . but feels he has locked her in a closet while he remains free.

How careful was I when I took my way
Each trifle under truest bars to thrust,
That to my use it might unused stay [307]
From hands of falsehood, in sure wards of trust.
But thou, to whom my jewels trifles are,
Most worthy comfort, now my greatest grief,
Thou, best of dearest and mine only care,
Art left the prey of every vulgar thief.
Thee have I not locked up in any chest,
Save where thou art not, though I feel thou art,

---

[307] She has tried to hide all evidence (verses / letters) of what was passing between them.

Within the gentle closure of my breast,
From whence at pleasure thou mayst come and part;
And even thence thou wilt be stol'n I fear,
For truth proves thievish for a prize so dear.

49 She prepares for the day she will lose him.

Against that time (if ever that time come)
When I shall see thee frown on my defects,
Whenas thy love hath cast his utmost sum,
Called to that audit by advised respects;
Against that time when thou shalt strangely pass,
And scarcely greet me with that sun thine eye,
When love converted from the thing it was
Shall reasons find of settled gravity;
Against that time do I ensconce me here
Within the knowledge of mine own desert,
And this my hand against myself uprear,
To guard the lawful reasons on thy part.
To leave poor me thou hast the strength of laws,
Since why to love I can allege no cause.

50 She makes another long journey. .[308]

How heavy[309] do I journey on the way,
When what I seek (my weary travel's end)
Doth teach that ease and that repose to say
'Thus far the miles are measured from thy friend'
The beast that bears me, tired with my woe,
Plods duly on, to bear that weight in me,
As if by some instinct the wretch did know
His rider loved not speed being made from thee.

---

[308] In Mary's will she leaves to her daughter, Elizabeth Lougher, the leases on her property in Pinkeston or Kinteston at Kilgelly in Pembrokeshire. Note that this was *her* gift, not that of her late husband's. Were these properties on either the Pembroke or the Talbot family estates? Digging deeper I discovered in Pembrokeshire two places, Kilgetty 3.5 miles north of Tenby and Rinaston near Ambleston, eight miles N.N.E. of Haverfordwest. Kilgetty is on the coast. Mary's brother Edward's wife, was Anne c1571-1644, daughter and co-heiress of James Barrett of Tenby co. Pembroke. James Barrett's brother's wife was Anne, daughter of a Thomas Lougher. Knowing these facts one senses that Mary was near Tenby so it was a delightful surprise subsequently to read the introduction of maritime:
59.6 Let this sad int'rim like the ocean be, which parts the shore where two contracted-new
60.1 Like as the waves make towards the pebbled shore, so do our minutes hasten to their end.
64.5 When I have seen the hungry ocean gain advantage on the kingdom of the shore,
    In *Urania*, *Antissia* is frowned upon for having entered into a relationship with a man she met on a beach. *A Lover's Complaint* starts *"From off a hill whose concave womb re-worded"*. Concave womb looks like an anagram of Cwmafon (near Port Talbot) or Cwmavon (near Pontypool), both in South Wales.
[309] Heavy can be used to denote pregnancy.

The bloody spur cannot provoke him on
That sometimes anger thrusts into his hide,
Which heavily he answers with a groan
More sharp to me than spurring to his side;
For that same groan doth put this in my mind:
My grief lies onward, and my joy behind.
51
Thus can my love excuse the slow offence
Of my dull bearer when from thee I speed:
From where thou art why should I haste me thence?
Till I return, of posting is no need.
O what excuse will my poor beast then find,
When swift extremity can seem but slow?
Then should I spur though mounted on the wind,
In winged speed no motion shall I know.
Then can no horse with my desire keep pace;
Therefore desire, of perfect'st love being made,
Shall neigh, no dull flesh in his fiery race;
But love, for love, thus shall excuse my jade:
Since from thee going he went wilful slow,
Towards thee I'll run, and give him leave to go.

52 . . and feels suppressed in her new home.

So am I as the rich whose blessed key
Can bring him to his sweet up-locked treasure,
The which he will not ev'ry hour survey
For blunting the fine point of seldom pleasure.[310]
Therefore are feasts so solemn and so rare,
Since seldom coming in the long year set[311],
Like stones of worth they thinly placed are,
Or captain jewels in the carcanet[312].
So is the time that keeps you as my chest,
Or as the wardrobe which the robe doth hide,
To make some special instant special blest
By new unfolding his imprisoned pride.
Blessed are you whose worthiness gives scope
Being had, to triumph, being lacked, to hope.

53 She tries to imagine what he is doing.

What is your substance, whereof are you made,
That millions of strange shadows on you tend?
Since everyone hath, every one, one shade,
And you, but one, can every shadow lend.

---

[310] She knows she will rarely see him.
[311] She hardly sees him for a year - sonnet 52 (weeks in a year) - but she *does* see him.
[312] Ornamental collar.

Describe Adonis, and the counterfeit
Is poorly imitated after you;
On Helen's cheek all art of beauty set,
And you in Grecian tires are painted new.[313]
Speak of the spring and foison of the year:
The one doth shadow of your beauty show,
The other as your bounty doth appear,
And you in every blessed shape we know.
In all external grace you have some part,
But you like none, none you, for constant heart.

54 She compares him to a rose that can live on through its perfume.

O, how much more doth beauty beauteous seem
By that sweet ornament which truth doth give!
The rose looks fair, but fairer we it deem
For that sweet odour which doth in it live.
The canker blooms[314] have full as deep a dye
As the perfumed tincture of the roses,
Hang on such thorns, and play as wantonly
When summer's breath their masked buds discloses;
But, for their virtue only is their show,
They live unwooed, and unrespected fade,
Die to themselves. Sweet roses do not so;
Of their sweet deaths are sweetest odours made.
And so of you, beauteous and lovely youth,
When that shall vade, by verse distills your truth.

55 Her love, through her verses, will make William eternal.

Not marble nor the gilded monuments
Of princes shall outlive this powerful rhyme,
But you shall shine more bright in these contents
Than unswept stone, besmeared with sluttish time.
When wasteful war shall statues overturn,
And broils root out the work of masonry,
Nor Mars his sword nor war's quick fire shall burn
The living record of your memory.
'Gainst death and all-oblivious enmity
Shall you pace forth; your praise shall still find room
Even in the eyes of all posterity
That wear this world out to the ending doom.
So, till the judgment that yourself arise,
You live in this, and dwell in lovers' eyes.

---

[313] It would be nice to find a portrait of William in Grecian attire confirming that Mary was getting news of William, but early Pembroke paintings were destroyed by fires in 1647 and 1666.
[314] Katherine Duncan Jones suggests that the canker bloom is the colloquial name for the wild, red poppy.

56 She tells him to enjoy sex, and then intimates that, for the moment, she has a friend.

Sweet love, renew thy force; be it not said
Thy edge should blunter be than appetite,
Which but today by feeding is allayed,
Tomorrow sharpened in his former might.
So, love, be thou, although today thou fill
Thy hungry eyes even till they wink with fullness,
Tomorrow see again, and do not kill
The spirit of love with a perpetual dullness.
Let this sad int'rim like the ocean be
Which parts the shore where two contracted-new
Come daily to the banks, that when they see
Return of love, more blest may be the view;
Or call it winter, which, being full of care,
Makes summer's welcome thrice more wished, more rare.

57 Mary waits for him without questioning . .[315]

Being your slave, what should I do but tend
Upon the hours and times of your desire?[316]
I have no precious time at all to spend,
Nor services to do, till you require;
Nor dare I chide the world-without-end hour
Whilst I, my sovereign, watch the clock for you,
Nor think the bitterness of absence sour,
When you have bid your servant once adieu;
Nor dare I question with my jealous thought
Where you may be, or your affairs suppose,
But like a sad slave stay and think of nought
Save where you are how happy you make those.
So true a fool is love that, in your Will
(Though you do anything) he thinks no ill.

58 . . tentatively telling him that she is still his slave but he should have a life of his own . .

That God forbid, that made me first your slave,
I should in thought control your times of pleasure,
Or at your hand th'account of hours to crave,
Being your vassal bound to stay your leisure.
O let me suffer, being at your beck,
Th'imprisoned absence of your liberty,
And patience, tame to sufferance, bide each check

---

[315] It appears she was saying *that what is sauce for the goose* ....

[316] Was there an understanding between them that they would eventually be together; or was Mary simple living the role of a man's mistress waiting on his pleasure?

Without accusing you of injury.
Be where you list, your charter is so strong
That you yourself may privilege your time
To what you will; to you it doth belong
Yourself to pardon of self-doing crime.
I am to wait, though waiting so be hell,
Not blame your pleasure, be it ill or well.

59 – 60 . . and wonders whether time will have changed them.

If there be nothing new, but that which is,
Hath been before, how are our brains beguiled,
Which, labouring for invention, bear amiss
The second burthen[317] of a former child!
O that record could with a backward look,
Even of five hundred[318] courses of the sun,
Show me your image in some antique book,
Since mind at first in character was done.
That I might see what the old world could say
To this composed wonder of your frame,
Whether we are mended, or whe'er better they,
Or whether revolution be the same.
O sure I am the wits of former days,[319]
To subjects worse have given admiring praise.

60 Watching a minute hand, the hour dies and is born again.

Like as the waves make towards the pebbled[320] shore,
So do our minutes hasten to their end,
Each changing place with that which goes before,
In sequent toil all forwards do contend.
Nativity, once in the main of light,
Crawls to maturity, wherewith being crowned,
Crooked eclipses 'gainst his glory fight,
And Time that gave doth now his gift confound.
Time doth transfix the flourish set on youth,
And delves the parallels in beauty's brow,
Feeds on the rarities of nature's truth,
And nothing stands but for his scythe to mow.
And yet to times in hope my verse shall stand,
Praising thy worth despite his cruel hand.

---

[317] burden

[318] Difficult to work out any chronology; Sixteen months; if they started their romance in May 1600 this would be November 1601; or if they parted early in May 1601 it would now be the Autumn of 1602, which I favour. The 500 could be purely figurative.

[319] *In former times I helped you with my ideas, and worse ideas have been greatly praised.* Could William and Mary have been involved in writing Shakespeare's As You Like It?

[320] This is quite specific, pebbles - not sandy or rocky - she seems to be by the sea.

Sonnets From Afar, 18 – 126

61 Mary is watchful of him, but she feels he is jealous.

Is it thy will thy image should keep open
My heavy eyelids to the weary night?
Dost thou desire my slumbers should be broken,
While shadows like to thee do mock my sight?
Is it thy spirit that thou send'st from thee
So far from home into my deeds[321] to pry,
To find out shames and idle hours in me,
The scope and tenure of thy jealousy?
O no; thy love, though much, is not so great;
It is my love that keeps mine eye awake,
Mine own true love that doth my rest defeat,
To play the watchman ever for thy sake.
For thee watch I, whilst thou dost wake elsewhere,
From me far off, with others all too near.

62 She likes herself but her face is weather-beaten . .

Sin of self-love possesseth all mine eye,
And all my soul, and all my every part;
And for this sin there is no remedy,
It is so grounded inward in my heart.
Methinks no face so gracious is as mine,
No shape so true, no truth of such account,
And for myself mine own worth do define,
As I all other in all worths surmount.
But when my glass shows me myself indeed,
Beated and chopt with tanned antiquity,[322]
Mine own self-love quite contrary I read;
Self so self-loving were iniquity.
'Tis thee (my self) that for myself I praise,
Painting my age with beauty of thy days.

63 . . and reminds herself that he too is growing older.

Against my love shall be as I am now,
With time's injurious hand crushed and o'erworn
When hours have drained his blood and filled his brow
With lines and wrinkles; when his youthful morn
Hath travailed on to age's steepy[323] night,
And all those beauties whereof now he's king
Are vanishing or vanished out of sight,
Stealing away the treasure of his Spring.
For such a time do I now fortify

---

[321] *Deeds* followed by *tenure* two lines later. Was William jealous and spying on her?
[322] Reads as if she has a good old fashioned seaside holiday tan!
[323] Steep

Against confounding age's cruel knife,
That he shall never cut from memory
My sweet love's beauty, though my lover's life.
His beauty shall in these black lines be seen,
And they shall live, and he in them still green.

64 – 65 She fears losing him . .[324]

When I have seen by time's fell hand defaced
The rich proud cost of outworn buried age;
When sometime lofty towers[325] I see down-razed,
And brass eternal slave to mortal rage;
When I have seen the hungry ocean gain
Advantage on the kingdom of the shore,
And the firm soil win of the watry main,
Increasing store with loss, and loss with store;
When I have seen such interchange of state,
Or state it self confounded to decay,
Ruin hath taught me thus to ruminate:
That Time will come and take my love away.
This thought is as a death, which cannot choose
But weep to have, that which it fears to lose.

65 . . to the inevitability of Time.

Since brass, nor stone, nor earth, nor boundless sea,
But sad mortality o'ersways their power,
How with this rage shall beauty hold a plea,
Whose action is no stronger than a flower?
O how shall summer's honey breath hold out
Against the wrackful[326] siege of batt'ring days,
When rocks impregnable are not so stout,
Nor gates of steel so strong, but time decays?
O fearful meditation, where, alack,
Shall time's best jewel from Time' chest lie hid?
Or what strong hand can hold his swift foot back,
Or who his spoil of beauty can forbid?
O, none, unless this miracle have might,
That in black ink my love may still shine bright.

---

[324] Cavanagh p72: In *Urania, Antissia* (Fitton) hears a rumour of *Amphilanthus* (Pembroke) having died.
[325] A ruined castle or abbey nearby?
[326] wrack = wreck

66 Mary feels suicidal . .[327]

Tired with all these, for restful death I cry:
As to behold desert a beggar born,
And needy nothing trimmed in jollity,
And purest faith unhappily forsworn,
And gilded honour shamefully misplaced,
And maiden virtue rudely strumpeted,
And right perfection wrongfully disgraced,
And strength by limping sway disabled,
And art made tongue-tied by authority,[328]
And folly, doctor-like, controlling skill,
And simple truth miscalled simplicity,
And captive-good attending Captain ill. [329]
Tired with all these, from these would I be gone,
Save that to die I leave my love alone.

67 . . and starts to describe a man's ageing, (William Polewhele or Richard Leveson?) and complains of her dependency on what he has gained.[330]

Ah! wherefore with infection should he live
And with his presence grace impiety,
That sin by him advantage should achieve,
And lace itself with his society?
Why should false painting imitate his cheek,
And steal dead seeing of his living hue?
Why should poor beauty indirectly seek
Roses of shadow, since his rose is true?
Why should he live, now Nature bankrupt is,
Beggared of blood to blush through lively veins?
For she hath no exchequer now but his,
And proud of many[331], lives upon his gains.
O, him she stores, to show what wealth she had
In days long since, before these last so bad.

---

[327] The content of this sonnet is reminiscent of the content of Hamlet's *To be or not to be...*
[328] Was she not allowed to write?
[329] Who was Captain ill? Mary's husband, William Polewhele, was captain of The Lyon's Whelp, that sailed under her cousin Sir Richard Leveson; the date here being about 1606.
[330] See her mother's letter of 1607. She marries Polewhele before February 1607. She could be describing Leveson but at first sight this does not seem to fit with Leveson's portrait at Arbury Hall.
[331] Envied by many?

68 She continues her description of him bemoaning the use of aids such as wigs to try to recover former glory.[332]

Thus is his cheek the map of days outworn,
When beauty lived and died as flowers do now,
Before these bastard signs of fair were borne,
Or durst inhabit on a living brow;
Before the golden tresses of the dead,
The right of sepulchres, were shorn away
To live a second life on second head,
Ere beauty's dead fleece made another gay.
In him those holy antique hours are seen
Without all ornament, itself and true,
Making no summer of another's green,
Robbing no old to dress his beauty new;
And him as for a map doth Nature store,
To show false Art what beauty was of yore.

69 – 70 She writes to Pembroke about a slander [333]

Those parts of thee that the world's eye doth view
Want nothing that the thought of hearts can mend;
All tongues (the voice of souls) give thee that due
Utt'ring bare truth even so as foes commend.
Thy outward thus with outward praise is crowned,
But those same tongues that give thee so thine own
In other accents do this praise confound[334]
By seeing farther than the eye hath shown.
They look into the beauty of thy mind,
And that in guess they measure by thy deeds;
Then, churls, their thoughts, although their eyes were kind
To thy fair flower add the rank smell of weeds.
But why thy odour matcheth not thy show,
The soil is this: that thou dost common grow.[335]

70

That thou art blamed[336] shall not be thy defect,
For slander's mark was ever yet the fair;
The ornament of beauty is suspect,
A crow that flies in heaven's sweetest air.
So thou be good, slander doth but approve
Thy worth the greater, being wooed of time;

---

[332] She describes her husband as having a worn face flattered by cosmetics and his being bald, he wears a wig.

[333] An accusation that she is pregnant by Pembroke?

[334] Mary tells William that the people who praise him are two-faced.

[335] She is saying that he was becoming common knowledge. Soyle (Solye) could mean shit.

[336] For what? If Mary was pregnant and gossip made him into the putative father then there must be some knowledge that William Herbert and Mary Fitton still have sight of each other.

For canker-vice the sweetest buds doth love,
And thou present'st a pure unstained prime.
Thou hast passed by the ambush of young days,
Either not assailed, or victor being charged,
Yet this thy praise cannot be so thy praise,
To tie up envy, evermore enlarged,
If some suspect of ill masked not thy show,
Then thou alone kingdoms of hearts shouldst owe.

71 – 76 Mary (pregnant?) accepts she might die . .[337]

No longer mourn for me when I am dead
Than you shall hear the surly sullen bell
Give warning to the world that I am fled
From this vile world with vildest [338]worms to dwell.
Nay, if you read this line remember not
The hand that writ it, for I love you so
That I in your sweet thoughts would be forgot
If thinking on me then should make you woe.
O, if, I say, you look upon this verse
When I perhaps compounded am with clay,
Do not so much as my poor name rehearse,
But let your love even with my life decay;
Lest the wise world should look into your moan,
And mock you with me after I am gone.

72 . . and no one will ever know the truth;

O, lest the world should task you to recite
What merit lived in me that you should love
After my death, dear love, forget me quite;
For you in me can nothing worthy prove,
Unless you would devise some virtuous lie
To do more for me than mine own desert,
And hang more praise upon deceased I
Than niggard truth would willingly impart.
O, lest your true love may seem false in this,
That you for love speak well of me untrue,
My name be buried where my body is,
And live no more to shame nor me nor you;
For I am shamed by that which I bring forth,[339]
And so should you, to love things nothing worth.

---

[337] This sonnet talking of a possibility of her death, perhaps by illness or, more likely, she is about to go into labour. The writer is not that ill that she cannot create a sonnet.
[338] Most reviled; vilest. See the 1607 letter from Mary's mother [5.31].
[339] pregnant?

73 – 76 She feels she is fading away.

That time of year thou mayst in me behold
When yellow leaves, or none, or few, do hang
Upon those boughs which shake against the cold, [340]
Bare ruined choirs[341] where late the sweet birds sang.
In me thou seest the twilight of such day
As after sunset fadeth in the west,
Which by and by black night doth take away,
Death's second self, that seals up all in rest.
In me thou seest the glowing of such fire
That on the ashes of his youth doth lie,
As the death-bed whereon it must expire,
Consumed with that which it was nourished by.
This thou perceiv'st which makes thy love more strong,
To love that well which thou must leave ere long.

74

But be contented when that fell arrest
Without all bail shall carry me away;
My life hath in this line some interest,
Which for memorial still with thee shall stay.
When thou reviewest this, thou dost review
The very part was consecrate to thee.
The earth can have but earth, which is his due;
My spirit is thine, the better part of me.
So then thou hast but lost the dregs of life,
The prey of worms, my body being dead,
The coward conquest of a wretch's knife,
Too base of thee to be remembered.
The worth of that is that which it contains,
And that is this, and this with thee remains.

75

So are you to my thoughts as food to life,
Or as sweet-seasoned showers are to the ground;
And for the peace of you I hold such strife
As 'twixt a miser and his wealth is found:
Now proud as an enjoyer, and anon
Doubting the filching age will steal his treasure;
Now counting best to be with you alone,
Then bettered that the world may see my pleasure;
Sometimes all full with feasting on your sight,
And by and by[342] clean starved for a look;
Possessing or pursuing no delight
Save what is had or must from you be took.

---

[340] Is this an echo of Sonnet 18, "Rough winds do shake the darling buds of May"?
[341] Both Wilton House and Arbury Hall are on the sites of former monasteries.
[342] *By and by* appears in Pecunia.

Sonnets From Afar, 18 – 126

Thus do I pine and surfeit day by day,
Or gluttoning on all, or all away.
76
Why is my verse so barren of new pride,
So far from variation or quick change?
Why with the time do I not glance aside
To new-found methods and to compounds strange?
Why write I still all one, ever the same,
And keep invention in a noted weed,[343]
That every word[344] doth almost tell my name,
Showing their birth and where they did proceed?
O know, sweet love, I always write of you,
And you and love are still my argument;
So all my best is dressing old words new,
Spending again what is already spent;
For as the sun is daily new and old,
So is my love, still telling what is told.

77 Her writing will remind him how things once were.

Thy glass will show thee how thy beauties wear,
Thy dial how thy precious minutes waste;
The vacant leaves[345] thy mind's imprint will bear,
And of this book[346] this learning mayst thou taste:
The wrinkles which thy glass will truly show
Of mouthed graves will give thee memory;
Thou by thy dial's shady stealth mayst know
Time's thievish progress to eternity;
Look what thy memory cannot contain
Commit to these waste blanks, and thou shalt find
Those children nursed, delivered from thy brain,[347]
To take a new acquaintance of thy mind.
These offices, so oft as thou wilt look,
Shall profit thee, and much inrich thy book.

---

[343] Literary style
[344] This line shows the wish to retain anonymity but occasionally Mary could not resist slipping cryptic clues into her sonnets are that give names; but this is not one. Writing with a quill pen Mary must have noticed that her *every* looks like *mary* . [PLATE 6, bottom, is an electronic composite of her *ever* (from never) and her *y*]. Every researcher or investigator reading this line, just as I did, immediately starts to look for an anagram but the reality was that Mary was sitting at a writing table, without her computer, simply looking at the words she had just written.
[345] There are empty pages left in the book....
[346] ... and she appears to be writing into a copy book and not on to loose leaves.
[347] Verse or plays

78 Mary tells him he is her inspiration.

So oft I invoked thee for my Muse,
And found such fair assistance in my verse
As every alien pen hath got my use,
And under thee their poesy disperse.
Thine eyes, that taught the dumb on high to sing,
And heavy ignorance aloft to fly,
Have added feathers to the learned's wing,
And given grace a double majesty.
Yet be most proud of that which I compile,
Whose influence is thine, and born of thee;
In others' works thou dost but mend the style,[348]
And arts with thy sweet graces graced be;
But thou art all my art, and dost advance
As high as learning my rude ignorance.

79 She gives a warning about the vanity of patronage when Pembroke patronises another poet.

Whilst I alone did call upon thy aid,
My verse alone had all thy gentle grace;
But now my gracious numbers are decayed,
And my sick Muse doth give an other place.[349]
I grant, sweet love, thy lovely argument
Deserves the travail of a worthier pen,
Yet what of thee thy poet doth invent [350]
He robs thee of, and pays it thee again.
He lends thee virtue, and he stole that word
From thy behaviour; beauty doth he give,
And found it in thy cheek; he can afford
No praise to thee but what in thee doth live.
Then thank him not for that which he doth say,
Since what he owes thee thou thyself dost pay.

80 The baby is born. Is it Pembroke's?[351]

O, how I faint when I of you do write,
Knowing a better spirit[352] doth use your name[353],

---

[348] He clearly puts the finishing touches to other writers' works.

[349] Mary could be collaborating with another poet (Barnfield?) Or, more likely, was she pregnant with his child; line-seven could be a taunt.

[350] Asking how does this poet flatter him?

[351] The maritime phrases appear to make fun of her husband, a ship's captain.

[352] A better spirit than me...

[353] The baby was baptised William, the same name as both her husband and Pembroke. Mary's sister, Anne, records in her household accounts for 1607 the costs of being at Perton, Mary's home, including two shillings for, *"my sister's nurse."* Mary's children by Leveson are called

And in the praise thereof spends all his might
To make me tongue-tied, speaking of your fame.
But since your worth, wide as the ocean is,
The humble as the proudest sail doth bear,
My saucy bark, inferior far to his,
On your broad main[354] doth wilfully appear.
Your shallowest help will hold me up afloat,
Whilst he upon your soundless deep doth ride;
Or, being wrecked, I am a worthless boat,
He of tall building[355] and of goodly pride.
Then if he thrive and I be cast away,
The worst was this: my love was my decay.[356]

81 Mary begins to feel better.

Or I shall live your epitaph to make,
Or you survive when I in earth am rotten;
From hence your memory death cannot take,
Although in me each part will be forgotten.
Your name from hence immortal life shall have,
Though I, once gone, to all the world must die;
The earth can yield me but a common grave,
When you entombed in men's eye shall lie.
Your monument shall be my gentle verse,
Which eyes not yet created shall o'er-read
And tongues to be your being shall rehearse
When all the breathers of this world are dead.
You still shall live (such virtue hath my pen)
Where breath most breathes, even in the mouths of men.

82 Her attitude towards William Herbert cools a little. She alone will tell him the truth.

I grant thou wert not married to my Muse[357],
And therefore mayst without attaint o'erlook
The dedicated words which writers use
Of their fair subject, blessing every book.
Thou art as fair in knowledge as in hue,
Finding thy worth a limit past my praise, [358]
And therefore art enforced to seek anew

William and Anne but he died in 1605.

[354] I think meaning *he looks mostly like you.*

[355] He is tall and strong.

[356] Cf. Sonnet 73.14 *Consumed with that which it was nourished by.* If she died would she have lost her life because of her love for William Herbert, suggesting, perhaps, that was he the father?

[357] A heterosexual statement.

[358] If Mary Wroth was on the scene than I think Mary Fitton was saying that Pembroke was going too far.

Some fresher stamp of the time-bettering days.
And do so love, yet when they have devised
What strained touches rhetoric can lend,
Thou, truly fair, wert truly sympathised
In true plain words by thy true-telling friend.
And their gross painting might be better used
Where cheeks need blood, in thee it is abused.

83 She has news from him (by a short letter) and responds.

I never saw that you did painting[359] need,
And therefore to your fair no painting set;
I found (or thought I found) you did exceed
The barren tender of a poet's debt;
And therefore have I slept in your report,
That you yourself being extant well might show
How far a modern quill doth come too short,
Speaking of worth,[360] what worth in you doth grow.
This silence for my sin you did impute,
Which shall be most my glory, being dumb;
For I impair not beauty, being mute[361],
When others would give life, and bring a tomb.
There lives more life in one of your fair eyes
Than both your poets[362] can in praise devise.

**84 A touch of jealousy of the man Pembroke
patronises and accuses him of being vain.**

Who is it that says most, which can say more
Than this rich praise, that you alone are you,
In whose confine immured is the store
Which should example where your equal grew?
Lean penury within that pen doth dwell
That to his subject lends not some small glory;
But he that writes of you, if he can tell
That you are you, so dignifies his story.
Let him but copy what in you is writ,
Not making worse what nature made so clear,
And such a counterpart shall fame his wit,
Making his style admired everywhere.
You to your beauteous blessings add a curse,
Being fond on praise, which makes your praises worse.

---

[359] *I never once thought that you needed to use cosmetics.*
[360] A pun on Wroth?
[361] A swan is mute.
[362] Mary Fitton and the other poet he patronised. Mary Sidney Wroth also wrote sonnets.

85 She points out this sycophancy,

My tongue-tied Muse in manners holds her still,
While comments of your praise, richly compiled,
Reserve their character with golden quill
And precious phrase by all the Muses filed.
I think good thoughts whilst other write good words,
And, like unlettered clerk, still cry 'amen'
To every hymn that able spirit affords
In polished form of well-refined pen.
Hearing you praised, I say *'tis so, 'tis true'*
And to the most of praise add something more;
But that is in my thought, whose love to you
(Though words come hindmost) holds his rank before.
Then others for the breath of words respect,
Me for my dumb thoughts, speaking in effect.

86 She feels rejected, and that she has been wasting her time.

Was it the proud full sail of his great verse,
Bound for the prize of all-too-precious you,[363]
That did my ripe thoughts in my brain inhearse,
Making their tomb the womb wherein they grew?
Was it his spirit, by spirits taught to write
Above a mortal pitch, that struck me dead?
No, neither he nor his compeers[364] by night
Giving him aid my verse astonished.[365]
He nor that affable familiar ghost[366]
Which nightly gulls him with intelligence,
As victors, of my silence cannot boast;
I was not sick of any fear from thence.
But when your countenance filled up his line,
Then lacked I matter, that enfeebled mine.

87 They now fall out with each other.
Everything appears as if it has been but a dream.

Farewell, thou art too dear for my possessing,
And like enough thou know'st thy estimate.
The charter of thy worth gives thee releasing;
My bonds in thee are all determinate.[367]

---

[363] Nautical terms and analogy. Hunting prizes was what Richard Leveson did.
[364] Colleagues
[365] I sense William has been passing off her work as his, as if she does not exist or showing them to his colleagues without acknowledging the author.
[366] Hamlet's father?
[367] Terminated or written in legal documents.

For how do I hold thee but by thy granting?[368]
And for that riches where is my deserving?
The cause of this fair gift in me is wanting,
And so my patent back again is swerving.
Thyself thou gav'st thy own worth then not knowing,
Or me, to whom thou gav'st it, else mistaking;
So thy great gift, upon misprision growing,
Comes home again, on better judgment making.
Thus have I had thee as a dream doth flatter:
In sleep a king, but waking no such matter.

88-90 Mary gives him his freedom, but loves him so much that she will absorb any of his faults to make his life easier.

When thou shalt be disposed to set me light,
And place my merit in the eye of scorn,
Upon thy side against myself I'll fight,
And prove thee virtuous, though thou art forsworn.
With mine own weakness being best acquainted,
Upon thy part I can set down a story
Of faults concealed, wherein I am attainted,
That thou in losing me shalt win much glory.
And I by this will be a gainer too,
For, bending all my loving thoughts on thee,
The injuries that to myself I do,
Doing thee vantage, double-vantage me.
Such is my love, to thee I so belong,
That for thy right myself will bear all wrong.

89 She gives him excuses to forsake her, and says she will conduct herself in his presence as if he does not exist.

Say that thou didst forsake me for some fault,
And I will comment upon that offence;
Speak of my lameness, and I straight will halt,
Against thy reasons making no defence.
Thou canst not, love, disgrace me half so ill,
To set a form upon desired change,
As I'll myself disgrace, knowing thy will.
I will acquaintance strangle, and look strange,
Be absent from thy walks, and in my tongue
Thy sweet beloved name no more shall dwell,
Lest I, too much profane, should do it wrong,
And haply of our old acquaintance tell.
For thee, against myself I'll vow debate,
For I must ne're love him whom thou dost hate.

---

[368] While the child was alive she had a physical bond with William. Now dead, the bond was only of William's granting. She cannot afford him emotionally, but if he is supporting her financially she cannot afford to be without him.

90 She asks him to leave her now; to delay would cause a problem for himself in the future.

Then hate me when thou wilt; if ever, now,
Now while the world is bent my deeds to cross,
Join with the spite of fortune, make me bow,
And do not drop in for an after-loss.
Ah, do not, when my heart hath scaped this sorrow,
Come in the rearward of a conquered woe;
Give not a windy night a rainy morrow,
To linger out a purposed overthrow.
If thou wilt leave me, do not leave me last,
When other petty griefs have done their spite,
But in the onset come; so shall I taste
At first the very worst of fortune's might;
And other strains of woe, which now seem woe,
Compared with loss of thee will not seem so.

91 His love is the greatest of assets, she fears it will be taken away.

Some glory in their birth, some in their skill,
Some in their wealth, some in their body's force,
Some in their garments though newfangled ill:
Some in their hawks and hounds, some in their horse;
And every humour hath his adjunct pleasure,
Wherein it finds a joy above the rest;
But these particulars are not my measure;
All these I better in one general best.
Thy love is better than high birth to me,
Richer than wealth, prouder than garments' cost,
Of more delight than hawks and horses be;
And having thee, of all men's pride I boast.
Wretched in this alone: that thou mayst take
All this away, and me most wretched make.

92 She would die happy knowing he still loves her,

But do thy worst to steal thyself away,
For term of life thou art assured mine;
And life no longer than thy love will stay,
For it depends upon that love of thine.
Then need I not to fear the worst of wrongs,
When in the least of them my life hath end.
I see a better state to me belongs
Than that which on thy humour doth depend.
Thou canst not vex me with inconstant mind,
Since that my life on thy revolt doth lie.

O what a happy title do I find,
Happy to have thy love, happy to die!
But what's so blessed-fair that fears no blot?
Thou mayst be false, and yet I know it not.

**93 . . and will assume that he does love her even though
she accepts he may be deceiving her.**

So shall I live, supposing thou art true,
Like a deceived husband; so love's face
May still seem love to me, though altered new:
Thy looks with me, thy heart in other place.
For there can live no hatred in thine eye,
Therefore in that I cannot know thy change.
In many's looks the false heart's history
Is writ in moods and frowns and wrinkles strange;
But heaven in thy creation did decree
That in thy face sweet love should ever dwell;
Whate'er thy thoughts or thy heart's workings be,
Thy looks should nothing thence but sweetness tell.
How like Eve's apple doth thy beauty grow,
If thy sweet virtue answer not thy show!

**94 The beauty of a flower is one thing but an
infected lily can smell worse than a weed.**

They that have power to hurt and will do none,
That do not do the thing they most do show,
Who moving others are themselves as stone,
Unmoved, cold, and to temptation slow:
They rightly do inherit heaven's graces,
And husband nature's riches from expense;
They are the lords and owners of their faces,
Others but stewards of their excellence.
The summer's flower is to the summer sweet,
Though to itself it only live and die;
But if that flower with base infection meet,
The basest weed outbraves his dignity;
For sweetest things turn sourest by their deeds:
Lilies that fester smell far worse than weeds.[369]

---

[369] This same line appears in *The reign of King Edward the Third* printed in 1596. One other occasion of direct plagiarism occurs in *As You Like It* where "Who ever loved, that loved not at first sight," derives from Christopher Marlowe. [Ardern Sonnets].

95 Her words turn bittersweet. If he continues in his lasciviousness things are likely to go wrong for him.

How sweet and lovely dost thou make the shame
Which like a canker in the fragrant rose
Doth spot the beauty of thy budding[370] name!
O, in what sweets dost thou thy sins enclose!
That tongue that tells the story of thy days,
Making lascivious comments on thy sport,
Cannot dispraise, but in a kind of praise,
Naming thy name, blesses an ill report.
O, what a mansion have those vices got
Which for their habitation chose out thee,
Where beauty's veil doth cover every blot,
And all things turns to fair that eyes can see!
Take heed, dear heart, of this large privilege;
The hardest knife ill-used doth lose his edge.

96 The loving links between them are not quite severed. She tells him he is taking advantage of his good looks and his position.

Some say thy fault is youth, some wantonness;
Some say thy grace is youth and gentle sport.
Both grace and faults are loved of more and less;
Thou mak'st faults graces that to thee resort.
As on the finger of a throned queen
The basest jewel will be well esteemed,
So are those errors that in thee are seen
To truths translated and for true things deemed.
How many lambs might the stern wolf betray,
If like a lamb he could his looks translate!
How many gazers mightst thou lead away,
If thou wouldst use the strength of all thy state!
But do not so; I love thee in such sort
As, thou being mine, mine is thy good report.

97 – 100 They start to make up and become friends. A year appears to have passed. Was she again pregnant? [371]

How like a winter hath my absence been
From thee, the pleasure of the fleeting year!
What freezings have I felt, what dark days seen!
What old December's bareness everywhere!
And yet this time removed was summer's time,
The teeming autumn, big with rich increase,

---

[370] The name William has will in it and she may be saying "chuffing".

[371] This sonnet has many allusions to birth; *big with rich increase; bearing; the wanton burden; widowed wombs; abundant issue; orphans; unfathered.* In Sonnet 98 are *heavy Saturn; proud lap pluck them where they grew; drawn after you; I with these did play.*

Bearing the wanton burden of the prime,
Like widowed wombs after their lords' decease; [372]
Yet this abundant issue seemed to me
But hope of orphans and unfathered fruit,
For summer and his pleasures wait on thee,
And, thou away, the very birds are mute;
Or if they sing, 'tis with so dull a cheer
That leaves look pale, dreading the winter's near.

98

From you have I been absent in the spring,
When proud-pied April, dressed in all his trim,
Hath put a spirit of youth in everything,
That heavy Saturn laughed and leaped with him.
Yet nor the lays of birds nor the sweet smell
Of different flowers in odour and in hue
Could make me any summer's story tell,
Or from their proud lap pluck them where they grew;
Nor did I wonder at the lily's white,
Nor praise the deep vermilion in the rose;
They were but sweet, but figures of delight,
Drawn after you, you pattern of all those.
Yet seemed it winter still, and, you away,
As with your shadow I with these did play.

99 [373]

The forward violet thus did I chide,
Sweet thief, whence didst thou steal thy sweet that smells,
If not from my love's breath, the purple pride
Which on thy soft cheek for complexion dwells?
In my love's veins thou hast too grossly dyed,
The lily I condemned for thy hand,
And buds of marjoram had stol'n thy hair;
The roses fearfully on thorns did stand,
Our blushing shame, another white despair;
A third, nor red nor white, had stol'n of both,
And to his robb'ry had annexed thy breath;
But, for his theft, in pride of all his growth
A vengeful canker eat him up to death.
More flowers I noted, yet I none could see
But sweet or colour it had stol'n from thee.

---

[372] Is she here saying that she expects her lover or husband soon to die? This could be a reference to Richard Leveson who was rumoured to have fathered two of her children. Leycester says there were two bastard daughters, but a boy, William, died in 1609. Mary could well have been pregnant when Leveson died if one reads into the unnamed bequests in Leveson's Will. She was again pregnant, this time to her husband William Polewhele, of Perton, Co. Stafford, around 1607, and pregnant again when he made his will on 19th September 1609 (proved 23rd June 1610).

[373] This sonnet contains an extra fifteenth line.

100-102 After a break she starts to compose again. The verse is neutral, non threatening.

Where art thou, Muse, that thou forget'st so long
To speak of that which gives thee all thy might?
Spend'st thou thy fury on some worthless song,
Dark'ning thy power to lend base subjects light?
Return, forgetful Muse, and straight redeem
In gentle numbers[374] time so idly spent;
Sing to the ear that doth thy lays esteem
And gives thy pen both skill and argument.
Rise, resty Muse, my love's sweet face survey
If time have any wrinkle graven there;
If any, be a *Satire* to decay
And make time's spoils despised everywhere.
Give my love fame faster than Time wastes life;
So thou prevene'st his scythe and crooked knife.

101

O truant Muse, what shall be thy amends
For thy neglect of truth in beauty dyed?
Both truth and beauty on my love depends;
So dost thou too, and therein dignified.
Make answer, Muse, wilt thou not haply say
`Truth needs no colour with his colour fixed,*
Beauty no pencil beauty's truth to lay,
But best is best, if never intermixed'
Because he needs no praise, wilt thou be dumb?
Excuse not silence so, for't lies in thee
To make him much outlive a gilded tomb
And to be praised of ages yet to be.
Then do thy office, Muse, I teach thee how,
To make him seem long hence, as he shows now.

102 She wants to reminds him of when their love was new and how she used to sing to him like a nightingale.

My love is strengthened, though more weak in seeming;
I love not less, though less the show appear;
That love is merchandised whose rich esteeming
The owner's tongue doth publish everywhere.[375]
Our love was new, and then but in the spring,
When I was wont to greet it with my lays,
As *Philomel*[376] in summer's front doth sing,

---

[374] poems

[375] Shakespeare plays before 1598 were published anonymously, those after carried the *William Shakespeare* name.

[376] Here is autobiography that she composed lays, poems designed to be sung. How delightful for a woman in love to sing to the man she loves. In 1595 Richard Barnfield published an Ode

And stops her pipe in growth of riper days.
Not that the summer is less pleasant now
Than when her mournful hymns did hush the night,
But that wild music burdens every bough,
And sweets grown common lose their dear delight.
Therefore, like her, I sometime hold my tongue,
Because I would not dull you with my song.

103 She finds it difficult to compose well.

Alack, what poverty my Muse brings forth,
That, having such a scope to show her pride,
The argument all bare is of more worth
Than when it hath my added praise beside.
Oh blame me not if I no more can write!
Look in your glass, and there appears a face
That over-goes my blunt invention quite,
Dulling my lines, and doing me disgrace.
Were it not sinful then striving to mend,
To mar the subject that before was well?
For to no other pass my verses tend
Than of your graces and your gifts to tell;
And more, much more than in my verse can sit
Your own glass shows you, when you look in it.

104 She counts the years and notices he is ageing.[377]

To me, fair friend, you never can be old,
For as you were when first your eye I eyed,
Such seems your beauty still. Three[378] winters cold
Have from the forests shook three summers' pride,
Three beauteous springs to yellow autumn turned
In process of the seasons have I seen,
Three April perfumes in three hot Junes burned,
Since first I saw you fresh, which yet are green.
Ah, yet doth beauty, like a dial hand,
Steal from his figure, and no pace perceived;

in which *Philomel* appears. Another *Philomel* Ode appears in 1598 in his *Pecunia* which was
printed in *The Passionate Pilgrim* in 1599. In Ovid's *Metamorphoses*, Philomela, the Greek
Nightingale, was raped by Tereus, her brother-in-law, who cut out her tongue to ensure her
silence. Tereus told his wife that Philomela was dead but Philomela made her story known by
weaving it into a robe, (Mary Fitton made her story known in *A Lover's Complaint*). The gods
eventually changed Tereus into a hawk, his wife into a swallow and Philomela into a nightingale.
Was Mary Fitton hinting that the Ode was hers and that, like Philomel, she has remained quiet?
[377] Which would imply she has seen him.
[378] Lines 3-7 may have been changed from a higher number to three, or that these sonnets have
been transposed or that three was written in as a smokescreen. Three years would be respectable
since William married in 1604 while a higher figure would be increasingly reprehensible
especially when William's wife did not produce an heir.

So your sweet hue, which methinks still doth stand,
Hath motion, and mine eye may be deceived.
For fear of which, hear this, thou age unbred:
Ere you were born was beauty's summer dead.

105 She still praises his virtues.

Let not my love be called Idolatry,
Nor my beloved as an Idol show,
Since all alike my songs and praises be
To one, of one, still such, and ever so.
Kind is my love today, tomorrow kind,
Still constant in a wondrous excellence;
Therefore my verse, to constancy confined,
One thing expressing, leaves out difference.
Fair, kind, and true,[379] is all my argument,
Fair, kind, and true, varying to other words,
And in this change is my invention spent,
Three themes in one, which wondrous scope affords.
Fair, kind, and true, have often lived alone,
Which three till now, never kept seat in one.

106 She continues to praise his looks.

When, in the chronicle of wasted time,
I see descriptions of the fairest wights,[380]
And beauty making beautiful old rhyme
In praise of Ladies dead and lovely Knights,
Then, in the blazon of sweet beauty's best,
Of hand, of foot, of lip, of eye, of brow,
I see their antique pen would have expressed
Even such a beauty as you master now.
So all their praises are but prophecies
Of this our time, all you prefiguring,
And for they looked but with divining eyes,
They had not skill enough your worth to sing;
For we, which now behold these present days,
Have eyes to wonder but lack tongues to praise.

107 Is she pregnant again?

Not mine own fears, nor the prophetic soul
Of the wide world dreaming on things to come,
Can yet the lease of my true love control,
Supposed as forfeit to a confined doom.

---

[379] Hamlet 3.1 asks Ophelia whether she is *honest and fair.*
[380] people

The mortal Moon hath her eclipse endured,[381]
And the sad Augurs mock their own presage;
Incertainties now crown themselves assured,
And peace proclaims Olives of endless age.
Now with the drops of this most balmy time
My love looks fresh, and death to me subscribes,[382]
Since spite of him I'll live in this poor rhyme,
While he insults o'er dull and speechless tribes;
And thou in this shalt find thy monument,
When tyrants' crests and tombs of brass are spent.

108 She still loves him although Time is taking its toll.

What's in the brain that Ink may character,[383]
Which hath not figured to thee my true spirit,
What's new to speak, what now to register,
That may express my love or thy dear merit?
Nothing, sweet boy,[384] but yet, like prayers divine,
I must each day say o'er the very same,
Counting no old thing old, thou mine, I thine,
Even as when first I hallowed thy fair name.
So that eternal love in love's fresh case
Weighs not the dust and injury of age,
Nor gives to necessary wrinkles place,
But makes antiquity for aye his page,
Finding the first conceit of love there bred,
Where time and outward form would shew it dead.

109 Their love could carry on as if they parted yesterday.

O Never say that I was false of heart,
Though absence seemed my flame to qualify,
As easy might I from myself depart,
As from my soul, which in thy breast doth lie:
That is my home of love, if I have ranged,
Like him that travels I return again,
Just to the time, not with the time exchanged,
So that my self bring water for my stain:
Never believe, though in my nature reigned
All frailties that besiege all kinds of blood,
That it could so preposterously be stained
To leave for nothing all thy sum of good;
For nothing this wide universe I call
Save thou, my rose, in it thou art my all.

---

[381] Her menstrual cycle has extended into a new month.
[382] She has heard that William looks fresh while she senses death. Perhaps another pregnancy.
[383] express
[384] A term of endearment, or perhaps a reminder of a former flirtation with homosexuality, or Oscar Wilde's view that Mr. W.H. played boy's, that is female roles in Shakespeare's plays.

110 Mary admits to there having been others.

Alas 'tis true, I have gone here and there
And made myself a motley to the view,
Gored mine own thoughts, sold cheap what is most dear,
Made old offences of affections new.
Most true it is that I have looked on truth
Askance and strangely; but, by all above,
These blenches[385] gave my heart another youth,
And worse essays proved thee my best of love.
Now all is done, have what shall have no end;
Mine appetite I never more will grind [386]
On newer proof, to try an older friend,
A god in love, to whom I am confined.
Then give me welcome, next my heaven the best,
Even to thy pure and most most loving breast.

111–112 She has been stained by the public's opinion of her.

O, for my sake do you wish[387] fortune chide,
The guilty goddess of my harmful deeds,
That did not better for my life provide,
Than public means which public manners breeds.
Thence comes it that my name receives a brand,
And almost thence my nature is subdued
To what it works in, like the Dyer's hand.
Pity me then, and wish I were renewed,
Whilst like a willing patient I will drink
Potions of Eisel[388] 'gainst my strong infection;
No bitterness that I will bitter think,
Nor double penance to correct correction.
Pity me then, dear friend, and I assure ye
Even that your pity is enough to cure me.

112

Your love and pity doth th' impression fill
Which vulgar scandal stamped upon my brow;
For what care I who calls me well or ill,
So you o'er-green my bad, my good allow? [389]
You are my all-the-world, and I must strive
To know my shames and praises from your tongue,
None else to me, nor I to none alive,

---

[385] Turnings aside; straying
[386] Whet; physically love. I think she now lives at Perton, renting her home from her cousin Richard Leveson (who dies in 1605) and perhaps now married or committed to Polewhele.
[387] Q has *wish* not *with*.
[388] Vinegar from the juice of the crab-apple. Eisel appears in Hamlet 5.1.
[389] Let grass grow over my bad but still allow my good to show.

Sonnets From Afar, 18 – 126

That my steeled sense or [390]changes right or wrong.
In so profound *Abisme* I throw all care
Of others' voices that my Adder's sense[391]
To critic and to flatterer stopped are:
Mark how with my neglect I do dispense:
You are so strongly in my purpose bred,
That all the world besides methinks y'are dead.

113 – 114 She sees him everywhere in her mind's eye.[392]

Since I left you mine eye is in my mind,
And that which governs me to go about
Doth part his function and is partly blind,
Seems seeing, but effectually is out;
For it no form delivers to the heart
Of bird, of flower, or shape, which it doth latch;[393]
Of his quick objects hath the mind no part,
Nor his own vision holds what it doth catch;
For if it see the rud'st or gentlest sight,
The most sweet-favour or deformed'st creature,
The mountain or the sea, the day or night,
The crow or dove, it shapes them to your feature.
Incapable of more, replete with you,
My most true mind thus maketh mine eye untrue.

114

Or whether doth my mind, being crown'd with you,
Drink up the monarch's plague, this flattery?
Or whether shall I say mine eye saith true,
And that your love taught it this *Alchemy,*
To make of monsters and things indigest
Such cherubins as your sweet self resemble,
Creating every bad a perfect best
As fast as objects to his beams assemble?
Oh, 'tis the first, 'tis flattery in my seeing,
And my great mind most kingly drinks it up.
Mine eye well knows what with his gust is 'greeing
And to his palate doth prepare the cup.
If it be poisoned, 'tis the lesser sin
That mine eye loves it, and doth first begin.

115 Her lines fail to express how much she loves him.

Those lines that I before have writ do lie,
Even those that said I could not love you dearer;

---

[390] Over; line-9 is difficult to understand.

[391] deaf ears - as deaf as an adder.

[392] Is this demonstrating a madness within?

[393] Q has *lack*.

Yet, then my judgment knew no reason why,
My most full flame should afterwards burn clearer.
But reckoning time, whose millioned accidents
Creep in twixt vows and change decrees of Kings,
Tan sacred beauty, blunt the sharp'st intents,
Divert strong minds to th' course of altring things:
Alas, why, fearing of time's tyranny,
Might I not then say now I love you best,
When I was certain o'er in-certainty,
Crowning the present, doubting of the rest?
Love is a babe; then might I not say so,
To give full growth to that which still doth grow.[394]

**116 Mary philosophises on true love's being
unalterable, or fooled by sex or Time.**

Let me not to the marriage of true minds
Admit impediments; love is not love
Which alters when it alteration finds,
Or bends with the remover to remove.
O no, it is an ever fixed mark
That looks on tempests and is never shaken;[395]
It is the star to every wandring bark,
Whose worth's unknown, although his height be taken.
Love's not Time's fool, though rosy lips and cheeks
Within his bending sickle's compass come;[396]
Love alters not with his brief hours and weeks,
But bears it out even to the edge of doom:
If this be error and upon me proved,
I never writ, nor no man ever loved.

**117 – 118 Begging forgiveness for straying,
and trying to rationalise what she has done.** [397]

Accuse me thus, that I have scanted all
Wherein I should your great deserts repay,
Forgot upon your dearest love to call
Whereto all bonds do tie me day by day;
That I have frequent been with unknown minds,
And given to time your own dear-purchased right;

---

[394] Could she be pregnant? She has six or seven children between 1601 and 1610.
[395] These four lines are convoluted and contain "shake", "pe" in tempest, and "ere" elsewhere.
[396] Lines 9-10; Love is not fooled by sexual acts. Compass = penis.
[397] Mary asks William's forgiveness but couches it as if these have been infidelities of the mind and not of the body. Well, have they? Rereading Sonnets 110-112 I sense matter over mind; e.g. 112.2 *Which vulgar scandal stamped upon my brow.* We know that she had at least eight children by four men; Pembroke (1); Leveson (2); Polewhele (3); Lougher (2) and two, possibly three, marriages.

That I have hoisted sail to all the winds
Which should transport me farthest from your sight.
Book both my wilfulness and errors down,
And on just proof surmise accumulate;
Bring me within the level of your frown,
But shoot not at me in your wakened hate:
Since my appeal says I did strive to prove
The constancy and virtue of your love.

118

Like as to make our appetites more keen
With eager compounds we our palate urge;
As to prevent our maladies unseen,
We sicken to shun sickness when we purge.
Even so, being full of your ne'er cloying sweetness,
To bitter sauces did I frame my feeding,
And, sick of welfare, found a kind of meetness
To be diseased ere that there was true needing.
Thus policy in love, t'anticipate
The ills that were not, grew to faults assured,
And brought to medicine a healthful state
Which rank of goodness would by ill be cured.
But thence I learn, and find the lesson true,
Drugs poison him that so fell sick of you.

119 She admits she has paid heavily for her experience.

What potions have I drunk of *Siren* tears
Distilled from Lymbecks[398] foul as hell within,
Applying fears to hopes, and hopes to fears,
Still losing when I saw myself to win?
What wretched errors hath my heart committed,
Whilst it hath thought itself so blessed never?
How have mine eyes out of their spheres been fitted
In the distraction of this madding fever?
O benefit of ill! Now I find true
That better is by evil still made better,
And ruined love when it is built anew
Grows fairer than at first, more strong, far greater.
So I return rebuked to my content,
And gain by ills thrice more than I have spent.

---

[398] Stills

120 They have hurt each other,
and now they must forgive each other.

That you were once unkind befriends me now,
And for that sorrow which I then did feel
Needs must I under my transgression bow,
Unless my nerves were brass or hammered steel.
For if you were by my unkindness shaken
As I by yours, you've passed a hell of Time,
And I, a tyrant, have no leisure taken
To weigh how once I suffered in your crime.
O that our night of woe might have remembered
My deepest sense how hard true sorrow hits,
And soon to you, as you to me, then tendered
The humble salve which wounded bosoms fits!
But that your trespass now becomes a fee;
Mine ransoms yours, and yours must ransom me.

121 She pities the world of falsehood, wantonness and evil.

'Tis better to be vile than vile esteemed,[399]
When not to be, receives reproach of being,
And the just pleasure lost, which is so deemed,
Not by our feeling, but by others' seeing.
For why should others' false adulterate eyes
Give salutation to my sportive[400] blood?
Or on my frailties why are frailer spies,
Which in their wills[401] count bad what I think good?
No, I am that I am, and they that level
At my abuses, reckon up their own;
I may be straight though they themselves be bevel
By their rank thoughts, my deeds must not be shown
Unless this general evil they maintain,
All men are bad and in their badness reign.

---

[399] Echoes Sonnet 71 and also her mother's letter [5.31] which notes that Mary Fitton was considered a vile woman.
[400] Wanton; this sonnet beautifully describes her character and the hypocasy of living in a man's world. She admits she enjoys sex, but whereas she is honest or straightforward, other people are oblique in their approaches.
[401] Sexuality. Note that Will sits above I-am in the next line.

122 The copy book with her sonnets has been passed to William but before she lets go she includes 122–126.

TThy gift,,[402] thy tables, are within my brain
Full charactered with lasting memory,
Which shall above that idle rank remain
Beyond all date, even to eternity;
Or, at the least, so long as brain and heart
Have faculty by nature to subsist;
Till each to razed oblivion yield his part
Of thee, thy record never can be missed.
That poor retention could not so much hold,
Nor need I tallies thy dear love to score;
Therefore to give them from me was I bold,[403]
To trust those tables that receive thee more.
To keep an adjunct to remember thee
Were to import forgetfulness in me.

123 A final cryptic clue gives her name.

No! Time, thou shalt not boast that I do change.
Thy pyramyds [404] built up with newer might
To me are nothing novel, nothing strange,
They are but dressings of a former sight.
Our dates are brief, and therefore we admire
What thou dost foist upon us that is old,
And rather make them born to our desire
Than think that we before have heard them told.[405]
Thy registers[406] and thee I both defy,
Not wondring at the present nor the past,
For thy records and what we see doth lie,
Made more or less by thy continual haste.
This I do vow, and this shall ever be:
I will be true despite thy scythe and thee.

---

[402] Q starts the line with TT and two commas after gift; Table / tablets to be written on. Taking the F from the first word of the second line with TThy from the first we can construct a phonetic Fyth-T-on. The double commas appear to be an "alert". The YF my at the start of the next sonnet again seems to hint at her name.

[403] It seems clear that she has given her Sonnets to William.

[404] Norton, p2006, n9; mentions pyramids erected in 1603 for James's 1604 coronation. I felt (probably wrongly) that chronologically we were around 1606-7. Alerted by a disparity, I noticed that **Thy Pyram**yds contains the name MARY and PYHT and an T & NO can be found at the start of the sonnet. These are exactly the same letters Mary uses to spells her surname, Phytton, in her letter [5.12]. Newdigate [op. cit. p28] observed the phrase, *time that limits all things* in the letter looks Shakespearean.. It was!

[405] Which makes us rather bear those evils we have,
    Than fly to others that we know not of.   (Hamlet's soliloquy, Q1.)

[406] Church registers of burials – she appears to be addressing Time.

124 Love will always be constant . .

YF my dear love were but the child of state,
It might for fortune's bastard be unfathered,
As subject to time's love or to time's hate,
Weeds among weeds, or flowers with flowers gathered.
No, it was builded far from accident;
It suffers not in smiling pomp, nor falls
Under the blow of thralled discontent,
Whereto th'inviting time our fashion calls.
It fears not policy, that *Heretic*
Which works on leases of short-numbered hours,
But all alone stands hugely politic, [407]
That it nor grows with heat nor drowns with showers.
To this I witness call the fools of time,
Which die for goodness, who have lived for crime.

125 . . and will rise above the vicissitudes of daily life. [408]

Were't aught to me I bore the canopy,[409]
With my extern the outward honouring,
Or laid great bases for eternity,
Which proves more short than waste or ruining?
Have I not seen dwellers on form and favour
Lose all, and more, by paying too much rent
For compound sweet; Forgoing simple savour,
Pitiful thrivers in their gazing spent?
No, let me be obsequious in thy heart,
And take thou my oblation, poor but free,
Which is not mixed with seconds, knows no art,
But mutual render, only me for thee.
Hence, thou suborned *Informer*, a true soul
When most impeached, stands least in thy control.[410]

126 So Time will out, and she sets him free.

O Thou, my lovely boy, [411] who in thy power,
Dost hold time's fickle glass, his sickle hour:
Who hast by waning grown, and therein show'st,
Thy lovers withering, as thy sweet self grow'st.

---

[407] prudent

[408] This is the last of the 108 sonnets after Sonnet 17. The next poem has only twelve lines and the expected, final couplet appears to be missing.

[409] A reference to Pembroke being one of the Knights of the Garter who carried the canopy that covered the King during the Coronation Procession in the summer of 1604.

[410] You will find that a true soul, when most threatened, will no longer be in your control.

[411] Meaning child or homosexual or how she first knew him? Perhaps she is reminding William of homosexual flirtations or a time when he acted female parts.

If Nature (sovereign mistress over wrack)
As thou goest onwards still will pluck thee back,
She keeps thee to this purpose: that her skill
May time disgrace, and wretched minutes kill.
Yet fear her, O thou minion of her pleasure,
She may detain, but not still keep, her treasure.
Her *Audit* (though delay'd) answer'd must be,
And her *Quietus*[412] is to render thee.

Mary Fitton, having completed the classical number of 108 sonnets (18-125), finished with 126, a verse of just six couplets. The rhyme is aa-bb-cc-dd-ee-ff compared with ab-ab-cd-cd-ef-ef-gg throughout the rest of the sonnets. Missing a seventh and final couplet, one short of a sonnet, frustrated any expectancy of a continuation. This told the reader that this *was* the end. The last four words are a double message with an anagram; *storie end(s) there* – and so it did.

Mary Fitton's life must have changed at this point. William Herbert had married in November 1604. Sir Richard Leveson had died in August 1605. Her father, Sir Edward Fitton, was buried on 4th March 1606 and, since there was no echo of his death in her poetry, it may be that the sonnets were completed around this date. Not only were the two men who had looked after her both dead, Sir William Knollys who had repeatedly avowed that he wanted to marry her, turned his back on her and in 1605 married a girl of eighteen.[413]

Within a year of her father's death, Mary, who had been used to having the protection of a man around her, married William Polewhele.

---

[412] Settlement. Is Qui-es-tu (French, *who are you?*) a stretch of the imagination?
[413] Chapter 5.28; 5.29.

CHAPTER NINE

THE LAST WORDS

In the end, Mary Fitton handed over her copybook to the man she loved, William Herbert, Earl Pembroke; we can read this in Sonnet 122. This may well have been three or four years before the book's contents were printed in 1609. The actual year of the hand-over and the specific reason will remain a matter of conjecture but, in the wrong hands, the contents of the book could have caused yet another scandal and very serious embarrassment to the Pembrokes. From Mary's point of view, the safest time to hand over the book would have been before she married William Polewhele as, on marriage, all her property would have passed into the hands of her husband. It would certainly have become Polewhele's property if Mary had died in childbirth. Pembroke may indeed have anticipated or pre-empted a potential conflict of ownership.[414] If, in 1609, he heard that Mary thought Polewhele was terminally ill, he may have registered and printed Mary's *Sonnets* and *A Lover's Complaint* just to make sure that he controlled the intellectual property, adding his own *Dark Lady* sonnets for good measure.

The Sonnets were registered in London on 20th May 1609; William Polewhele was buried on 26th September 1609. The Sonnets were reprinted in 1640 the same year that Mary Fitton (Mary Lougher[415]) made her will. These coincidences should be noted as should Mary Wroth's recording that *Antissia* (Mary Fitton), upset by *Amphilanthus* (Pembroke) rejecting her love, enlisted one *Dolorindus* to murder *Amphilanthus*. When the plot failed *Dolorindus* allied himself with *Amphilanthus* but eventually married *Antissia*. Taking this element of Wroth's *Urania* at its simplest, *Dolorindus* might have been John Lougher, Mary Fitton's second husband.

Shakespeareans easily dismiss the idea that Mr.W.H., in the Dedication, is William Herbert saying that before he succeeded to the Pembroke title, which happened to be in his twenty-first year, he was formally referred to as Lord Herbert and possibly as Sir William Herbert. In riposte, if the dedication had said either Ld.W.H or Sr.W.H his identity would have become apparent to all. Yet the whole concourse of the sonnets has specifically hidden the lovers' identities, almost as if the love affair was still extant at the time Mary released William in Sonnet 126. For years Mary was still in love with him, and for some reason she thought that he was in love with her; perhaps she never forgot those first intimate months, her working alongside William to develop *As You Like It* and her first experience of sex. By allowing the Dedication to stand when it was published, William Herbert would have known that he could not be identified

---

[414] This had happened when his uncle, Philip Sidney, died and his sister, Mary Sidney Herbert had assumed ownership of Philip's poetry ahead of his Philip's widow.

[415] Her will first named her as Mary Polewhele, but the Polewhele was struck out and Lougher inserted.

The Last Words

by it; people would be looking for a commoner. Further if William had not recognised there was a cipher in the Dedication, or he had not managed to break it, he would not have tampered with wording or punctuation.

I still muse why William Herbert did not have legitimate children. He was not impotent as he sired bastard children before and during his marriage to Mary Talbot. His supposedly misshapen wife conceived late in the marriage but lost her child – perhaps she was unable to have healthy children or she suffered miscarriages. Apart from the wealth that his wife's dowry brought, she was genetically a rotten choice if he wanted progeny as the Herberts (Pembrokes) and the Talbots (Shrewsburys) had been intermarrying for centuries. If he had wanted progeny, Mary Fitton would have provided a fecund partner; she appears to have had at least eight pregnancies. Would William Herbert have married Mary Fitton if their baby had lived? I think not – she was at least his intellectual equal but had a wildness of spirit with which he may not have wanted to ally himself.

William Herbert, as a young man, avoided marriage for nearly a decade; if there was some truth in the story that he was not the genetic son of the ageing 2nd Earl then the threat of being exposed was so great that it would be better for the family's reputation that he allowed his younger brother to succeed him. If in the wildest possibility his real father were Christopher Marlowe a lot would be explained – why Marlowe went to university almost as an afterthought at the age of eighteen[416]; why William was such a gifted poet; why Venus & Adonis[417] (an inferior version of Marlowe's Hero & Leander) appeared so shortly after Marlowe appeared to be stabbed to death at Deptford; why there was a rumour that Marlowe had returned to the country and was hidden at Wilton.[418]

It is quite clear that the writers of the Sonnets, poems and plays either wanted, or needed to hide their identity; and they did so, most successfully, for over 400 years. Shake-Speare just had to be a pen-name, a fact which in itself eliminates William Shakespeare of Stratford-upon-Avon. But if William Herbert "owned" the Sonnets in 1609, it does not lie well with the fact that the Shakespeare name was floating around by implication from about 1593 when

---

[416] Most young men had *left* University by the time they were 17.

[417] V&A is thought to have been set in the County of Kent in 1580, the year of William Herbert's birth. In late Summer 1579 both Marlowe (26 February 1564, son of a cobbler) and Mary Sidney (27 November 1561) were supposedly in Canterbury (Urry; *Christopher Marlowe and Canterbury*).

[418] In *As You Like It*, written post-Marlowe, a fleeting character called Sir Oliver Mar-text is introduced when there already is a substantial character called Oliver. This must relate to the *Marprelate Pamphlets* to which Marlowe is thought to have contributed and was definitely printed by his friend, John Penry. I would guess that Penry was known as the *Shepherd* at University since he came from a remote farm in Wales. I believe the author of *As You Like It* knew that John Penry's body had been switched to allow Christopher Marlowe to escape arrest, torture and death. Hence the lines which I believe relate to John Penry:
"Dead shepherd, now I find thy saw of might:
Who ever loved that loved not at first sight?"

The Last Words

William Herbert was only thirteen. However, if the intellectual property of the Shakespeare Plays and Poems was vested in the Sidney-Herbert family then, on the Countess's death, the heir to the legacy would have been the heir to the Earl of Pembroke, William Herbert at the time. Perhaps, once the Dowager Countess had died, the publishing of the *Shakespeare* plays in a single folio signalled the family divesting itself of the responsibility. This may have been either a pragmatic, financial or political decision, or simply bringing together the plays as a gift to the world. You may recall that Ben Jonson, in his poem facing the title page of the *First Folio,* told the reader to, *look not on his Picture, but his Book.* The title page being, of course, the door (dor) that opens to reveal the plays inside.

If the Stratford Shakespeare was not the author then the question remains *who was?* Was it possible that a thirteen-year-old boy working with an exceptional tutor or under the tutelage of his gifted mother could have produced *Venus & Adonis* and *The Rape of Lucrece*? I guess that William Herbert was wanting to compete with the nineteen-year-old Henry Wriothesley and wishing to emulate his uncle, Sir Philip Sidney, who died when William was six and at his most impressionable. Whoever worked with William Herbert, whether his mother or his tutor Samuel Daniel, it looks as if William was allowed to take the credit under the pen name William Shakespeare; "*the first heir of my invention*" would now make sense.

Research has not revealed a named writer or writers of the plays, whether William Shakespeare or anyone else. My feeling is that the conduit through which the plays emerged was the Sidney-Herberts, either through patronage, or having written plays themselves, or having modified existing or embryo plays. Mary Sidney Herbert was known to have placed herself very much in the thick of things. She was involved with a large number of literary personages who had the ability to write plays, but even closer to home were a brother, Robert Sidney, Mary Wroth's father, and a Sir William Herbert of Powis. Drama was certainly an art and a culture that the Sidneys and the Herberts enjoyed and supported. It is hardly conceivable that their College was not involved with the development of dramatic plays.

All roads seem to lead back to the Sidney family and the Countess Pembroke in particular. The introduction to the Ardern Shakespeare *King Richard II* nicely explains the subtleties of dabbling in the theatre. On 7th February 1601, four weeks after the gala performance of *Twelfth Night,* supporters of Robert Devereux, Lord Essex, paid for Shakespeare's Company to perform *Richard II* with *its deposing and killing of the king,* at the Globe Theatre. They reasoned that the play's propaganda would help serve them in their attempt, the following day, to seize control of London and hence the Crown. The play was *good,* but not that good; and they did not gain public support. Lord Essex, William Knolly's nephew, was executed. So, one can see that to publish and perform an English historical drama held an inherent risk as the plot inevitably involved a change of sovereign and with it associated propaganda that might work for or against the existing monarch. Even a benign play under

The Last Words

one monarch could become malign under the next. The Lord Chamberlain's remit was to ensure that the public would not become restless, hence the subtlety of his role. It was a wise author and a wise patron who did not ascribe their names to a historical play. As Hamlet said, *The play's the thing wherein I'll catch the conscience of the king.*

For Scrabble® players the combination of the three higher value letters H, P and K should stir the mind; all three are in HERBERT PEMBROKE and in SHAKESPEARE.

To transmute one into another one must remove the letters R O B B E R T and add A A S S and one is still left with an M. However good an actor or director William Shakespeare was, it is easy to perceive how a young Earl who stole a man's name could also consider the man an ass. Equally, the Sidney emblem of an arrow looks like a playing-card Ace, written then as AS or AAS; or a pun on *arse*.

My favourite explanation is to draw a cross with the two names HARBERTS[419] and PEMBROKES using the common letter B as the centre. Remove ROBERT and one is left with HARS PEM KES which yields M SHEKSPEAR – the M being either Master or Mary.

Another choice is to again remove ROBERT from HERBERT PEMBROKES AAS. This gives M. SHAKESPEARE. Mary Herbert Sidney, the (mute) Swan of Avon – who watched over it all and nothing was said.

She signed her letters, *M. Pembroke.*

Two fires, one big, the other great, have caused considerable frustration to historians. The first in 1647 destroyed most of the Pembroke home at Wilton. The other, the 1666 Great Fire, destroyed Baynards Castle, the Pembroke's London home on the bank of the Thames. Between them all the Pembrokes Tudor portraits were lost and countless books and documents, including, probably, hand-written scripts of the Shake-Speare plays, went up in smoke. Was this the destiny of the copybook containing Mary Fitton's Sonnets or dare we romanticise that her impassioned scribbles are collecting dust, like her painting, in some forgotten archive? We end with two epilogues. The first is from *As You Like It* and is spoken by Rosalind having stepped out of her robes as Ganymede;[420] (Could Mary Fitton have played this part as Gwenyth Paltrow played Juliet in *Shakespeare in Love?*).

---

[419] Harbert and Penbroke were often used.

[420] Even having stepped out of male robes, the actor who played Rosalind would still have been a boy or young man. History may yet throw a dart when a new generation of Shakespeareans conclude that Rosalind is the fiery spirit of Mary Fitton.

The Last Words

It is not the fashion to see the lady the epilogue; but it is no more unhandsome than to see the lord the prologue. If it be true that good wine needs no bush, 'tis true that a good play needs no epilogue; yet to good wine they do use good bushes, and good plays prove the better by the help of good epilogues. What a case am I in then, that am neither a good epilogue nor cannot insinuate with you in the behalf of a good play! I am not furnished like a beggar, therefore to beg will not become me. My way is to conjure you; and I'll begin with the women. I charge you, O women, for the love you bear to men, to like as much of this play as please you; and I charge you, O men, for the love you bear to women – as I perceive by your simpering none of you hates them – that between you and the women the play may please. If I were a woman, I would kiss as many of you as had beards that pleased me,[421] complexions that liked me, and breaths that I defied not; and, I am sure, as many as have good beards, or good faces, or sweet breaths, will, for my kind offer, when I make curtsy, bid me farewell.

Epilogue

Mary Wroth's *The Countess of Montgomery's Urania* is an extensive allegory on the Court and social life around her. In two parts, the first book was so libellous that she was forced to withdraw it; the second was printed only recently. When the first part was published in 1621 Mary Wroth had an open relationship with William Herbert and was mother to their two children[422] – despite William still being married to Mary Talbot who lost an infant in 1620.

In brief, Countess Montgomery was the wife of Philip, William Herbert's brother. The book's many characters were all given contrived names but obviously represented real people. Mary Wroth was *Pamphilia* and Pembroke was *Amphilanthus, the Emperor*. Mary Fitton was *Antissia* – meaning *opponent* – and Mary Fitton *had been* Mary Wroth's opponent for William's love. In fact, in *Urania* a mock marriage took place between *Pamphilia* and *Amphilanthus* with *Antissia* one of a number of witnesses. This must have been before 1600 when William was 20 and his cousin 14. This love for his cousin may have been another reason why William Herbert was trying to avoid marriage. The following comment in Chapter 5 [5.20] now might make more sense.

---

[421] Francis Beaumont wrote of Abigal, (Chapter Five); "She loved all the players in the last Queen's time once over. She was struck when they acted lovers, and forsook some when they played murthers."

[422] Their first child, William, was born in the spring of 1620 and became a colonel in Ireland during the 1642-51 Civil War. The second, Katherine, married a Mr. Lovel of Oxfordshire.

The Last Words

"One Mrs Martin who dwelt at the Chopping Knife near Ludgate told me that she hath seen priests marry gentlewomen at the Court, in that time when that Mrs Fitton was in great favour, ..."

From Sheila T Cavanagh's *Cherished Torment the emotional geography of Lady Mary Wroth's Urania* there are many instances where Antissia is described but, on page 72, when Antissia hears false reports of Amphilanthus' death she: *put on mourning . . . and betaking herself to a Castle, not far from the sea, where she beheld nothing but Rocks, hills of Sand, as bare as her content: Waves raging like her Sorrow.* [423]

Mary Wroth's words are an echo of Sonnets 64 and 65, yet published 12 years apart and nearly twenty years after the event. So I conclude with these two sonnets, written over four hundred years ago. Mary is in South Wales. As she walks along a deserted beach near Tenby Castle she fears the loss of the man she adores.

Sonnet 64

When I have seen by time's fell hand defaced
The rich proud cost of outworn buried age;
When sometime lofty towers I see down-razed,
And brass eternal slave to mortal rage;
When I have seen the hungry ocean gain
Advantage on the kingdom of the shore,
And the firm soil win of the watry main,
Increasing store with loss, and loss with store;
When I have seen such interchange of state,
Or state it self confounded to decay,
Ruin hath taught me thus to ruminate:
That Time will come and take my love away.
This thought is as a death, which cannot choose
But weep to have, that which it fears to lose.

Sonnet 65

Since brass, nor stone, nor earth, nor boundless sea,
But sad mortality o'ersways their power,
How with this rage shall beauty hold a plea,
Whose action is no stronger than a flower?
O how shall summer's honey breath hold out
Against the wrackful siege of batt'ring days,

---

[423] It has been suggested that *Antissia* (Mary Fitton) suffered from post-traumatic stress.

The Last Words

When rocks impregnable are not so stout,
Nor gates of steel so strong, but time decays?
O fearful meditation, where, alack,
Shall time's best jewel from Time' chest lie hid?
Or what strong hand can hold his swift foot back,
Or who his spoil of beauty can forbid?
O, none, unless this miracle have might,
That in black ink my love may still shine bright.

Well, that should have been the end except there is one last twist. I believe William Herbert and, or Mary Fitton set out to fool us! Every analyst of the Sonnets has concurred with there being a third person, the *Dark Lady*, and I have supported the candidature of Aemelia Lanier as being *most compelling.* We also know that Sonnets 138 and 144 appeared in the *Passionate Pilgrim* in 1599, *before* the scandal with Mary Fitton, so it would appear that the author of the Sonnets addressed two different people.

William Herbert was described by his tutor as a man who could not *bear injury, or cross in reputation.* This is borne out in his emotional cocktail of sadness, frustration, love, frenzy and anger in his *Dark Lady* sonnets. But what if this was his response to Mary Fitton's love, and to her perceived betrayal, such as around 1604, in finding that she was carrying Leveson's child, or in 1606-7 when she closed the door in his face by marrying Polewhele? By the inclusion of just two sonnets from the *Passionate Pilgrim*, published *before* 1600, whoever arranged to have these poems printed would have put up a brilliant smokescreen, shifting the time-window, and hiding the fact that the relationship between Mary Fitton and William Herbert continued until well after his marriage; so fooling his wife, society, historians and posterity.

It would have been difficult for Mary Fitton's sonnets to have been written in isolation - they needed an external stimulus. I had thought, throughout, that Mary was reacting simply to gossip about her ex-lover, brought to her by people such as her new lover, Sir Richard Leveson, and the occasional meeting with William Herbert. Then, having done the extensive research and the writing, I reread Sonnets 127-152, (excluding 138 and 144), and found the appropriateness with which William Herbert's sonnets could be addressed to, or respond to, Mary Fitton and her sonnets. For instance, the three *Williams* of Sonnet 135 can be explained from William Polewhele, William Herbert, Leveson's bastard child, named William, or Polewhele's legitimate son, named William.

William Herbert and Mary Fitton led us *all* astray. They led the world to perceive, on face-value, that *William Shakespeare* had, or wanted, a homosexual relationship with a young man; before or after addressing sonnets of love to his dark mistress; with the poem, *A Lover's Complaint,* standing

The Last Words

alone and having no relevance. It was just as plausible to accept that Aemelia Lanier was that *Dark Lady* whom William Herbert lusted after, before his affair with Mary Fitton. But the probable truth is that there were only two lovers in the Sonnets, William Herbert and Mary Fitton – who at some time may simply have been in mourning, looked sad, worn a black wig or used mascara.

Before we go our separate ways, I ask you, kindly, please return to Chapter Three and reread the so-called *Dark Lady* Sonnets. Knowing all the history, you should find it surprisingly easy to sense what had been happening. Then read how Sonnet 8 responds to Sonnet 128; how 135 & 136 fit after 110 or before 111; and Sonnet 131 before 110. (Appendix Six helps bring all the Sonnets together).

Having eliminated the *compelling* Aemelia Lanier from the puzzle, we can pick up the last piece in this four-hundred year-old jigsaw, and know it is going to fit-on,

whose *Quietus* is to render thee –

and end the story here.

A Lover's Complaint

Appendix 1 – A Lover's Complaint by William Shake-Speare

1 From off a hill whose concave womb[424] re-worded
  A plaintful story from a sistering vale,
  My spirits to attend this double voice accorded,
  And down I laid to list the sad-tuned tale;
  Ere long espied a fickle maid full pale,
  Tearing of papers, breaking rings a-twain,
  Storming her world with sorrow's wind and rain.

2 Upon her head a platted hive of straw,
  Which fortified her visage from the sun,
  Whereon the thought might think sometime it saw
  The carcass of beauty spent and done:
  Time had not scythed all that youth begun,
  Nor youth all quit; but, spite of heaven's fell rage,
  Some beauty peep'd through lattice of sear'd age.

3 Oft did she heave her napkin to her eyne,
  Which on it had conceited characters,
  Laundering the silken figures in the brine
  That season'd woe had pelleted in tears,
  And often reading what contents it bears;
  As often shrieking undistinguish'd woe,
  In clamours of all size, both high and low.

4 Sometimes her levell'd eyes their carriage ride,
  As they did battery to the spheres intend;
  Sometime diverted their poor balls are tied
  To the orbed earth; sometimes they do extend
  Their view right on; anon their gazes lend
  To every place at once, and, nowhere fix'd,
  The mind and sight distractedly commix'd.

5 Her hair, nor loose nor tied in formal plait,
  Proclaim'd in her a careless hand of pride
  For some, untuck'd, descended her sheaved hat,
  Hanging her pale and pined cheek beside;
  Some in her threaden fillet still did bide,
  And true to bondage would not break from thence,
  Though slackly braided in loose negligence.

---

[424] Why has she not used *sides* and *echoed?* Looks like an anagram of Cwmafon (near Port Talbot) or Cwmavon (near Pontypool), both in South Wales.

A Lover's Complaint

6 A thousand favours from a maund[425] she drew
   Of amber, crystal, and of beaded jet,
   Which one by one she in a river threw,
   Upon whose weeping margent[426] she was set,
   Like usury, applying wet to wet,
   Or monarch's hands that let not bounty fall
   Where want cries some, but where excess begs all.

7 Of folded schedules had she many a one,
   Which she perused, sigh'd, tore, and gave the flood;
   Crack'd many a ring of posied gold and bone
   Bidding them find their sepulchres in mud;
   Found yet more letters sadly penn'd in blood,
   With sleided silk feat and affectedly
   Enswathed, and seal'd to curious secrecy.

8 These often bathed she in her fluxive eyes,
   And often kiss'd, and often gan to tear:
   Cried 'O false blood, thou register of lies,
   What unapproved witness dost thou bear!
   Ink would have seem'd more black and damned here!'
   This said, in top of rage the lines she rents,
   Big discontent so breaking their contents.

9 A reverend man that grazed his cattle nigh,
   Sometime a blusterer, that the ruffle knew
   Of court, of city, and had let go by
   The swiftest hours, observed as they flew,
   Towards this afflicted fancy fastly drew,
   And, privileged by age, desires to know
   In brief the grounds and motives of her woe.

10 So slides he down upon his grained bat,
   And comely-distant sits he by her side;
   When he again desires her, being sat,
   Her grievance with his hearing to divide:
   If that from him there may be aught applied
   Which may her suffering ecstasy assuage,
   'Tis promised in the charity of age.

11 'Father,' she says, 'though in me you behold
   The injury of many a blasting hour,
   Let it not tell your judgment I am old;
   Not age, but sorrow, over me hath power.
   I might as yet have been a spreading flower,
   Fresh to myself, If I had self-applied
   Love to myself and to no love beside.

---

[425] basket
[426] bank of the river.

A Lover's Complaint

12 'But, woe is me! too early I attended
A youthful suit; it was to gain my grace;
Of one by nature's outwards so commended
That maidens' eyes stuck over all his face:
Love lack'd a dwelling, and made him her place;
And when in his fair parts she did abide,
She was new lodged and newly deified.

13 'His browny locks did hang in crooked curls;
And every light occasion of the wind
Upon his lips their silken parcels hurls.
What's sweet to do, to do will aptly find:
Each eye that saw him did enchant the mind,
For on his visage was in little drawn
What largeness thinks in Paradise was sawn.

14 'Small show of man was yet upon his chin;
His phoenix down[427] began but to appear
Like unshorn velvet on that termless skin
Whose bare out-bragg'd the web it seem'd to wear:
Yet show'd his visage by that cost more dear;
And nice affections wavering stood in doubt
If best were as it was, or best without.

15 'His qualities were beauteous as his form,
For maiden-tongued he was, and thereof free;
Yet, if men moved him, was he such a storm
As oft 'twixt May and April is to see,
When winds breathe sweet, untidy though they be.[428]
His rudeness so with his authorized youth
Did livery falseness in a pride of truth.

16 'Well could he ride, and often men would say
'That horse his mettle from his rider takes:
Proud of subjection, noble by the sway,
What rounds, what bounds, what course, what stop he makes!'
And controversy hence a question takes,
Whether the horse by him became his deed,
Or he his manage by the well-doing steed.

17 'But quickly on this side the verdict went:
His real habitude gave life and grace
To appertainings and to ornament,
Accomplish'd in himself, not in his case:
All aids, themselves made fairer by their place,
Came for additions; yet their purposed trim
Pieced not his grace, but were all graced by him.

---

[427] This shows how young the man was.
[428] These two lines reflect *the rough winds that blow the darling buds of Maie.* Sonnet 18.

A Lover's Complaint

18 'So on the tip of his subduing tongue
   All kinds of arguments and question deep,
   All replication prompt, and reason strong,
   For his advantage still did wake and sleep:
   To make the weeper laugh, the laugher weep,
   He had the dialect and different skill,
   Catching all passions in his craft of will.

19 'That he did in the general bosom reign
   Of young, of old; and sexes both enchanted
   To dwell with him in thoughts, or to remain
   In personal duty, following where he haunted:
   Consents bewitch'd, ere he desire, have granted;
   And dialogued for him what he would say,
   Ask'd their own wills, and made their wills obey.

20 'Many there were that did his picture get,
   To serve their eyes, and in it put their mind;
   Like fools that in th' imagination set
   The goodly objects which abroad they find
   Of lands and mansions, theirs in thought assign'd;
   And labouring in moe pleasures to bestow them
   Than the true gouty landlord which doth owe them:

21 'So many have, that never touch'd his hand,
   Sweetly supposed them mistress of his heart.
   My woeful self, that did in freedom stand,
   And was my own fee-simple, not in part,
   What with his art in youth, and youth in art,
   Threw my affections in his charmed power,
   Reserved the stalk and gave him all my flower.

22 'Yet did I not, as some my equals did,
   Demand of him, nor being desired yielded;
   Finding myself in honour so forbid,
   With safest distance I mine honour shielded:
   Experience for me many bulwarks builded
   Of proofs new-bleeding, which remain'd the foil
   Of this false jewel and his amorous spoil.

23 'But, ah, who ever shunn'd by precedent
   The destined ill she must herself assay?
   Or forced examples, 'gainst her own content,
   To put the by-past perils in her way?
   Counsel may stop awhile what will not stay;
   For when we rage, advice is often seen
   By blunting us to make our wits more keen.

24 'Nor gives it satisfaction to our blood,
   That we must curb it upon others' proof;
   To be forbode the sweets that seem so good,
   For fear of harms that preach in our behoof.
   O appetite, from judgment stand aloof!
   The one a palate hath that needs will taste,
   Though reason weep, and cry, 'It is thy last.'

25 'For further I could say 'This man's untrue,'
   And knew the patterns of his foul beguiling;
   Heard where his plants in others' orchards grew,
   Saw how deceits were gilded in his smiling;
   Knew vows were ever brokers to defiling;
   Thought characters and words merely but art,
   And bastards of his foul adulterate heart.

26 'And long upon these terms I held my city,
   Till thus he gan besiege me: 'Gentle maid,
   Have of my suffering youth some feeling pity,
   And be not of my holy vows afraid:
   That's to ye sworn to none was ever said;
   For feasts of love I have been call'd unto,
   Till now did ne'er invite, nor never woo.

27 "All my offences that abroad you see
   Are errors of the blood, none of the mind;
   Love made them not: with acture[429] they may be,
   Where neither party is nor true nor kind:
   They sought their shame that so their shame did find;
   And so much less of shame in me remains,
   By how much of me their reproach contains.

28 "Among the many that mine eyes have seen,
   Not one whose flame my heart so much as warm'd,
   Or my affection put to the smallest teen,
   Or any of my leisures ever charm'd:
   Harm have I done to them, but ne'er was harm'd;
   Kept hearts in liveries, but mine own was free,
   And reign'd, commanding in his monarchy.

29 "Look here, what tributes wounded fancies sent me,
   Of paled pearls and rubies red as blood;
   Figuring that they their passions likewise lent me
   Of grief and blushes, aptly understood
   In bloodless white and the encrimson'd mood;
   Effects of terror and dear modesty,
   Encamp'd in hearts, but fighting outwardly.

---

[429] action

A Lover's Complaint

30 "And, lo! Behold these talents of their hair,
　　With twisted metal amorously impleach'd,
　　I have received from many a several fair,
　　Their kind acceptance weepingly beseech'd,
　　With th'annexions of fair gems enrich'd,
　　And deep-brain'd sonnets that did amplify
　　Each stone's dear nature, worth, and quality.

31 "The diamond, why, 'twas beautiful and hard,
　　Whereto his invised[430] properties did tend;
　　The deep-green emerald, in whose fresh regard
　　Weak sights their sickly radiance do amend;
　　The heaven-hued sapphire and the opal blend
　　With objects manifold: each several stone,
　　With wit well blazon'd, smiled or made some moan.

32 "Lo, all these trophies of affections hot,
　　Of pensived and subdued desires the tender,
　　Nature hath charged me that I hoard them not,
　　But yield them up where I myself must render,
　　That is, to you, my origin and ender;
　　For these, of force, must your oblations be,
　　Since I their altar, you empatron me.

33 "O, then, advance of yours that phraseless hand,
　　Whose white weighs down the airy scale of praise;
　　Take all these similes to your own command,
　　Hallow'd with sighs that burning lungs did raise;
　　What me your minister, for you obeys,
　　Works under you; and to your audit comes
　　Their distract parcels in combined sums.

34 "Lo, this device was sent me from a nun,
　　Or sister sanctified, of holiest note,
　　Which late her noble suit in court did shun,
　　Whose rarest havings made the blossoms dote;
　　For she was sought by spirits of richest coat,
　　But kept cold distance, and did thence remove,
　　To spend her living in eternal love.

35 "But, O my sweet, what labour is't to leave
　　The thing we have not, mastering what not strives,
　　Playing the place which did no form receive,
　　Playing patient sports in unconstrained gyves?
　　She that her fame so to herself contrives,
　　The scars of battle 'scapeth by the flight,
　　And makes her absence valiant, not her might.

---

[430] envied?

A Lover's Complaint

36 "O, pardon me, in that my boast is true:
   The accident which brought me to her eye
   Upon the moment did her force subdue,
   And now she would the caged cloister fly:
   Religious love put out Religion's eye:
   Not to be tempted, would she be immured,
   And now, to tempt, all liberty procured.

37 "How mighty then you are, O hear me tell!
   The broken bosoms that to me belong
   Have emptied all their fountains in my well,
   And mine I pour your ocean all among:
   I strong o'er them, and you o'er me being strong,
   Must for your victory us all congest,
   As compound love to physic your cold breast.

38 "My parts had power to charm a sacred nun,
   Who, disciplined, ay, dieted in grace,
   Believed her eyes when they to assail begun,
   All vows and consecrations giving place:
   O most potential love! vow, bond, nor space,
   In thee hath neither sting, knot, nor confine,
   For thou art all, and all things else are thine.

39 "When thou impressest, what are precepts worth
   Of stale example? When thou wilt inflame,
   How coldly those impediments stand forth
   Of wealth, of filial fear, law, kindred, fame.
   Love's arms are peace, 'gainst rule, 'gainst sense, 'gainst shame,
   And sweetens, in the suffering pangs it bears,
   The aloes of all forces, shocks, and fears.

40 "Now all these hearts that do on mine depend,
   Feeling it break, with bleeding groans they pine;
   And supplicant their sighs to you extend,
   To leave the battery that you make 'gainst mine,
   Lending soft audience to my sweet design,
   And credent soul to that strong-bonded oath
   That shall prefer and undertake my troth.'

41 'This said, his watery eyes he did dismount,
   Whose sights till then were levell'd on my face;
   Each cheek a river running from a fount
   With brinish current downward flow'd apace:
   O, how the channel to the stream gave grace!
   Who glazed with crystal gate the glowing roses
   That flame through water which their hue encloses.

A Lover's Complaint

42 'O father, what a hell of witchcraft lies
   In the small orb of one particular tear!
   But with the inundation of the eyes
   What rocky heart to water will not wear?
   What breast so cold that is not warmed here?
   O cleft effect! cold modesty, hot wrath,
   Both fire from hence and chill extincture hath.

43 'For, lo, his passion, but an art of craft,
   Even there resolved my reason into tears;
   There my white stole of chastity I daff'd,
   Shook off my sober guards and civil fears;
   Appear to him, as he to me appears,
   All melting; though our drops this difference bore,
   His poisoned me, and mine did him restore.

44 'In him a plenitude of subtle matter,
   Applied to cautels, all strange forms receives,
   Of burning blushes, or of weeping water,
   Or swooning paleness; and he takes and leaves,
   In either's aptness, as it best deceives,
   To blush at speeches rank to weep at woes,
   Or to turn white and swoon at tragic shows.

45 'That not a heart which in his level came
   Could 'scape the hail of his all-hurting aim,
   Showing fair nature is both kind and tame;
   And, veil'd in them, did win whom he would maim:
   Against the thing he sought he would exclaim;
   When he most burn'd in heart-wish'd luxury,
   He preach'd pure maid, and praised cold chastity.

46 'Thus merely with the garment of a grace
   The naked and concealed fiend he cover'd;
   That th' unexperient gave the tempter place,
   Which like a cherubin above them hover'd.
   Who, young and simple, would not be so lover'd?
   Ay me! I fell; and yet do question make
   What I should do again for such a sake.

47 'O, that infected moisture of his eye,
   O, that false fire which in his cheek so glow'd,
   O, that forced thunder from his heart did fly,
   O, that sad breath his spongy lungs bestowed,
   O, all that borrow'd motion seeming owed,
   Would yet again betray the fore-betray'd,
   And new pervert a reconciled maid.'

The Passionate Pilgrim

Appendix 2

THE PASSIONATE PILGRIM (1599)[431]

Did William Herbert have *The Passionate Pilgrim* printed, with its twenty-one poems on the subjects of love and women, as a gift to a woman? Here is a summary of the poems.

PP1	Shake-Speare Sonnet 138
PP2	Shake-Speare Sonnet 144
PP3	Shakespeare – Love's Labour Lost
PP4	William Shakespeare – Venus and Adonis
PP5	Shakespeare – Love's Labour Lost
PP6	William Shakespeare – Venus and Adonis
PP7	not yet attributed
PP8	Richard Barnfield
PP9	William Shakespeare – Venus and Adonis
PP10	not yet attributed
PP11	Bartholomew Griffin, from his sequence Fidessa, 1596.
PP12	Thomas Deloney (1543- 600)
PP13	not yet attributed
PP14, PP15	not yet attributed
PP16	not yet attributed
PP17	Shakespeare – Love's Labour Lost
PP18	not yet attributed
PP19	Thomas Weelkes (1576-1623)
PP20	Christopher Marlowe / Walter Raleigh
PP21	Richard Barnfield – Philomel (Nightingale)

Is it possible that the hitherto unpublished poems, PP7, 10, 13, 14, 15, 16 and 18 were composed by William Herbert? [432]

---

[431] PP7, 10, 13, 14, 15, 16 and 18 are not attributed. PP14 and PP15 run together.

[432] During PP's subsequent printings poems were taken out and others put in. In 1600 there was an edition called *A book of amours by John Davies with certain sonnets by William Shakespeare*. In 1612 Thomas Heywood wrote: *Here likewise, I must necessarily insert a manifest injury done me in that work, by taking the two Epistles of Paris to Helen, and Helen to Paris, and printing them in a lesse(r) volume, under the name of another, which may put the world in opinion I might steal them from him; and he to doe himself right, hath since published them in his own name: but as I must acknowledge my lines not worthy his patronage, under whom he hath publisht them, so the Author I know much offended with M. Jaggard that (altogether unknown to him) presumed to make so bold with his name.* An Apology for Actors, Epistle.

The Passionate Pilgrim

PP1 Modified by 1609 to become Shake-speare's Sonnet 138

When my love swears that she is made of truth,
I do believe her, though I know she lies,
That she might think me some untutored youth,
Unskilful in the world's false forgeries.
Thus vainly thinking that she thinks me young,
Although I know my years be past the best,
I smiling credit her false-speaking tongue,
Outfacing faults in love with love's ill rest.
But wherefore says my love that she is young?
And wherefore say not I that I am old?
O, love's best habit's in a soothing tongue,
And age in love loves not to have years told.
Therefore I'll lie with love, and love with me,
Since that our faults in love thus smothered be.

PP2 Modified slightly in 1609 to become Shake-Speares Sonnet 144

Two loves I have, of comfort and despair,
That like two spirits do suggest me still;
My better angel is a man right fair,
My worser spirit a woman coloured ill.
To win me soon to hell, my female evil
Tempteth my better angel from my side,
And would corrupt my saint to be a devil,
Wooing his purity with her fair pride.
And whether that my angle be turned fiend,
Suspect I may, yet not directly tell;
For being both to me, both to each friend,
I guess one angel in another's hell.
The truth I shall not know, but live in doubt,
Till my bad angel fire my good one out.

PP3 Love's Labour Lost – Shakespeare

Did not the heavenly rhetoric of thine eye,
'Gainst whom the world could not hold argument,
Persuade my heart to this false perjury?
Vows for thee broke deserve not punishment.
A woman I forswore;[433] but I will prove,
Thou being a goddess, I forswore not thee:
My vow was earthly, thou a heavenly love;
Thy grace being gained cures all disgrace in me.
My vow was breath, and breath a vapour is;
Then, thou fair sun, that on this earth doth shine,
Exhal'st this vapour vow; in thee it is:
If broken, then it is no fault of mine.
If by me broke, what fool is not so wise
To break an oath, to win a paradise?

---

[433] Has he now met the woman to whom he was in 1595 engaged to be married?

The Passionate Pilgrim

PP4 Venus and Adonis

Sweet Cytherea[434], sitting by a brook
With young Adonis, lovely, fresh and green,
Did court the lad with many a lovely look,
Such looks as none could look but beauty's queen.
She told him stories to delight his car;
She showed him favours to allure his eye;
To win his heart, she touched him here and there;
Touches so soft still conquer chastity.
But whether unripe years did want conceit,
Or he refused to take her figured proffer,
The tender nibbler would not touch the bait,
But smile and jest at every gentle offer:
Then fell she on her back, fair queen, and toward:
He rose and ran away; ah, fool too froward.

PP5 Love's Labour Lost – Shakespeare

If love make me forsworn, how shall I swear to love?
O never faith could hold, if not to beauty vowed:
Though to myself forsworn, to thee I'll constant prove;
Those thoughts, to me like oaks, to thee like osiers bowed.
Study his bias leaves, and makes his book thine eyes,
Where all those pleasures live that art can comprehend.
If knowledge be the mark, to know thee shall suffice;
Well learned is that tongue that well can thee commend:
All ignorant that soul that sees thee without wonder;
Which is to me some praise, that I thy parts admire.
Thine eye Jove's lightning seems, thy voice his dreadful thunder,
Which, not to anger bent, is music and sweet fire.
Celestial as thou art, O do not love that wrong,
To sing heaven's praise with such an earthly tongue.

PP6 Venus and Adonis

Scarce had the sun dried up the dewy morn
And scarce the herd gone to the hedge for shade,
When Cytherea, all in love forlorn,
A longing tarriance for Adonis made
Under an osier growing by a brook,
A brook where Adon used to cool his spleen.
Hot was the day; she hotter that did look
For his approach, that often there had been.
Anon he comes, and throws his mantle by,
And stood stark naked on the brook's green brim:
The sun looked on the world with glorious eye,

---

[434] Venus

The Passionate Pilgrim

Yet not so wistly as this queen on him.
He, spying her, bounced in whereas he stood;
'O Jove,' quoth she, 'why was not I a flood!'

PP7
Fair is my love, but not so fair as fickle;
Mild as a dove, but neither true nor trusty;
Brighter than glass, and yet, as glass is, brittle;
Softer than wax, and yet as iron rusty;
A lily pale, with damask dye to grace her;
None fairer, nor none falser to deface her.

Her lips to mine how often hath she joined,
Between each kiss her oaths of true love swearing!
How many tales to please me hath she coined,
Dreading my love, the loss thereof still fearing!
Yet in the midst of all her pure protestings
Her faith, her oaths, her tears, and all were jestings.

She burned with love, as straw with fire flameth;
She burned out love, as soon as straw out-burneth;
She framed the love, and yet she foiled the framing;
She bade love last, and yet she fell a-turning.
Was this a lover, or a lecher whether?
Bad in the best, though excellent in neither.

PP8 Richard Barnfield (see Chapter Four)

PP9 Venus and Adonis

Fair was the morn, when the fair queen of love,
[   ]
Paler for sorrow than her milk-white dove,
For Adon's sake, a youngster proud and wild,
Her stand she takes upon a steep-up hill,
Anon Adonis comes with horn and hounds;
She, silly queen, with more than love's good will,
Forbade the boy he should not pass those grounds.
'Once', quoth she, 'did I see a fair sweet youth
Here in these brakes deep-wounded with a boar,
Deep in the thigh, a spectacle of ruth!
See, in my thigh,' quoth she, 'here was the sore.'
She showed hers; he saw more wounds than one,[435]
And blushing fled, and left her all alone.

PP10
Sweet rose, fair flower, untimely plucked, soon vaded,
Plucked in the bud and vaded in the spring!

---

[435] Her period, he is embarrassed and flees.

The Passionate Pilgrim

Bright orient pearl, alack, too timely shaded!
Fair creature, killed too soon by death's sharp sting!
Like a green plum that hangs upon a tree,
And falls through wind before the fall should be.

I weep for thee and yet no cause I have;
For why thou left'st me nothing in thy will.
And yet thou left'st me more than I did crave,
For why I craved nothing of thee still:
O yes, dear friend, I pardon crave of thee,
Thy discontent thou didst bequeath to me.[436]

PP11 Bartholomew Griffin from his sequence Fidessa.
Venus with young Adonis sitting by her
Under a myrtle shade began to woo him;
She told the youngling how god Mars did try her,
And as he fell to her, so fell she to him.
'Even thus', quoth she, the warlike god embraced me',
And then she clipped Adonis in her arms;
'Even thus', quoth she, 'the warlike god unlaced me',
As if the boy should use like loving charms;
'Even thus', quoth she, 'he seized on my lips',
And with her lips on his did act the seizure;
And as she fetched breath, away he skips,
And would not take her meaning nor her pleasure.
Ah, that I had my lady at this bay,
To kiss and clip me till I run away!

PP12 Thomas Deloney
Crabbed age and youth cannot live together:
Youth is full of pleasance, age is full of care;
Youth like summer morn, age like winter weather;
Youth like summer brave, age like winter bare.
Youth is full of sport, age's breath is short;
Youth is nimble, age is lame;
Youth is hot and bold, age is weak and cold;
Youth is wild and age is tame.
Age, I do abhor thee; youth, I do adore thee;
O, my love, my love is young!
Age, I do defy thee. O, sweet shepherd, hie thee,
For methinks thou stay too long.

PP13
Beauty is but a vain and doubtful good,
A shining gloss that vadeth suddenly,
A flower that dies when first it 'gins to bud,
A brittle glass that's broken presently;
A doubtful good, a gloss, a glass, a flower,

---

[436] He has caught something (syphilis?) off this young woman. Has the woman died?

The Passionate Pilgrim

Lost, vaded, broken, dead within an hour.

And as goods lost are seld[437] or never found,
As vaded gloss no rubbing will refresh,
As flowers dead lie witherid on the ground,
As broken glass no cement can redress:
So beauty blemished once, for ever lost,
In spite of physic, painting, pain and cost.

PP14

Good night, good rest: ah, neither be my share;
She bade good night that kept my rest away;
And daffed me to a cabin hanged with care,
To descant on the doubts of my decay.
'Farewell,' quoth she, 'and come again to-morrow.'
Fare well I could not, for I supped with sorrow.

Yet at my parting sweetly did she smile,
In scorn or friendship nill I conster whether;
'T may be, she joyed to jest at my exile,
'T may be, again to make me wander thither:
'Wander', a word for shadows like myself,
As take the pain, but cannot pluck the pelf.[438]

PP15

Lord, how mine eyes throw gazes to the east!
My heart doth charge the watch; the morning rise
Doth cite each moving sense from idle rest,
Not daring trust the office of mine eyes.
While Philomela[439] sings, I sit and mark,
And wish her lays were tuned like the lark.

For she doth welcome daylight with her ditty,
And drives away dark dreaming night:
The night so packed, I post unto my pretty;
Heart hath his hope and eyes their wished sight;
Sorrow changed to solace and solace mixed with sorrow;
For why, she sighed, and bade me come tomorrow.

Were I with her, the night would post too soon,
But now are minutes added to the hours;
To spite me now, each minute seems a moon;
Yet not for me, shine sun to succour flowers!
Pack night, peep day; good day, of night now borrow;
Short night, tonight, and length thyself tomorrow.

---

[437] seldom
[438] reward
[439] See Sonnet 102

The Passionate Pilgrim

PP16

It was a lording's daughter, the fairest one of three,
That liked of her master as well as well might be,
Till looking on an Englishman, the fairest that eye could see,
Her fancy fell a-turning.
Long was the combat doubtful that love with love did fight,
To leave the master loveless, or kill the gallant knight;
To put in practice either, alas, it was a spite
Unto the silly damsel!
But one must be refused; more mickle was the pain
That nothing could be used to turn them both to gain,
For of the two the trusty knight was wounded with disdain:
Alas, she could not help it!
Thus art with arms contending was victor of the day,
Which by a gift of learning[440] did bear the maid away:
Then, lullaby, the learned man hath got the lady gay;
For now my song is ended.

PP17 Love's Labour Lost

On a day, alack the day!
Love, whose month was ever May,
Spied a blossom passing fair,
Playing in the wanton air.
Through the velvet leaves the wind
All unseen 'gan passage find,
That the lover, sick to death,
Wished himself the heaven's breath,
'Air', quoth he, 'thy cheeks may blow;
Air, would I might triumph so!
But, alas! my hand hath sworn
Ne'er to pluck thee from thy thorn;
Vow, alack! for youth unmeet,
Youth, so apt to pluck a sweet.
Thou for whom Jove would swear
Juno but an Ethiope were;
And deny himself for Jove,
Turning mortal for thy love.'

PP18 (Barnfield?)

My flocks feed not, my ewes breed not,
My rams speed not, all is amiss;
Love is dying, faith's defying,
Heart's denying, causer of this.
All my merry jigs are quite forgot,

---

[440] Frances Sidney willed £5,000 to found Sidney Sussex College, Cambridge; but there were six daughters.

The Passionate Pilgrim

All my lady's love is lost, God wot;
Where her faith was firmly fixed in love,
There a nay is placed without remove.
One silly cross wrought all my loss;
O frowning Fortune, cursed fickle dame!
For now I see inconstancy
More in women than in men remain.
In black mourn I, all fears scorn I,
Love hath forlorn me, living in thrall:
Heart is bleeding, all help needing,
O cruel speeding, fraughted with gall.
My shepherd's pipe can sound no deal;
My wether's bell rings doleful knell;
My curtal dog that wont to have played,
Plays not at all, but seems afraid;
My sighs so deep procures to weep,
In howling wise, to see my doleful plight.
How sighs resound through heartless ground,
Like a thousand vanquished men in bloody fight!
Clear wells spring not, sweet birds sing not,
Green plants bring not forth their dye;
Herds stand weeping, flocks all sleeping,
Nymphs back peeping[441] fearfully.
All our pleasure known to us poor swains,
All our merry meetings on the plains,
All our evening sport from us is fled,
All our love is lost, for Love is dead.
Farewell, sweet lass, thy like ne'er was
For a sweet content, the cause of all my moan:
Poor Corydon[442] must live alone;
Other help for him I see that there is none.

PP19 Thomas Weelkes (1576-1623)

When as thine eye hath chose the dame,
And stalled the deer that thou shouldst strike,
Let reason rule things worthy blame,
As well as fancy, partial might;
Take counsel of some wiser head,
Neither too young nor yet unwed.
And when thou com'st thy tale to tell,
Smooth not thy tongue with filed talk,
Lest she some subtle practice smell
A cripple soon can find a halt
But plainly say thou lov'st her well,
And set thy person forth to sell.
And to her will frame all thy ways;

---

[441] Nymphs back peeping - meaning what exactly? Unless M..y Ph... ?
[442] A rustic Shepherd

The Passionate Pilgrim

Spare not to spend, and chiefly there
Where thy desert may merit praise,
By ringing in thy lady's ear:
The strongest castle, tower and town,
The golden bullet beats it down.
Serve always with assured trust,
And in thy suit be humble true;
Unless thy lady prove unjust,
Press never thou to choose anew:
When time shall serve, be thou not slack
To proffer, though she put thee back.
What though her frowning brows be bent,
Her cloudy looks will calm ere night,
And then too late she will repent
That thus dissembled her delight;
And twice desire, ere it be day,
That which with scorn she put away.

What though she strive to try her strength,
And ban and brawl, and say thee nay,
Her feeble force will yield at length,
When craft hath taught her thus to say:
'Had women been so strong as men,
In faith, you had not had it then,'

The wiles and guiles that women work,
Dissembled with an outward show,
The tricks and toys that in them lurk,
The cock that treads them shall not know.
Have you not heard it said full oft,
A woman's nay doth stand for nought?

Think women still to strive with men,
To sin and never for to saint:
There is no heaven, by holy then,
When time with age shall them attaint.
Were kisses all the joys in bed,
One woman would another wed.

But, soft, enough, too much I fear,
Lest that my mistress hear my song;
She will not stick to round me on th' ear,
To teach my tongue to be so long,
Yet will she blush, here be it said,
To hear her secrets so bewrayed.

The Passionate Pilgrim

PP20 Christopher Marlowe / Walter Raleigh

Live with me, and be my love,
And we will all the pleasures prove
That hills and valleys, dales and fields,
And all the craggy mountains yield.

There will we sit upon the rocks,
And see the shepherds feed their flocks,
By shallow rivers, by whose falls
Melodious birds sing madrigals.
There will I make thee a bed of roses,
With a thousand fragrant posies,
A cap of flowers, and a kirtle
Embroider'd all with leaves of myrtle.
A belt of straw and ivy buds,
With coral clasps and amber studs;
And if these pleasures may thee move,
Then live with me and be my love.
LOVE'S ANSWER
If that the world and love were young,
And truth in every shepherd's tongue,
These pretty pleasures might me move
To live with thee and be thy love.

PP21 Richard Barnfield (see Chapter Four)

Appendix 3 – Aemelia Lanier

Biography compiled and written by Kari Boyd McBride.

Aemilia Lanyer was the daughter of Baptista Basano and Margaret Johnson, his common-law wife. Nothing is known about Aemilia's mother. Margaret may have been the aunt of Robert Johnson, a musician of Shakespeare's company, later attached to the court of Charles I (Boyd McBride 1). Baptista Bassano came to England from Venice with his four brothers; all became musicians at the English court. Baptista's first appearance as a musician for the court was at the coronation of Edward VI in 1547 (Greer et al., 44). Aemilia Basano was apparently born while her father was in the King's service. She was christened at St. Botolph, Bishopsgate on January 27, 1569. Lanyer's father died when she was seven. His will indicates that she had at least one sister, Angela, four years her junior. Her father's death, however, did not halt Aemilia's access to Elizabethan court circles. By the time of her mother's death in 1587, the eighteen-year-old Aemilia had found favour at court. The Queen's Lord Chamberlain,[443] a man forty-five years older than Aemilia, chose her to be his mistress. Lord Hunsdon and Aemilia Bassano enjoyed the arrangement for a number of years, until she became pregnant. Aemilia "apparently resented being married off to Alphonso Lanyer, a court musician" (Woods 213). The son by Lord Hunsdon, Henry, was born in 1593, soon after her marriage to Lanyer. Odillya, her daughter by Alphonso, was born in 1598, but died ten months later.

Much of what information is available on Lanyer's life comes from the records of Simon Forman, an astrologer whom she consulted during 1597. Forman's diary indicates that Lanyer was concerned about promotion to knighthood for her husband, who was serving as a soldier at the time (Woods 213). Forman also documents Lanyer's problem with miscarriages, as well as her missing the enjoyment of Queen Elizabeth's court. In his notes, Forman claims that Lanyer's need for his advice, coupled with her financial difficulties, led her to allow him some sort of familiarity. The implication that Forman was involved with Lanyer sexually is exaggerated, according to Woods and Greer, although he undoubtedly had that aim. Woods also refutes

---

[443] The various Lord Chamberlains were:
1557 William Howard, 1st. Lord Effingham; Richard Leveson's wife's grandfather.
1572 Thomas Radcliffe, 3rd Earl Sussex - married Katherine, Mary Sidney Herbert's sister.
1585 Henry Carey, 1st. Lord Hunsdon - Aemelia Lanier's lover
1596 William Brooke - (descendent of Sir John Oldcastle on whom Falstaff is based.)
1597 George Carey, 2nd. Lord Hunsdon - son of Henry.
1603 Thomas Howard, 1st Earl of Suffolk - William Knollys' father-in-law.
1613 Robert Carr, 1st Earl of Somerset
1615 William Herbert, 3rd. Earl of Pembroke; Mary Fitton's lover.
1625 Philip Herbert, 1st. Earl of Montgomery (William's brother & 4th. Earl of Pembroke.)
1641 Robert Devereux, 3rd Earl of Essex.

Aemelia Lanier

claim of historian A. L. Rowse that Lanyer was William Shakespeare's "dark lady," arguing that the notion comes from a misreading of Forman's diaries. No documentary evidence indicates Shakespeare and Lanyer knew one another.

Aemilia Lanyer published her only known volume of poems, Salve Deus Rex Judaeorum (Hail God, King of the Jews), in 1611. The book is remarkable both because women poets rarely published in Elizabethan and Jacobean England, and because of its groundbreaking women's perspective on religious issues. As Lewalski says, it "is a vigorous apologia for women's equality or superiority to men in spiritual and moral matters" (203). Lanyer was seeking support through patronage with the publication of the work, specifically female patronage. There is some suggestion "that the nine dedications to the volume may have been written in expectation of the usual £2 per dedication" (Greer 45). The desired funding was not forthcoming.

Lanyer's financial situation worsened after the death of her husband, in 1613. Alphonso Lanyer had received a hay-and-grain patent from King James in 1604, which entitled him to "six pence for every load of hay and three pence for every load of straw brought into London and Westminster" (Boyd McBride 1). Aemilia made over the grant to her brother-in-law, Innocent, apparently with an understanding of receiving partial proceeds herself. She later fought in court for her share of the income from the grant, with minimal success (Woods 214). Lanyer's financial problems were compounded by the fact that her son, Henry, predeceased her, leaving her with two grandchildren to raise. For a time, Lanyer ran a school for "noblemen and gentlemen's children" (Greer 45), but legal disputes with the landlord resulted in her being arrested on several occasions. As Boyd McBride says, an arrest would constitute "a scene not apt to inspire confidence among the parents of one's students", and Aemilia gave up the endeavour. Lanyer's monetary difficulties continued until her death, at age seventy-six.

Two Barnfield Poems

Appendix 4 – Two Barnfield's Poems

The Combat between Conscience and Covetousness

To his Worshipful good friend, Master *John Steventon,* [444]*of Dothill, in the County of Salop, Esquire.*

> *Sith Conscience (long since) is exiled the City,*
> *O let her in the Country, find some Pity:*
> *But if she be exiled, the Country too,*
> *O let her find, some favour yet of you.*

The Combat, between Conscience and Covetousness, in the mind of Man.[445]

> *Now had the coal-black steedes, of pitchy Night,*
> *(Breathing out Darkness) banisht cheerful Light,*
> *And sleep (the shadow of eternal rest)*
> *My several senses, wholly had possest.*
> *When lo, there was presented to my view,*
> *A vision strange, yet not so strange, as true.*
> *Conscience (me thought) appeared unto me,*
> *Cloth'd with good Deeds, with Trueth and Honesty,*
> *Her countenance demure, and sober sad,*
> *Nor any other Ornament she had.*
> *Then Covetousness did encounter her,*
> *Clad in a Cassock, like a Usurer,*
> *The Cassock, it was made of poor-men's skins,*
> *Lac'd here and there, with many several sins:*
> *Nor was it furd, with any common fur;*
> *Or if it were, himself he was the fur.*
> *A Bag of money, in his hand he held,*
> *The which with hungry eie, he still beheld.*
> *The place wherein this vision first began,*
> *(A spacious plain) was cald The Mind of Man.*

> *The Carle*[446] *no sooner, Conscience had espied,*
> *But swelling like a Toad, (puft up with pride)*
> *He straight began against her to invey;*
> *These were the words, which Covetise did say.*
> *Conscience (quoth he) how dar'st thou be so bold,*
> *To claim the place, that I by right do hold?*
> *Neither by right, nor might, thou canst obtain it:*
> *By might (thou knowst full well) thou canst not gain it.*
> *The greatest Princes are my followers,*

---

[444] No biography has been discovered, but he lived by the border with Wales.
[445] Starting with, from Virgil - *quid non mortalia pectora cogis; Auri sacra fames?*
[446] churl?

Two Barnfield Poems

The King in Peace, the Captain in the Wars:
The Courtier, and the simple Countryman:
The Judge, the Merchant, and the Gentleman:
The learned Lawyer, and the Politician:
The skilful Surgeon, and the fine Physician:
In brief, all sorts of men me entertain,
And hold me, as their Souls sole Sovereign,
And in my quarrel, they will fight and die,
Rather then I should suffer injury.
And as for title, interest, and right,
I'll prove its mine by that, as well as might.
Though Covetousness, were used long before,
Yet Judas Treason, made my Fame the more;
When Christ he caused, crucified to be,
For thirty pence, man sold his mind to me:
And now adaies, what tenure is more free,
Then that which purchas'd is, with Gold and fee?

Conscience.
With patience, have I heard thy large Complaint,
Wherein the Diuell, would be thought a Saint:
But wot ye what, the Saying is of old?
One tale is good, until anothers told.
Truth is the right, that I must stand upon,
(For other title, hath poor Conscience none)
First I will prove it, by Antiquity,
That thou art but an upstart, unto me;
Before that thou wast ever thought upon,
The mind of Man, belonged to me alone.
For after that the Lord, had Man Created,
And him in blissful Paradise had seated;
(Knowing his Nature was to vice inclined)
God gave me unto man, to rule his mind,
And as it were, his Governor to be,
To guide his mind, in Trueth, and Honesty.
And where thou sayst, that man did fell his soul;
That Argument, I quickly can control:
It is a fayned fable, thou doost tell,
That, which is not his own, he cannot sell;
No man can sell his soul, although he thought it:
Mans soule is Christs, for he hath dearly bought it.
Therefore usurping Covetise, be gone,
For why, the mind belongs to me alone.

Covetousness.
Alas poor Conscience, how thou art deceav'd?
As though of senses, thou wert quite bereaved.
What wilt thou say (that thinkst thou canst not err)
If I can prove my self the ancienter?
Though into Adams mind, God did infuse thee,
Before his fall, yet man did never use thee.

Two Barnfield Poems

What was it else, but Avarice in Eve,
(Thinking thereby, in greater Bliss to live)
That made her taste, of the forbidden fruit?
Of her Desire, was not I the root?
Did she not covet? (tempted by the Devil)
The Apple of the Tree, of good and evil?
Before man used Conscience, she did covet:
Therefore by her Transgression, here I prove it,
That Covetousness possest the mind of man,
Before that any Conscience began.

Conscience.
Even as a counterfeited precious stone,
Seems to be far more rich, to look upon,
Then doeth the right: But when a man comes near,
His baseness then, doeth evident appear:
So Covetise, the Reasons thou doost tell,
Seem to be strong, but being weighed well,
They are indeed, but only mere Illusions,
And do inforce but very weak Conclusions.
When as the Lord (fore-knowing his offence)
Had given man a Charge, of Abstinence,
And to refrain, the fruit of good and ill:
Man had a Conscience, to obey his will,
And never would be tempted thereunto,
Until the Woman, she, did work man woe.
And made him break, the Lords Commandment,
Which all Mankind, did afterward repent:
So that thou seest, thy Argument is vain,
And I am prov'd, the elder of the twain.

Covetousness.
Fond Wretch, it was not Conscience, but fear,
That made the first man (Adam) to forbear
To taste the fruit, of the forbidden Tree,
Lest, if offending he were found to be,
(According as Jehovah said on high,
For his so great Transgression, he should dye.
Fear curbed his mind, it was not Conscience then,
(For Conscience freely, rules the harts of men)
And is a godly motion of the mind,
To every virtuous action inclined,
And not enforc'd, through fear of Punishment,
But is to virtue, voluntary bent:
Then (simple Trul) be packing presently,
For in this place, there is no room for thee.
Conscience.
Aye me, (distressed Wight) what shall I do?
Where shall I rest? Or whither shall I go?
Unto the rich? (woes me) they, do abhor me:

Two Barnfield Poems

Unto the poor? (alas) they, care not for me:
Unto the Old-man? he; hath me forgot:
Unto the Young-man? yet he, knows me not:
Unto the Prince? he; can dispense with me:
Unto the Magistrate? that, may not be:
Unto the Court? for it, I am too base:
Unto the Country? there, I have no place:
Unto the City? thence, I am exiled:
Unto the Village? there; I am reviled:
Unto the Bar? the Lawyer there, is bribed?
Unto the War? there, Conscience is derided:
Unto the Temple? there; I am disguised:
Unto the Market? there, I am despised:
Thus both the young and old, the rich and poor,
Against me (silly Creature) shut their door.
Then, sith each one seeks my rebuke and shame,
I'll go again to Heaven (from whence I came.)

This said (me thought) making exceeding moan,
She went her way, and left the Carle alone,
Who vaunting of his late-got victory,
Aduaunc'd himself in pomp and Majesty:
Much like a Cock, who having killed his foe,
Brisks up himself, and then begins to crow.
So Covetise, when Conscience was departed,
Gan to be proud in mind, and haughty hearted:
And in a stately Chair of state he set him,
(For Conscience banisht) there was none to let him,
And being but one entry, to this Plain,
(Whereof as king and Lord, he did remain)
Repentance cald, he caused that to be kept,
Lest Conscience should return, whilst as he slept:
Wherefore he caused it, to be wacht and warded
Both night and Day, and to be strongly guarded:
To keep it safe, these three he did intreat,
Hardness of heart, with Falsehood, and Deceit:
And if at any time, she chaunc'd to venter,
Hardness of heart, denied her still to enter.
When Conscience was exiled the mind of Man,
Then Covetise, his government began.
This once being seen, what I had seen before,
(Being only seen in sleep) was seen no more;
For with the sorrow, which my Soul did take
At sight hereof, forthwith I did awake.   *FINIS.*

Two Barnfield Poems

AN ODE

Nights were short, and daies were long;
Blossoms on the Hauthorn's hung:
Philomæle (Night-Musiques King)
Told the comming of the spring.
Whose sweet silver-sounding voice
Made the little birds rejoice:
Skipping light from spray to spray,
Till Aurora shew'd the day.
Scarce might one see, when I might see
(For such chaunces sudden be)
By a well of Marble-stone,
A Shepheard lying all alone.
Weep he did; and his weeping
Made the fading flowers spring.
Daphnis was his name (I ween)
Youngest Swaine of Summers Queen.
When Aurora saw t'was he.
Weep she did for companie:

Weep she did for her sweet son,
That (when antique Troy was wonne)
Suffer'd death by luckless fate,
Whom she now laments too late:
And each morning (by Cocks crew)
Showers down her silver dew.
Whose tears (falling from their spring)
Give moysture to each living thing,
That on earth increase and grow,
Through power of their friendlie foe.
Whose effect when Flora felt,
Tears, that did her bosom melt,
(For who can resist tears often,
But She whom no tears can soften?)
Peering strait above the banks,
Shew'd herself to give her thanks.
Wondring thus at Natures work,
(Wherein many maruailes lurke)

Me thought I heard a doleful noise,
Consorted with a mournful voice,
Drawing nie to hear more plain,
Hear I did, unto my pain,
(For who is not pain'd to hear
Him in grief whom heart holds dear?)
Silly swain (with grief ore-gone)
Thus to make his piteous moan.
Love I did, (alas the while)
Love I did, but did beguile
My dear love with loving so,

Two Barnfield Poems

(Whom as then I did not know.)
Love I did the fairest boy,
That these fields did ere enjoy.
Love I did faire Ganymed;
(Venus darling, beauties bed:)
Him I thought the fairest creature;
Him the quintessence of Nature:

But yet (alas) I was deceiu'd,
(Love of reason is bereau'd)
For since then I saw a Lass,
(Lass) that did in beauty pass,
(Pass) faire Ganymede as far
As Phoebus doth the smallest star.
Love commanded me to love;
Fancy bade me not remove
My affection from the swain
Whom I never could obtain:
(For who can obtain that favour,
Which he cannot graunt the crauer?)
Love at last (though loath) prevailde;
(Love) that so my heart assailde;
Wounding me with her faire eies,
(Ah how Love can subtelize,
And devize a thousand shifts,
How to work men to his drifts)

Her it is, for whom I mourn;
Her, for whom my life I scorn;
Her, for whom I weep all day;
Her, for whom I sigh, and say,
Either She, or else no creature,
Shall enjoy my love: whose feature
Though I never can obtain,
Yet shall my true love remain:
Till (my body turn'd to clay)
My poor soul must pass away,
To the heavens; where (I hope)
Hit shall find a resting scope:
Then since I loved thee (alone)
Remember me when I am gone.
Scarce had he these last words spoken,
But me thought his heart was broken;
With great grief that did abound,
(Cares and grief the heart confound)

In whose heart (thus riv'd in three)
Eliza written I might see:
In Caracters of crimson blood,
(Whose meaning well I understood.)
Which, for my heart might not behold,
I hyed me home my sheep to fold.

The Two Noble Kinsmen

Appendix 5 – The Two Noble Kinsmen

The Shakespeare First Folio did not include two plays, *Pericles,* and *The Two Noble Kinsmen.* The latter is thought to have been written mainly by John Fletcher (1579-1625). Since *Kinsmen* was a late play, and if William Herbert had a hand in it, logic suggested that there may be some autobiography written into it. Here in full, and retaining continuity, are the four main speeches of the Jailor's Daughter (scenes 2.4, 2.6, 3.2 and 3.4) who releases Prince Palamon from her father's custody.

2.4 Why should I love this gentleman? 'Tis odds
He never will affect me. I am base,
My father the mean keeper of his prison,
And he a prince. To marry him is hopeless,
To be his whore is witless. Out upon't,
What pushes are we wenches driven to
When fifteen once has found us? First, I saw him;
I, seeing, thought he was a goodly man;
He was as much to please a woman in him -
If he please to bestow it so – as ever
These eyes yet looked on. Next, I pitied him,
And so would any wench, o'my conscience,
That ever dreamed or vowed her maidenhead
To a young handsome man. Then, I loved him,
Extremely loved him, infinitely loved him -
And yet he had a cousin fair as he, too.
But in my heart was Palamon, and there,
Lord, what a coil he keeps! To hear him
Sing in the evening, what a heaven it is!
And yet his songs are sad ones. Fairer spoken
Was never gentleman. When I come in
To bring him water in a morning, first
He bows his noble body, then salutes me, thus:
"Fair, gentle maid, good morrow. May thy goodness
Get thee a happy husband." Once he kissed me -
I loved my lips the better ten days after.
Would he would do so every day! He grieves much,
And me as much to see his misery.
What should I do to make him know I love him?
For I would fain enjoy him. Say I ventured
To set him free? What says the law then? Thus much
For law or kindred! I will do it,
And this night; ere tomorrow he shall love me.

The Two Noble Kinsmen

2.6 Let all the dukes and all the devils roar
    He is at liberty! I have ventured for him,
    And out I have brought him. To a little wood
    A mile hence I have sent him, where a cedar
    Higher than all the rest spreads like a plane,
    Fast by a brook – and there he shall keep close
    Till I provide him files and food, for yet
    His iron bracelets are not off. O Love,
    What a stout-hearted child thou art! My father
    Durst better have endured cold iron than done it.
    I love him beyond love and beyond reason
    Or wit or safety. I have made him know it -
    I care not, I am desperate. If the law
    Find me and then condemn me for't, some wenches,
    Some honest-hearted maids, will sing my dirge
    And tell the memory my death was noble,
    Dying almost a martyr. That way he takes,
    I purpose, is my way too. Sure, he cannot
    Be so unmanly as to leave me here
    If he do, maids will not so easily
    Trust men again. And yet, he has not thanked me
    For what I have done – no, not so much as kissed me -
    And that, methinks, is not so well. Nor scarcely
    Could I persuade him to become a free man,
    He made such scruples of the wrong he did
    To me and to my father. Yet, I hope
    When he considers more, this love of mine
    Will take more root within him. Let him do
    What he will with me – so he use me kindly.
    For use me, so he shall, or I'll proclaim him
    And to his face, no man. I'll presently
    Provide him necessaries and pack my clothes up,
    And where there is a patch of ground I'll venture
    So he be with me. By him, like a shadow;
    I'll ever dwell. Within, this hour the hubbub
    Will be all o'er the prison – I am then
    Kissing the man they look for. Farewell, father:
    Get many more such prisoners and such daughters
    And shortly you may keep yourself. Now to him.

3.2 He has mistook the brake I meant is gone
    After his fancy. Tis now wellnigh morning,
    No matter – would it were perpetual night,
    And darkness lord o'th' world. Hark, 'tis a wolf!
    In me hath grief slain fear, and, but for one thing,
    I care for nothing – and that's Palamon.
    I reck not if the wolves would jaw me, so

The Two Noble Kinsmen

He had this file. What if I hollered for him?
I cannot holler. If I whooped, what then?
If he not answered, I should call a wolf
And do him but that serviced I have heard
Strange howls this livelong night – why may't not be
They have made prey of him? He has no weapons;
He cannot run; the jangling of his gyves
Might call fell things to listen; who have in them
A sense to know a man unarmed, and can
Smell where resistance is. I'll set it down.
He's torn to pieces: they howled many together
And then they fed on him. So much for that:
Be bold to ring the bell. How stand I then?
All's chared when he is gone. No, no, I lie;
My father's to be hanged for his escape,
Myself to beg, if I priced life so much
As to deny my act – but that I would not,
Should I try death by dozens. I am moped -
Food took I none these two days,
Sipped some water. I have not closed mine eyes
Save when my lids scoured off their brine. Alas,
Dissolve, my life: let not my sense unsettle,
Lest I should drown or stab or hang myself.
O state of nature, fail together in me
Since thy best props are warped. So which way now?
The best way is the next way to a grave,
Each errant step beside is torment. Lo,
The moon is down, the crickets chirp, the screech-owl
Calls in the dawn. All offices are done
Save what I fail in: but the point is this,
An end, and that is all.

3.4 I am very cold, and all the stars are out too
The little stars and all, that look like aglets -
The sun has seen my folly. Palamon!
Alas, no, he's in heaven. Where am I now?
Yonder's the sea and there's a ship – how't tumbles!
And there's a rock lies watching underwater -
Now, now, it beats upon it – now, now, now,
There's a leak sprung, a sound one-how they cry!
Open her before the wind – you'll lose all else.
Up with a course or two and tack about, boys,
Good night, good night, you're gone: I am very hungry.
Would I could find a fine frog – he would tell me
News from all parts o'th' world, then would I make
A carrack of a cockle-shell, and sail
By east and north-east to the King of Pygmies;

For he tells fortunes rarely. Now my father,
Twenty to one, is trussed up in a trice
Tomorrow morning, I'll say never a word.
(Sings)
For I'll cut my green coat, a foot above my knee.
And I'll clip my yellow locks, an inch below mine eye,
Hey nonny, nonny, nonny,
He s'buy me a white cut, forth for to ride,
And I'll go seek him, through the world that is so wide,
Hey nonny, nonny, nonny,
O for a prick now, like a nightingale,
To put my breast against. I shall sleep like a top else.

Although the Two Noble Kinsmen is a different story to Hamlet, we have the echoes of a prison, the passion of a besotted maid tricked by an indifferent prince, a father grossly wronged and a maid going mad.

In 1619, two months after the death of the actor Richard Burbage, William Herbert wrote while an after-dinner play was being put on by the Duke of Lennox,

> & even now the company are at a play, which I
> being tender harted could not endure to see so
> soone after the loss of my old acquaintance
> Burbadg."

The play was *Pericles*, the only other play missing from the First Folio!

Appendix Six

Appendix 6 – Marrying the Sonnets

As I understand, it the relationship and correspondence between Mary Fitton and William Herbert carried on at least until Mary married Polewhele. Mary kept copies of the sonnets she sent William Herbert in her copy book, but she received from him one sonnet, on a loose leaf, for every four she sent. Her sonnets were printed in sequence. His twenty-eight sonnets were printed out of sequence but in an order that seemed to give some sense of flow. The last two sonnets have a dreamlike feeling, as if to round everything off. The analysis below excludes Sonnets 138 & 144 and 153 & 154.

There are four types of letter in a correspondence. A responds to B; B responds to A; A creates a new subject; B creates a new subject. The difficulty with understanding exchanges of letters is that letters cross in the post and the delays in responding; a letter could bounce back with a messenger, or a letter may have to wait considerable time before a messenger was available. I have tried, below, to give a logic to the twenty-four of the twenty-eight sonnets composed by William Herbert. The order is based on key words, mood, events and locations. The order is subjective but one can see immediately how Sonnet 8 can be a response to Sonnet 128.

Sonnet 8 is a response to Sonnet 128.
Sonnet 9 responds to Sonnet 148.
Sonnet 145 responds to Sonnet 10.
Sonnet 140 responds to Sonnet 16.
Sonnet 132 responds to Sonnet 20.
Sonnet 133 responds to Sonnet 26.
Sonnet 147 responds to Sonnet 34.
Sonnet 35 responds to Sonnet 141.
Sonnet 40 responds to Sonnet 129.
Sonnet 139 responds to Sonnet 42.
Sonnet 54 responds to Sonnet 130.
Sonnet 137 responds to Sonnet 68.
Sonnet 71 responds to Sonnet 146.
Sonnet 83 responds to Sonnet 127.
Sonnet 87 responds to Sonnet 151.
Sonnet 89 responds to Sonnet 149.
Sonnet 109 responds to Sonnet 142.
Sonnet 110 responds to Sonnet 131.
Sonnets 135 & 136 follow Sonnet 131.
Sonnet 111 responds to Sonnets 135 & 136
Sonnet 112 responds to Sonnet 134.
Sonnet 150 responds to Sonnet 115.
Sonnet 152 responds to Sonnet 116.
Sonnet 126 responds to Sonnet 143.